THE ENTHUSIAST'S GUIDE TO NIGHT AND LOW-LIGHT PHOTOGRAPHY

50 Photographic Principles You Need to Know

ALAN HESS

THE ENTHUSIAST'S GUIDE TO NIGHT AND LOW-LIGHT PHOTOGRAPHY: 50 PHOTOGRAPHIC PRINCIPLES YOU NEED TO KNOW

Alan Hess

Editor: Jocelyn Howell
Project manager: Lisa Brazieal
Marketing coordinator: Mercedes Murray
Layout and type: WolfsonDesign
Design system and front cover design: Area of Practice
Front cover image: Alan Hess

ISBN: 978-1-68198-242-7
1st Edition (1st printing, June 2017)
© 2017 Alan Hess
All images © Alan Hess unless otherwise noted

Rocky Nook Inc.
1010 B Street, Suite 350
San Rafael, CA 94901
USA

www.rockynook.com

Distributed in the U.S. by Ingram Publisher Services
Distributed in the UK and Europe by Publishers Group UK

Library of Congress Control Number: 2016957325

Dedicated to Nadra Farina-Hess

ACKNOWLEDGMENTS

WRITING A BOOK about night and low-light photography means going out at night to take photos. This can create chaos when you're trying to make plans and live a normal life. It's a very good thing that my wife, Nadra, understands and supports this. None of this would be possible without her love and support.

Creating a book like this is a team effort and I am really pleased with the Rocky Nook team with whom I get to work. I want to thank all of the people responsible for turning my words and images into something that I am very proud to have worked on. Thank you to Scott Cowlin, Ted Waitt, Jocelyn Howell, Mercedes Murray, Lisa Brazieal and the whole Rocky Nook family for your great work and dedication to publishing quality photography books.

Thank you to my family and friends for understanding that the crazy hours and weird requests are not going to stop as I keep looking for new subjects.

The credit for the beautiful star trail photo on page 89 goes to my nephew Tyler Torwick, who got bitten by the photography bug and has captured some great views of the night sky. Thanks for allowing me to use your photo, Tyler.

I am lucky to know some great local photographers, and when I needed a shot of the moon rising over the San Diego skyline, I knew that the best example had already been taken by my friend Daniel Knighton of Pixel Perfect Images (page 87). Daniel and I have shot so many shows together I have lost count of them. I can't thank him enough for the use of his image. You can see his work at http://pixelperfectimages.net

A few years ago, I was teaching photography at the Photoshop World conference and I was asked by Kathy Siler if I could teach a class on how I used Photoshop to process my night and low-light images. That request led to me teaching about the Photoshop techniques I use and to chapter 5 of this book. Thank you, Kathy, for pushing me in that direction.

Being an instructor at the Photoshop World conference over the years has put me in contact with some of the best photographers, designers, and Photoshop experts in the world, many of whom I now call my friends. I am honored to have presented alongside these artists and each and every one of them has made me a better photographer and author. So thank you, Joe McNally, Moose Peterson, Glyn Dewis, Dave Clayton, Scott Kelby, Kaylee Greer, Ben Willmore, Dave Cross, Bert Monroy, Corey Barker, Rick Sammon, and Frank Doorhof.

Being an author is usually a solitary undertaking. I do spend long hours at the computer trying to get the words to sound just right. I am lucky in that I have great friends in the photography industry whom I can call for advice or encouragement. The amazing people at Nikon Professional Services keep my gear working and always have tech advice when I ask for it. Thank you, Scott Diussa, Mark Suban, Mike Corrado, Brien Aho, Mark Kettenhofen, Sara Wood, and JC Carey.

And lastly, a HUGE thank you to you, the reader, for picking up this book. I could not do this without your support.

CONTENTS

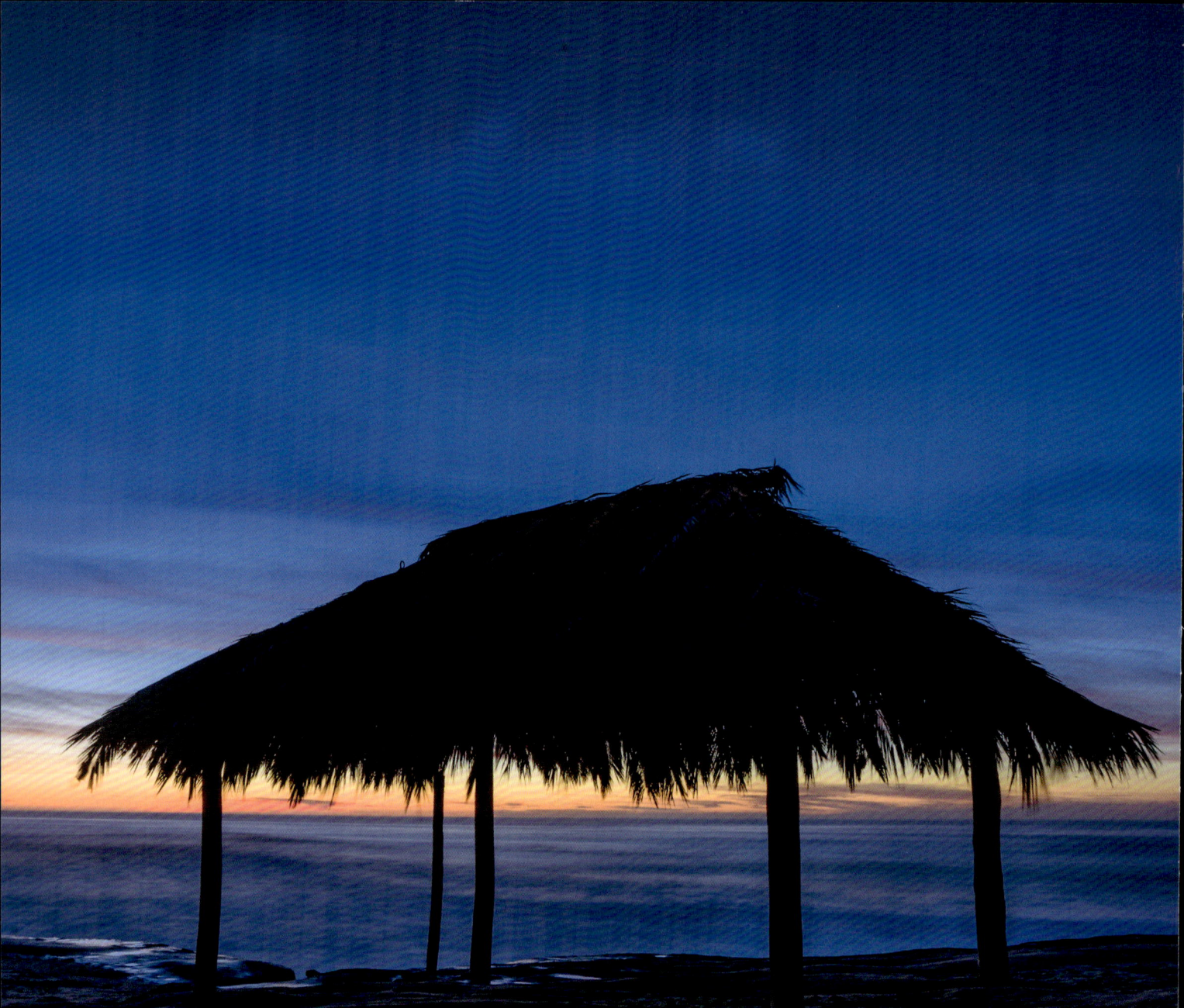

CONTENTS

1

NIGHT AND LOW-LIGHT PHOTOGRAPHY BASICS

CHAPTER 1

Photography is the act of capturing light that bounces off of a subject and recording it with a camera sensor or film. This is pretty easy when there is a lot of light, but it becomes much more difficult in low-light situations. This chapter explains why low-light photography is difficult and covers some general tools for getting the best images possible in low-light situations. I have broken night and low-light photography into two distinct categories: capturing action and capturing the scene. The issues with both types of subjects are the same—there is simply not enough light to make it easy to capture a good photograph—but the key difference is that you need a much higher shutter speed when you shoot action.

1. NIGHT AND LOW-LIGHT PHOTOGRAPHY IS DIFFICULT

PHOTOGRAPHING IN LOW LIGHT is difficult because there is not a lot of light—this seems pretty obvious. But the lack of abundant light can create a lot of different issues. In low-light situations it is more difficult to focus and much more difficult to achieve proper exposure. Shooting sports, action, and events in low light means shooting with a very shallow depth of field, making your focus critical. You also need to use a high ISO, which creates more digital noise, just to get a high enough shutter speed to freeze the action.

When you're shooting in low light, you can no longer trust your built-in light meter to give you the exposure you want. If you use any of the automatic exposure modes to photograph the night sky, the large areas of dark tones can cause the camera to record an overexposed image. It requires a lot of careful planning to shoot very long exposures using tripods and releases.

The following images show some different problems that can arise when shooting at night and in low light and how I addressed those problems. **Figures 1.1** and **1.2** both show low-light scenes that required me to use a long shutter speed to properly expose the scene. In **Figure 1.2**, you can see that the use of a long shutter speed caused the surfers in the water to become ghostly figures. In both scenarios, the camera was mounted on a tripod to make sure it didn't move.

Capturing action in low light is much more difficult than capturing a stationary scene because long shutter speeds cause moving objects to appear blurry or ghostlike. No one wants a wedding or concert photo to be out of focus. For **Figures 1.3** and **1.4**, the shutter speed had to be fast enough to freeze the action, which meant I needed to use a high ISO and a wide maximum aperture to let in enough light for a proper exposure.

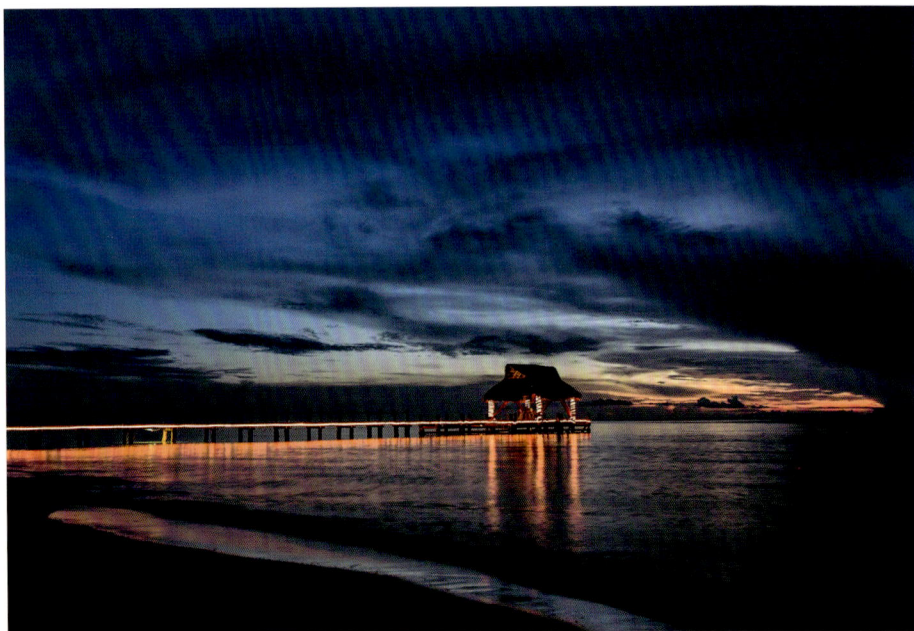

1.1 After the sun set, the lights on the jetty came on, making for a great photo. I needed to use a long shutter speed to let enough light enter the camera, so I mounted the camera on a small tripod that I set on a table to keep it steady for the exposure.
ISO 400; 2 sec.; f/5; 24mm

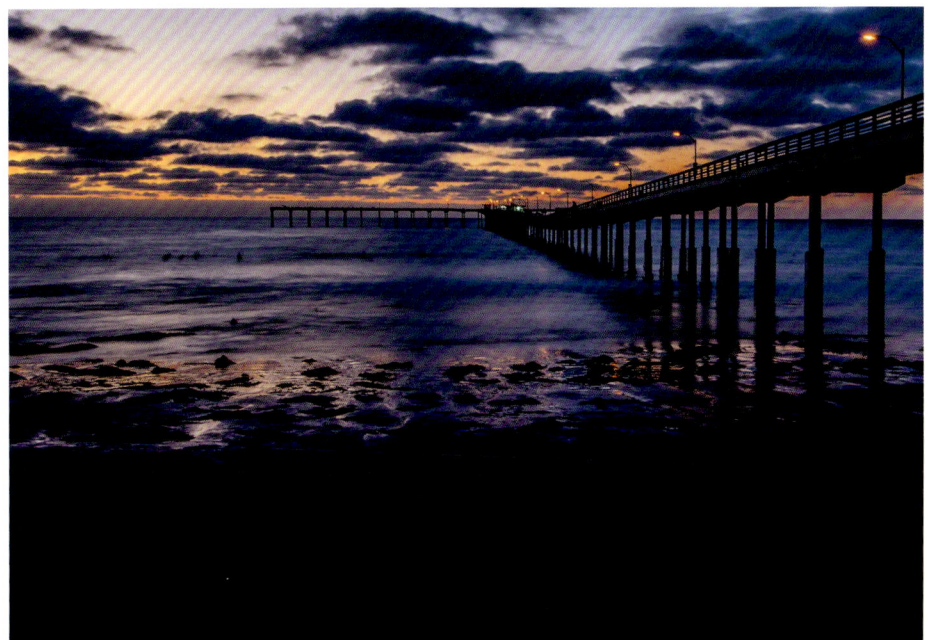

1.2 I used a long shutter speed of 10 seconds, which turned the surfers in the waves into ghostly shapes. **ISO 100; 10 sec.; f/16; 20mm**

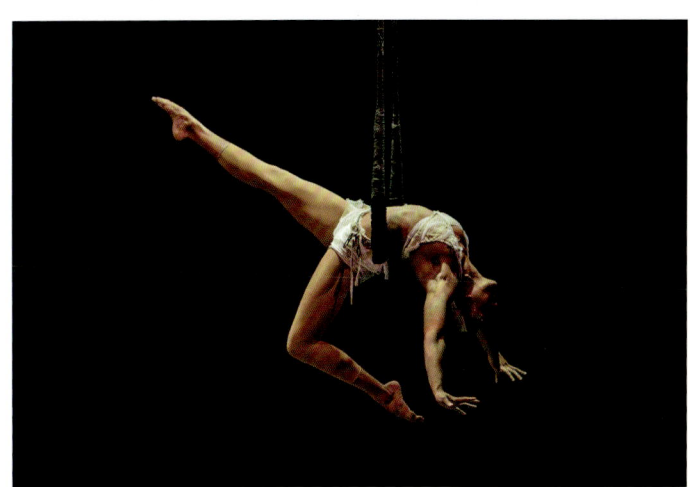

1.3 I needed to use a fast shutter speed to photograph this aerialist during a performance. **ISO 2500; 1/400 sec.; f/2.8; 130mm**

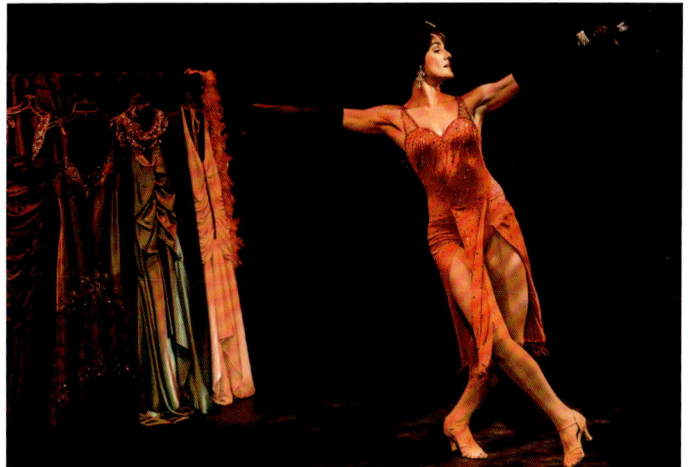

1.4 Photographing this dancer going through a routine on the ground didn't require me to use as fast of a shutter speed as I did for the aerialist, but I still used a shutter speed of 1/250 second to freeze the kick in action. **ISO 2000; 1/250 sec.; f/2.8; 200mm**

2. THE PROS AND CONS OF LONG EXPOSURES

THE SHUTTER SPEED controls the length of time the shutter is open, allowing light to reach the sensor in the camera. The longer the shutter is open, the more light is allowed in.

When you leave the shutter open for a long period of time, any movement by the subject or camera during the exposure can result in a blurred subject or image. This can be either a pro or a con, depending on the subject. If you are trying to freeze the action when you're taking a concert photo, then you probably don't want to use a long shutter speed. On the other hand, if you are trying to capture the light trails from car headlights as they go down the street, then a longer shutter speed is perfect because it will cause the light to blur.

There are a couple of things that are important to pay attention to when you use long shutter speeds. First, you need to make sure the camera is as stable as possible. Chapter 2 covers all the details of using a tripod or monopod, as well as other ways to keep the camera steady during the exposure. Second, you need to know what in the image will be moving.

Figures 2.1 and **2.2** show some of the pros of using a long shutter speed. It can be a great way to compress time into a single frame. On the other hand, using a long shutter speed means that you cannot capture any action photos or freeze your subject if it is moving.

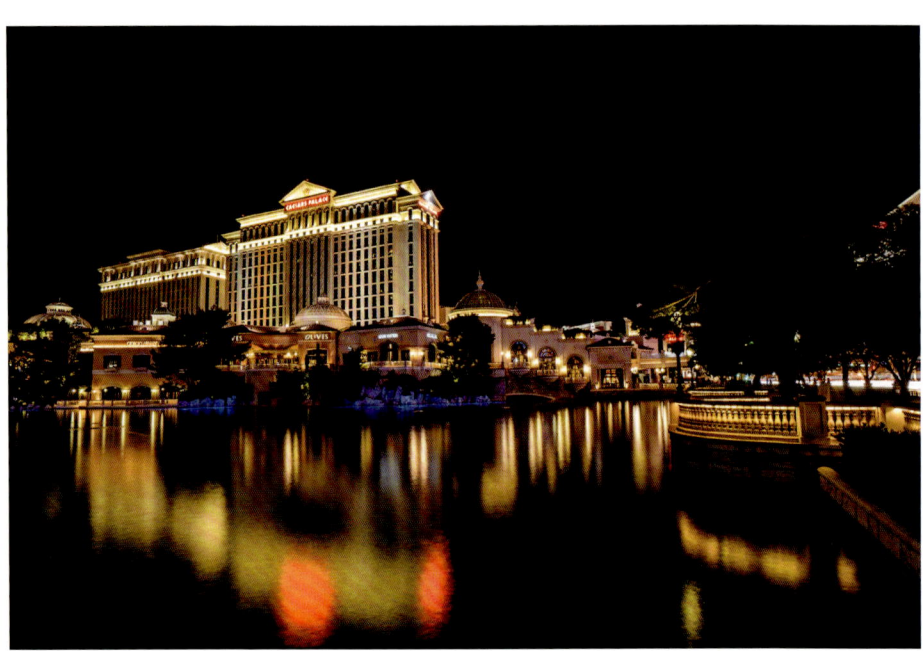

2.1 I used a 30-second shutter speed to make the water look smooth and to get those nice blurred reflections of the light.
ISO 100; 30 sec.; f/18; 20mm

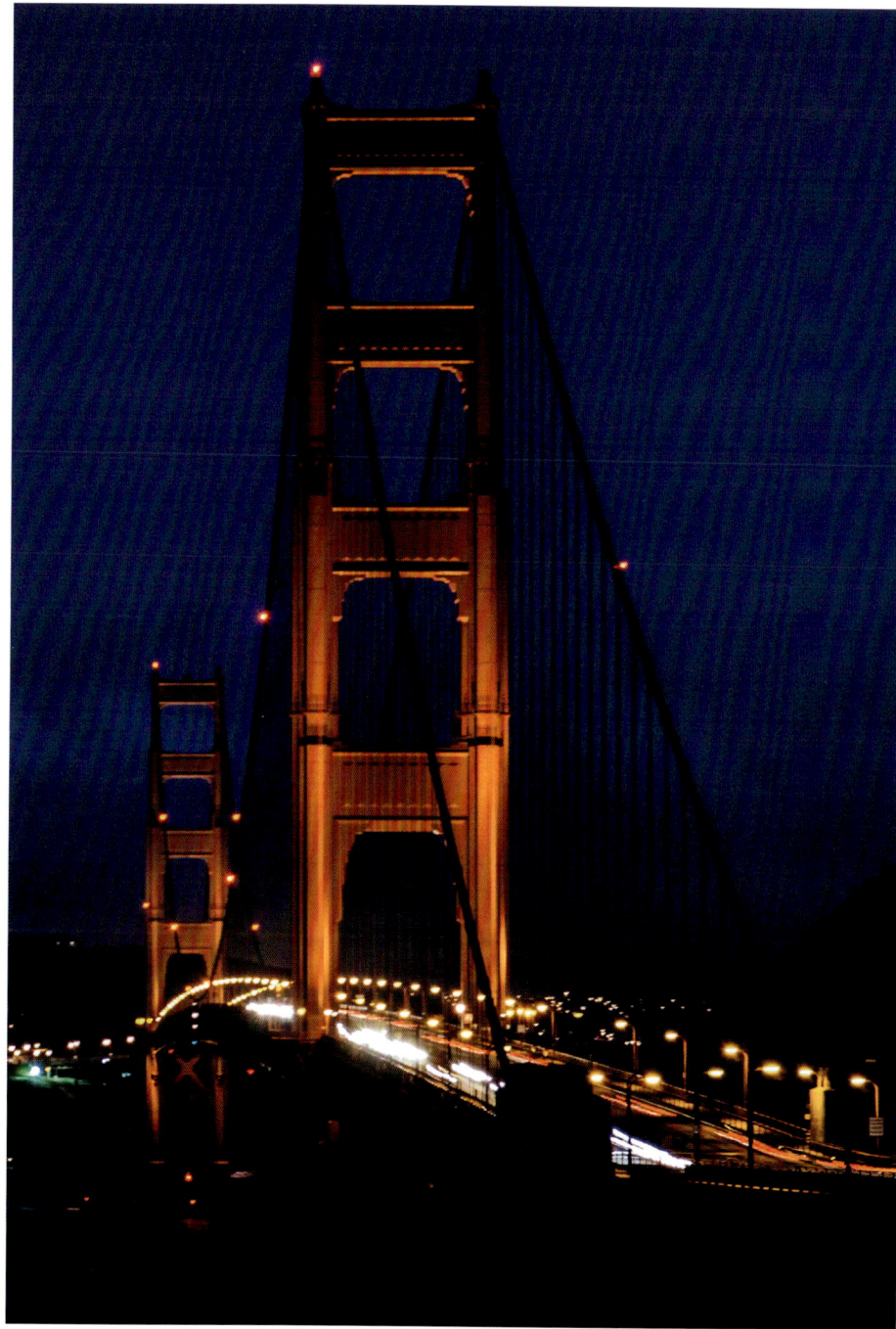

2.2 The lights of the cars driving across the bridge turn into colored streaks when a long shutter speed is used.

ISO 200; 2 sec.; f/5.6; 200mm

3. THE PROS AND CONS OF WIDE APERTURES

THE APERTURE IS the opening in the lens that lets light through to the sensor in the camera. The term aperture is also used to describe the size of the opening in the lens, which is represented by an f/stop number. Since the f/stop is a fraction, the smaller the denominator, the larger the opening, as seen in **Figure 3.1**.

When you're shooting images in low light and need to use a fast shutter speed to freeze the action—at a concert or sporting event, for example—you will want to use as wide of an aperture as possible. For example, I shoot most of my concert photos at f/2.8, which is a very wide aperture.

The aperture also controls the depth of field in an image—that is, how much of the image is in acceptable focus. This is key information to consider because when you shoot using a wide aperture to allow as much light as possible to reach the sensor, the images are going to have a shallow depth of field, meaning much of the background will be blurry. In **Figure 3.2**, you can see that the focus was on the face of the performer and the background (which was pretty close) is blurred.

I photographed the Mythos aerial show in a very dimly lit theater with an aperture of f/2.8 (**Figure 3.3**). This worked to keep the subject in focus, but if you look closely, you can see that his rear foot is blurred because it was further back than the rest of his body.

The downside to using a wide aperture and shallow depth of field is that you have to be very precise when focusing on your main subject because there is no wiggle room. Another issue is that lenses with a wide maximum aperture are expensive. For example, the Nikon 70–200mm f/2.8, a lens I use all the time, costs well over $2,000, while the 70–200mm f/4 costs around $1,400. That's more than $600 for 1 stop of light.

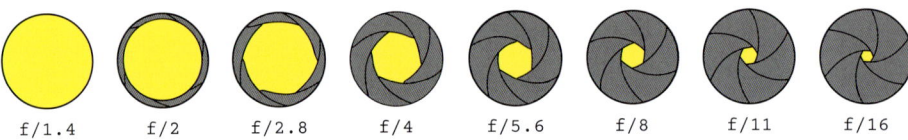

f/1.4   f/2   f/2.8   f/4   f/5.6   f/8   f/11   f/16

3.1 As you can see, the smaller the denominator, the larger the opening in the lens and the more light allowed in.

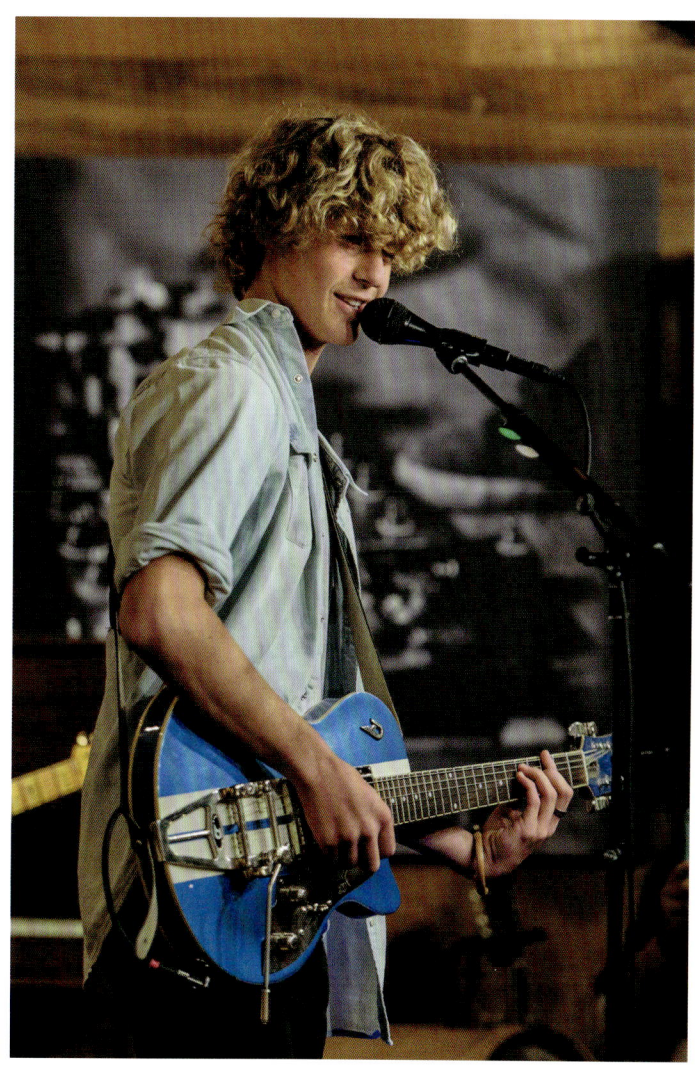

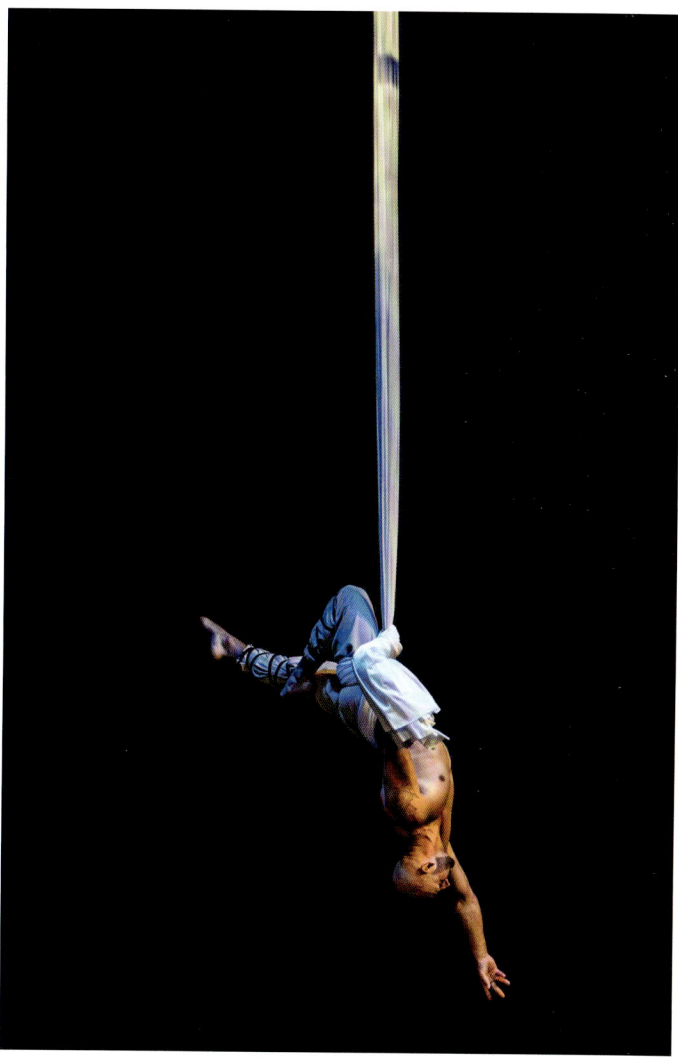

3.2 Cody Lovaas performing at the Bro-Am studio.
ISO 6400; 1/160 sec.; f/2.8; 125mm

3.3 The Mythos aerial show used low lighting to set the mood, which made it very difficult to photograph.
ISO 3200; 1/400 sec.; f/2.8; 70mm

4. USE THE ISO TO YOUR ADVANTAGE

THE ISO SETTING determines how sensitive the sensor in the camera acts. Since the actual sensitivity of the sensor doesn't change, the ISO really adjusts how the information from the sensor is amplified. The more amplification, the less light is needed. The downside to this is that when you raise the ISO there is more digital noise introduced into the image.

The good news for photographers who shoot at night or in low light is that camera manufacturers have made advances in reducing the amount of noise introduced into images by the use of high ISOs. The Nikon D750 allows me to use ISO settings that are much higher than what I could use with my first digital cameras. I routinely photograph sporting events and concerts at ISO 3200 and 6400 without even worrying about noise. As you can see in **Figure 4.1**, even at ISO 6400 there is very little noise, so I was able to use a high enough shutter speed to freeze the action.

There is a common belief among photographers that you have to use the lowest ISO possible to avoid digital noise at all costs. The reality is that the noise is usually not even noticed by people looking at the photo as long as the photo is interesting. Be brave, push that ISO.

I shot **Figure 4.2** at night and there was very little light, so I used ISO 6400 and f/2.8 just to get a shutter speed of 1/200 second. This worked fine when the players were swimming, but when the action increased, the shutter speed was not fast enough to freeze the action (**Figure 4.3**). If I could do it over, I would have pushed the ISO even higher to freeze the action and avoid the blur.

Even when it seems like there is enough light to capture a good photograph—in the early evening, for example—you may still need to rely on a higher ISO to get a fast enough shutter speed to freeze the action (**Figure 4.4**).

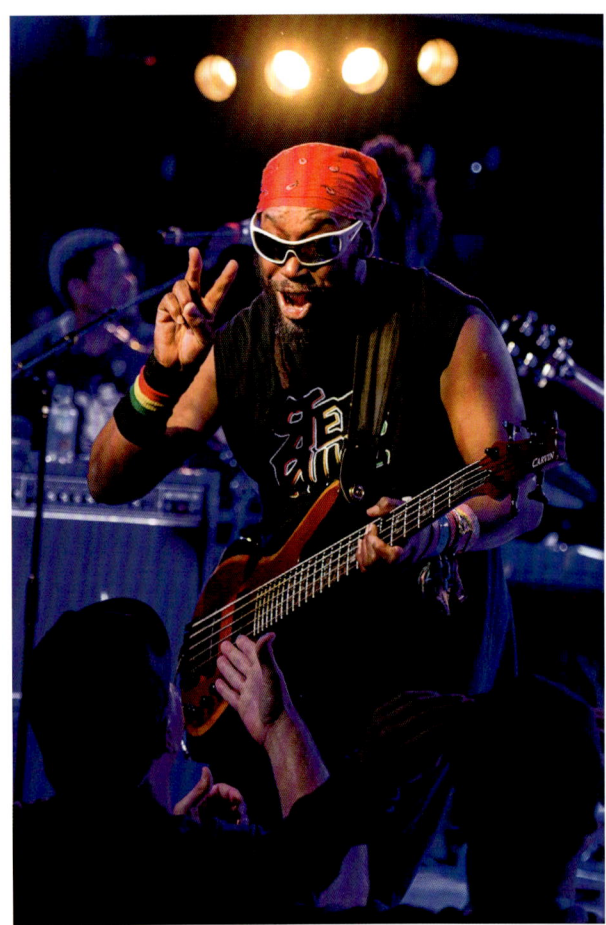

4.1 Shooting a concert often means using a high ISO to allow for a shutter speed that is fast enough to freeze the action.
ISO 6400; 1/250 sec.; f/2.8; 200mm

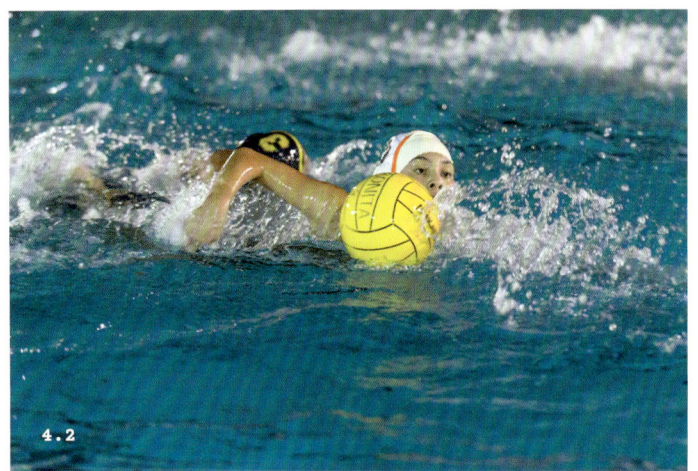

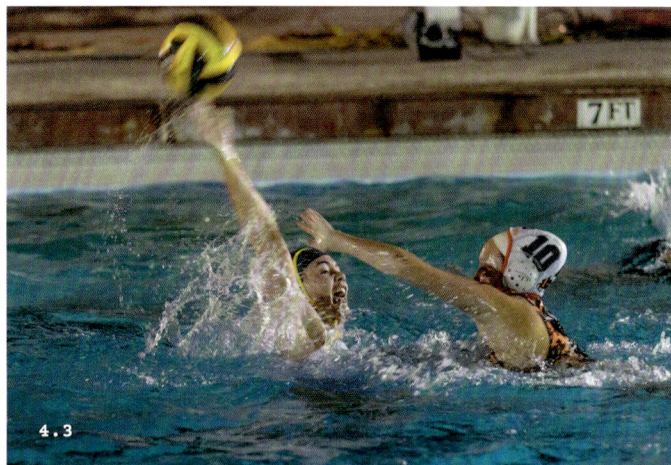

4.2 An ISO of 6400 and a shutter speed of 1/200 second worked fine when the players were swimming with the ball.
ISO 6400; 1/200 sec.; f/2.8; 200mm

4.3 When the action increased, ISO 6400 was not high enough to allow me to use action-freezing shutter speeds and the movement became a blur.
ISO 6400; 1/200 sec.; f/2.8; 200mm

4.4 It might seem like there is a lot of light at an early-evening horse race, but to freeze the horses I needed to use a shutter speed of 1/800, which meant I had to bump the ISO up to 1600.
ISO 1600; 1/1800 sec.; f/2.8; 200mm

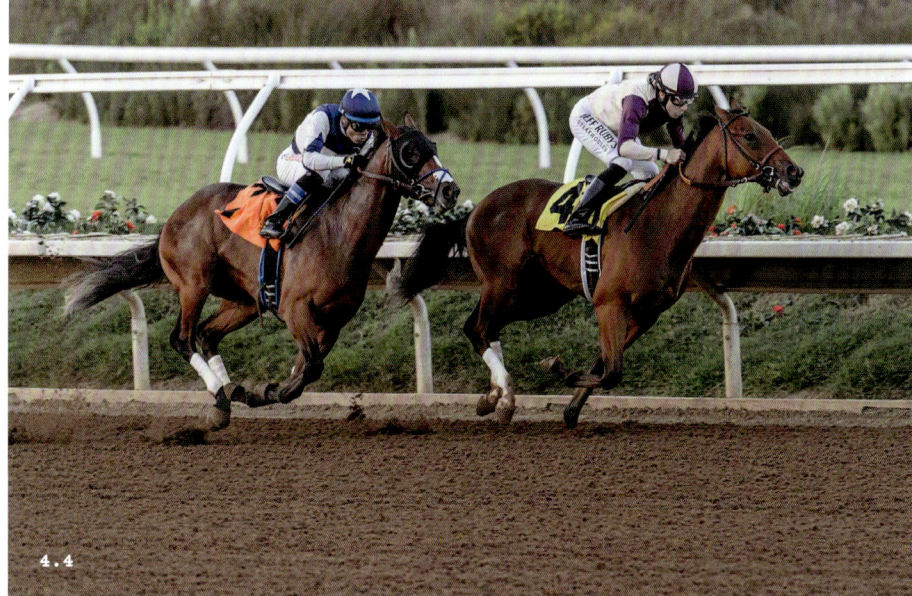

5. WHY EQUIVALENT EXPOSURES ARE IMPORTANT

THERE ARE THREE SETTINGS that allow you to adjust the exposure: shutter speed, aperture, and ISO. The combination of these three settings is what creates the exposure. To understand the idea behind equivalent exposures we need to quantify the amount of light that reaches the sensor and understand how that is determined by the relationship between the three exposure settings.

The unit of measurement used to describe the amount of light reaching the sensor is called a stop. When you double the size of the aperture and let in twice as much light, you are letting in an additional 1 stop of light. When you increase the shutter speed and halve the amount of light reaching the sensor, you decrease the amount of light by 1 stop. The same is true of the ISO; when you reduce the ISO from ISO 400 to ISO 200, you need twice as much light, or 1 stop of light more. A difference of 1 stop of light when adjusting the shutter speed is the same as 1 stop of light when adjusting the aperture or ISO. This allows you to create equivalent exposures, which is when the overall exposure is the same but the settings are different.

Figures 5.1 and **5.2** show the same scene captured with vastly different exposure settings, but the exposure is the same for both.

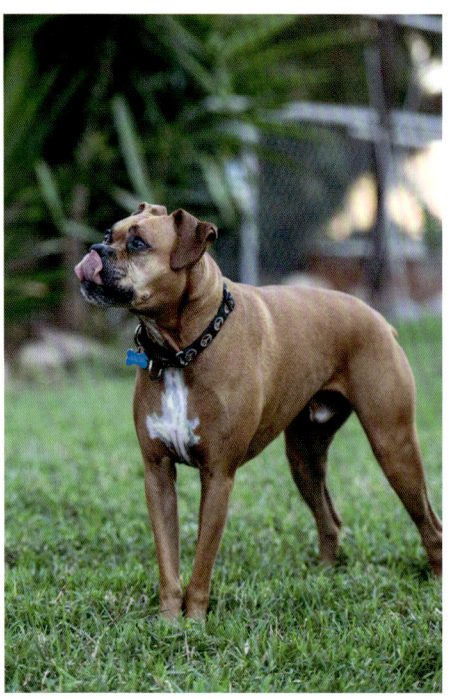

5.1 Using a wide aperture creates a very shallow depth of field.
ISO 400; 1/250 sec.; f/2.8; 24mm

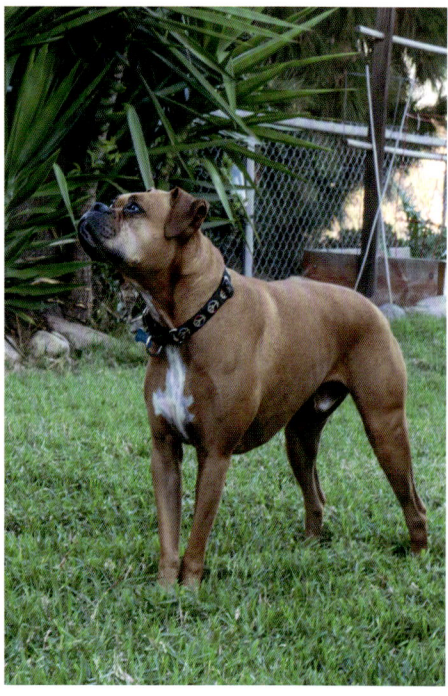

5.2 The equivalent exposure allows me to use a slower shutter speed and a deeper depth of field.
ISO 400; 1/8 sec.; f/16; 24mm

Knowing how to shoot equivalent exposures is important when it comes to photographing night and low-light scenes with long shutter speeds. You can start by shooting the scene with a much shorter shutter speed, a higher ISO, and a wider aperture. Then you can calculate what shutter speed to use when you use a lower ISO and smaller aperture.

Let's walk through the math to see how this works. To capture **Figure 5.3**, I used an ISO of 6400, an aperture of f/2.8, and a shutter speed of 1/15 second, which resulted in a properly exposed image. But as you can see, the water is not smooth and the depth of field is very shallow. To fix these issues, I needed to use a smaller aperture and a longer shutter speed.

I reduced the ISO from 6400 to 100, which is a difference of six stops of light (6400 to 3200 to 1600 to 800 to 400 to 200 to 100). This meant I had to adjust the shutter speed and aperture by a total of six stops to get back to the proper exposure. To increase the depth of field, I closed the aperture down from f/2.8 to f/5.6, which is two full stops of light (f/2.8 to f/4.0 to f/5.6). Then I adjusted the shutter speed by four stops of light, increasing the amount of time the shutter was open from 1/15 sec to 1/8 sec to 1/4 sec to 1/2 sec. The resulting image in **Figure 5.4** has the same exposure as **Figure 5.3**, but I used very different settings.

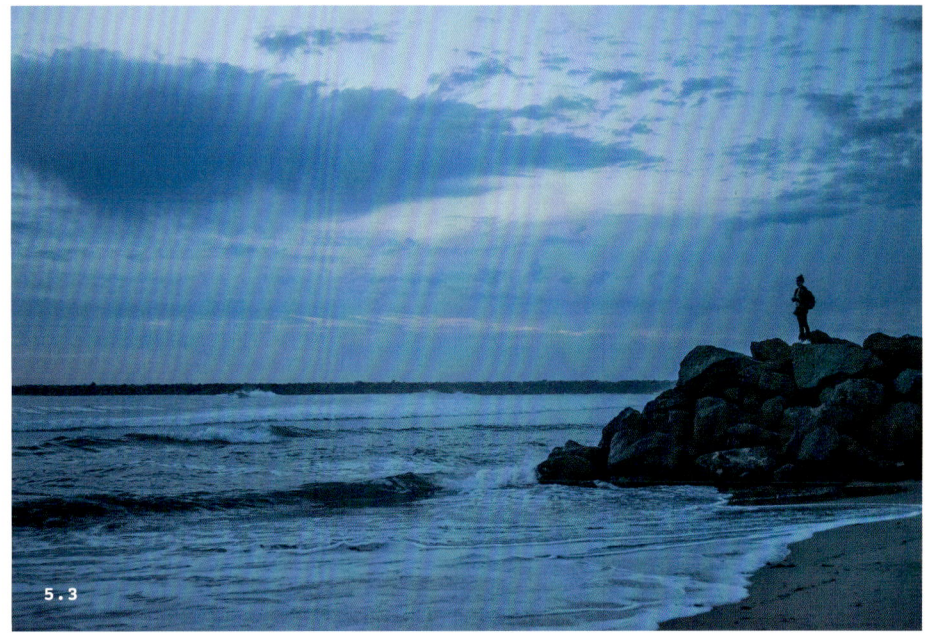

5.3

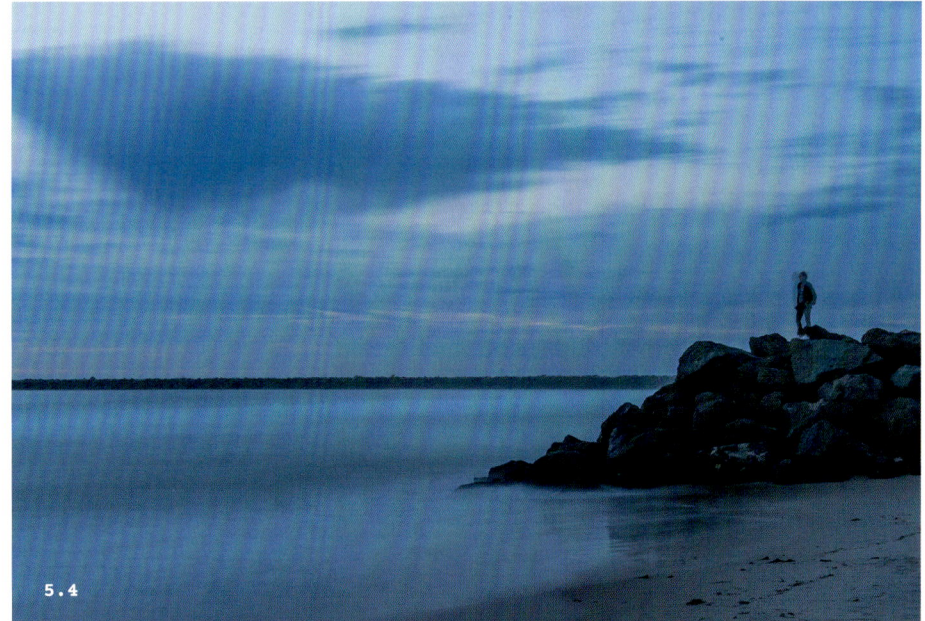

5.4

5.3 The exposure settings here result in a properly exposed image, but this isn't the look I wanted to capture.
ISO 6400; 1/15 sec.; f/2.8; 24mm

5.4 By working out the equivalent exposure settings, I was able to capture a properly exposed image and the look is closer to what I wanted.
ISO 100; 1/2 sec.; f/5.6; 24mm

To make your life easier, here is a chart that shows the full, half, and third stops for shutter speed, aperture, and ISO.

Shutter speed

Full Stop	Half Stop	Third Stop
1/8000		1/6400
	1/6000	1/5000
1/4000		1/3200
	1/3000	1/2500
1/2000		1/1600
	1/1500	1/1250
1/1000		1/800
	1/750	1/640
1/500		1/400
	1/350	1/320
1/250		1/200
	1/180	1/160
1/125		1/100
	1/90	1/80
1/60		1/50
	1/45	1/40
1/30		1/25
	1/20	1/20
1/15		1/13
	1/10	1/10
1/8		1/6
	1/6	1/5
1/4		1/3
	1/3	1/2.5
1/2		1/1.6
	1/1.5	1/1.3
1 sec.		1.3 sec.
	1.5 sec.	1.6 sec.
2 sec.		2.5 sec.
	3 sec.	3 sec.
4 sec.		5 sec.
	6 sec.	6 sec.
8 sec.		10 sec.
	10 sec.	13 sec.
15 sec.		20 sec.
	20 sec.	25 sec.
30 sec.		

Aperture

Full Stop	Half Stop	Third Stop
f/1.0		f/1.1
	f/1.2	f/1.2
f/1.4		f/1.6
	f/1.7	f/1.8
f/2.0		f/2.2
	f/2.4	f/2.4
f/2.8		f/3.2
	f/3.3	f/3.5
f/4.0		f/4.5
	f/4.8	f/5.0
f/5.6		f/6.3
	f/6.7	f/7.1
f/8.0		f/9.0
	f/9.5	f/10
f/11		f/13
	f/13	f/14
f/16		f/18
	f/19	f/20
f/22		f/25
	f/27	f/29
f/32		

ISO

Full Stop	Half Stop	Third Stop
100		125
	140	160
200		250
	280	320
400		500
	560	640
800		1000
	1100	1250
1600		2000
	2200	2500
3200		4000
	4500	5000
6400		8000
	9000	10000
12800		

6. ADD SOME LIGHT WHEN YOU NEED TO

SHOOTING LOW-LIGHT IMAGES doesn't mean you can't add some light when you need to. The key is to know what type of light to add and how much so that you don't ruin the low-light look of your images. This is especially true for portraits shot in low light where you want to shine a little light onto the subject. In **Figures 6.1** and **6.2** you can see the difference it made when I added a touch of light to my portrait of Sam. In this case, I used an off-camera flash with a softbox.

We'll cover photographing portraits in low light in more detail in chapter 3.

Share Your Best Low-Light Image!

Once you've captured your best low-light image, share it with the Enthusiast's Guide community! Follow *@EnthusiastsGuides* and post your image to Instagram with the hashtag *#EGLowLight.* Don't forget that you can also search that same hashtag to view all the posts and be inspired by what others are shooting.

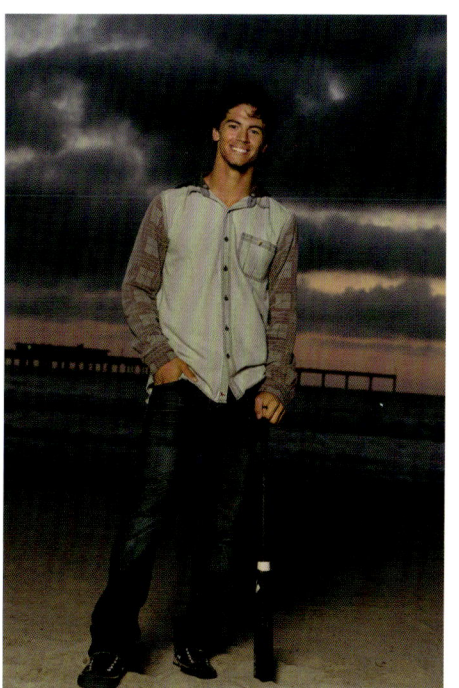

6.1 I shot this portrait of Sam at the beach a few minutes after the sun set.
ISO 800; 1/200 sec.; f/6.3; 70mm

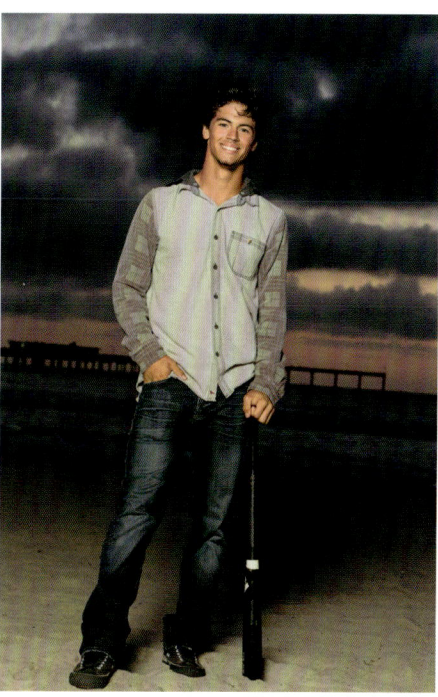

6.2 By adding just a touch of light, I got a better portrait.
ISO 800; 1/200 sec.; f/6.3; 70mm

YOUR CAMERA HAS at least four exposure modes that control how the shutter speed, aperture, and ISO are set. Three of these modes rely on the built-in light meter to look at the scene in front of the camera and determine the best settings. The fourth mode allows you to put in any settings you see fit. Let's take a closer look at the four main exposure modes—Program Auto, Shutter Speed Priority, Aperture Priority, and Manual—and see why Manual mode is my favorite. Most cameras have a dial that allows you to pick the exposure mode (**Figure 7.1**).

Program Auto Mode

When you use the Program Auto mode the camera uses the information from the built-in light meter to set the shutter speed and aperture for you. This mode gives the camera total control

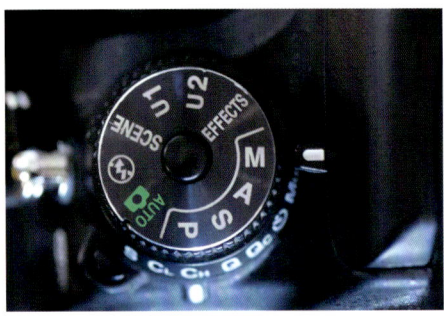

7.1 The exposure mode dial on my Nikon D750. Just turn the dial to pick the exposure mode you want to use. For me, that's usually Manual mode for low-light photography.

of the exposure and can reduce the best DSLR to an expensive point-and-shoot camera. If you use this mode to photograph at night or in low light, the resulting image will most likely be overexposed and blurry. For **Figure 7.2**, the camera was set to Program Auto with an ISO of 800. As you can see, the resulting image is too light and the shutter speed was too slow to freeze any action.

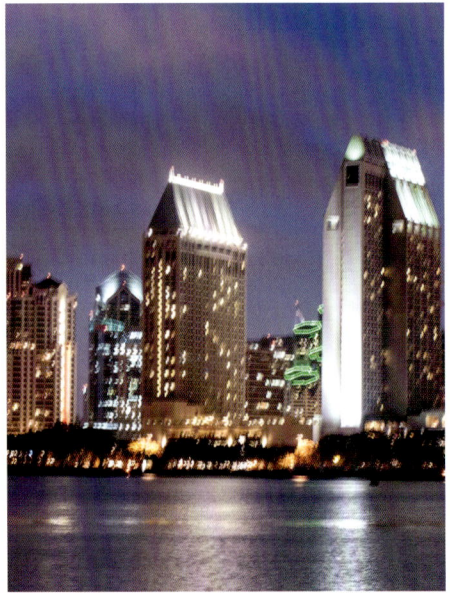

7.2 Using the Program Auto mode resulted in a slow shutter speed, making it impossible to keep the camera steady. The resulting image is both blurry and overexposed.
ISO 800; 2 sec.; f/5.6; 70mm

Shutter Speed Priority Mode

In Shutter Speed Priority mode, the photographer sets the shutter speed and the camera sets the aperture based on the shutter speed and information from the built-in light meter. This mode gives you a lot more control over how the subjects in your image are captured, but it still gives the camera the final say in determining the exposure. An important thing to note about this mode is that the camera can't use just any aperture; it is limited by the maximum aperture of the lens. For example, if you're shooting in a low-light situation and want to freeze the action by using a shutter speed of 1/250 second at ISO 800, then the camera will pick the widest possible aperture. With the 70–200mm f/2.8 lens, that would be f/2.8, but with the 28–300mm f/3.5-5.6 lens, it would be f/5.6 at 300mm. Chances are, that would create a image that is too dark. We will discuss more about lenses, focal lengths, and apertures in chapter 2.

Aperture Priority Mode

In Aperture Priority mode, the photographer sets the aperture and the camera sets the shutter speed based on the aperture and information from the built-in light meter. This gives you creative control over the depth of field in the image. You also have some control over the shutter speed because as you use wider apertures, you will end up with faster shutter speeds. Keep in mind that the maximum aperture is determined by which lens you're using.

Aperture Priority is a very popular exposure mode and it can give you great results if you understand how it works and pay attention to the information from the camera meter.

Manual Mode

In Manual mode, the photographer sets both the shutter speed and the aperture. The camera doesn't get to set anything, but it will show you whether the image will be over- or underexposed and to what degree. You should become comfortable shooting in Manual mode. If you aren't there yet, hopefully this section will get you started.

Manual mode gives you total control over the exposure process and the camera will not change anything. I shot most of the images in this book using Manual mode. It is the mode I use the most, especially when it comes to low-light images.

When you're using Manual mode, a quick and easy way to determine which shutter speed and aperture settings to use is to put your camera in Aperture Priority mode to get a good starting point. Then you can switch back to Manual mode, input the settings you got by using Aperture Priority mode, and adjust the exposure without the camera doing anything to thwart you. As you go through this book, especially the sections in chapters 3 and 5, you will see how I come up with my settings for Manual mode.

In **Figure 7.3** you can see a fast-moving subject—a football player running with the ball—photographed at night under stadium lights. Those lights are not as bright as you would think, and this image would have been overexposed and blurry if I hadn't used Manual mode. **Figure 7.4** shows a scene in which the lights of the city are really bright, but the background is dark, so the exposure settings could vary greatly depending on what area the camera uses to measure the light.

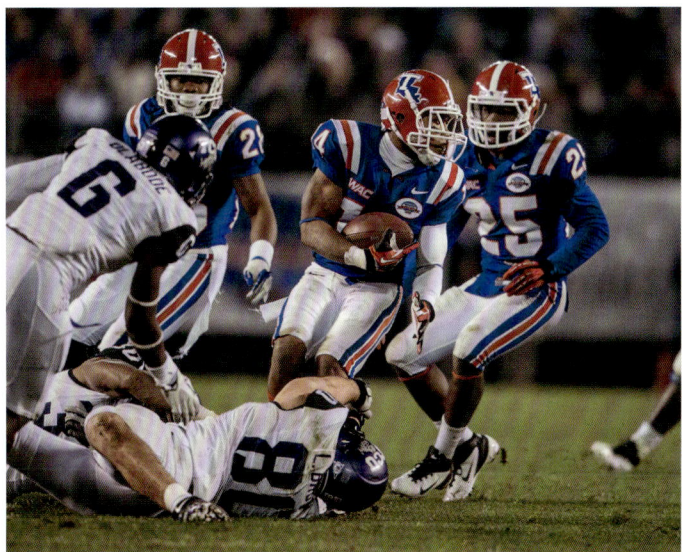

7.3 Sports photography requires the use of a fast shutter speed and high ISO.
ISO 3200; 1/1600; f/2.8; 400mm

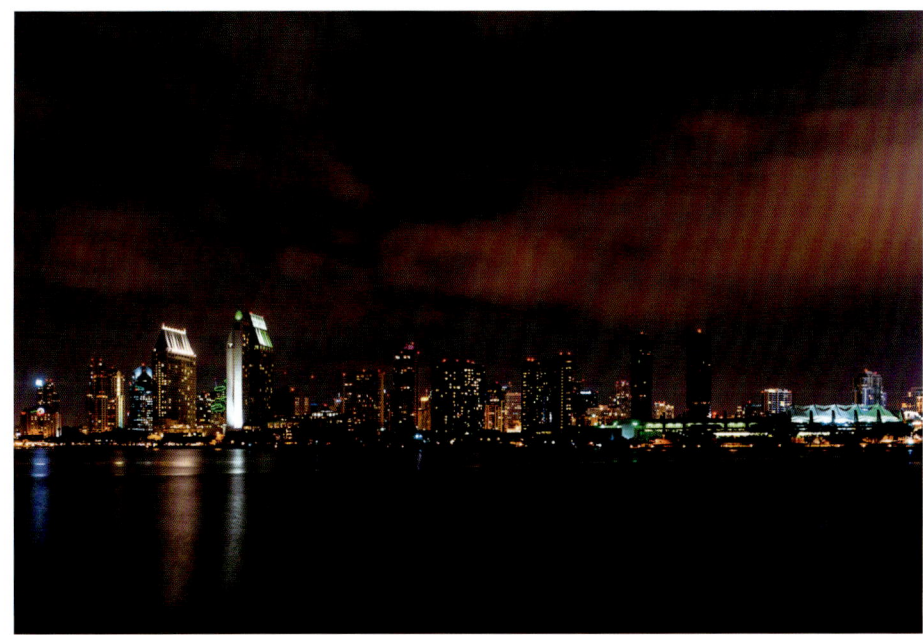

7.4 This image of the San Diego nighttime skyline captures both the dark sky and bright city lights. Using Manual mode allowed me to fine-tune the exposure without having to rely on a single spot in the image for metering.
ISO 400; 2 sec.; f/11; 24mm

Exposure Compensation

There is one more exposure control on your camera that needs to be discussed before we go any further, and that is exposure compensation. Exposure compensation allows you to use the automatic exposure modes and then tell the camera how much to over- or underexpose the image. This gives you just a tad more creative control over the automatic modes.

Exposure compensation is pretty easy to use; you just press the exposure compensation button and dial in either positive or negative compensation, usually in a range from –5 to +5 stops. When you select a positive number, the camera allows in more light, and with a negative number, the camera allows in less light. In **Figure 7.5** you can see that I have dialed in –3 exposure compensation. This setting reduces the amount of light let into the camera by three stops. You can see the difference this makes in **Figures 7.6** and **7.7**.

Exposure compensation is important for night and low-light photography. When you use an automatic exposure mode like Aperture Priority mode, the built-in light meter looks at all the dark tones in the night sky and tends to overexpose the image. Exposure compensation allows you to force the camera to use a shutter speed that lets in less light.

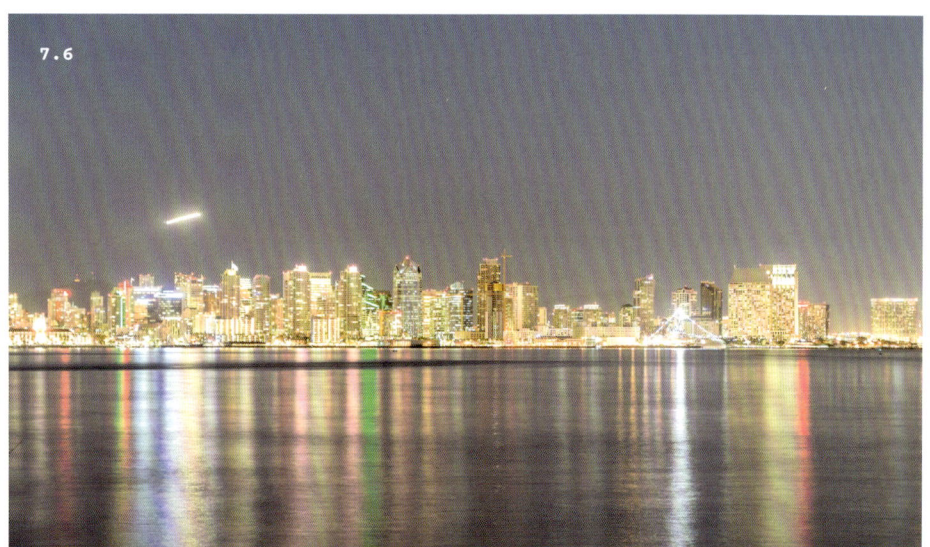

7.6

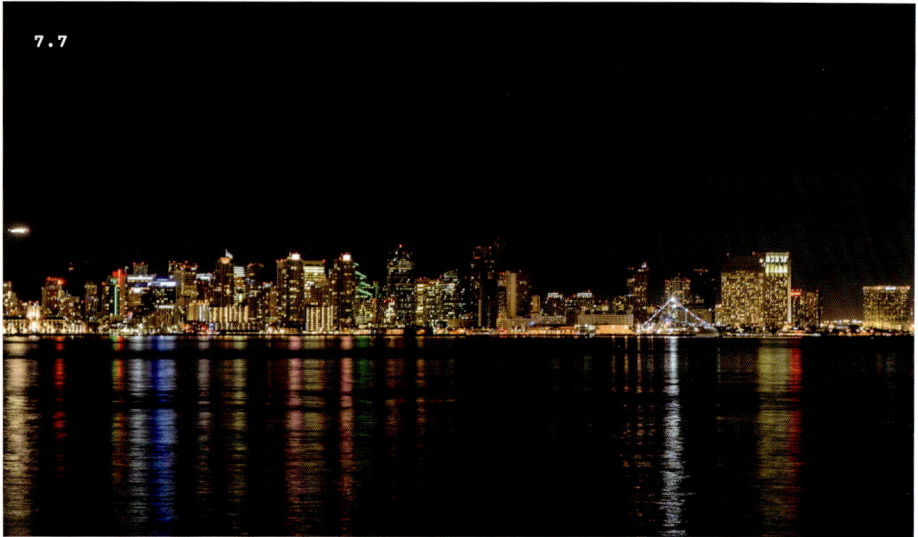

7.7

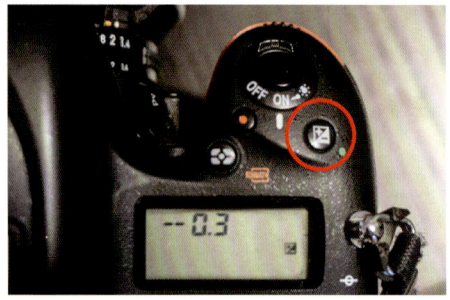

7.5 The exposure compensation button on the D750 with a setting of –3 exposure.

7.6 I shot this photo of downtown San Diego using Aperture Priority mode, which resulted in an overexposed image.
ISO 200; 15 sec.; f/4.0; 70mm

7.7 With –3 exposure compensation dialed in, the image looks a lot more like the scene in front of the camera. Since I was using Aperture Priority mode, the camera adjusted the shutter speed by three full stops.
ISO 200; 2 sec.; f/4.0; 70mm

8. SOMETIMES THE BUILT-IN LIGHT METER LIES

YOUR CAMERA HAS a built-in light meter that measures the light in the scene so that the camera knows what settings to use to create a proper exposure. The meter reads the brightness of the light reflected off the objects in the scene, and then, depending on the exposure mode you use, sets the shutter speed or aperture, or both.

The camera looks at the scene and averages the bright and dark areas to a neutral tone. This works great if the scene doesn't have huge areas of black or white. You can check this out easily by just taking a photo of a white piece of paper or a black piece of paper. The image of the white piece of paper will look gray and underexposed, and the photo of the black piece of paper will look gray and overexposed. You can see how an image that is mostly black, like an image of the night sky, will fool the built-in light meter.

Let's look at the different metering modes and how each one looks at the scene in different ways. Most cameras have three different metering (light measuring) modes: Spot, Center-Weighted, and Matrix or Evaluative.

Spot Metering

When you use the Spot metering mode, the camera only looks at a small part of the whole scene. This small area is usually right in the center of the frame, but some camera models tie the Spot metering area to the focus point, allowing you to measure the light at the same spot on which you are focusing.

This is the mode I use the most when I'm photographing concerts because it ignores the background and just measures the light on the subject. In **Figure 8.1**, you can see how much of the scene the Spot meter covers. The vast dark areas behind the performer are not taken into account when the camera reads the light from the scene.

Center-Weighted Metering

The Center-Weighted metering mode looks at the center portion of the frame and ignores the edges of the frame. Many camera models allow you to adjust the size of the center area. In **Figure 8.2**, you can see the area measured by the Center-Weighted meter. This mode works great if the subject in the middle of the frame is not too light or too dark.

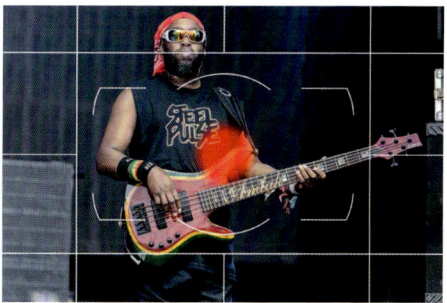

8.1 The red area is the portion of the scene that the Spot meter looks at to determine the correct exposure setting for the image. The meter ignores the rest of the scene.

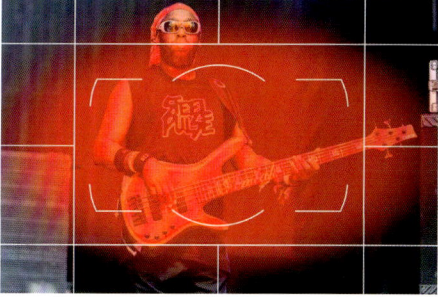

8.2 The red area is the portion of the scene that the Center-Weighted meter looks at.

Matrix or Evaluative Metering

The Matrix (Nikon) or Evaluative (Canon) metering mode looks at the whole scene in front of the camera and tries to determine what you are photographing and the proper exposure.

This metering mode works well for most situations. The camera breaks the whole scene into parts, and then checks the values of each part and how they are mapped against a database to determine the subject matter and proper exposure. Some cameras even have facial recognition software, so the camera can adjust the exposure if it thinks you are photographing people. This is very impressive technology that can result in well-exposed images. In **Figure 8.3**, you can see how the camera looks at the whole frame rather than just parts of the frame.

Metering Doesn't Always Work

When you're photographing subjects in low light, the metering system can easily be fooled, resulting in images that are not properly exposed. This happens because the built-in light meter wants to create a neutral gray average, which means that scenes with lots of black will be overexposed.

For example, **Figure 8.4** shows an image that I took using Aperture Priority mode and Matrix metering. As you can see, the image is way too bright and it does not accurately portray the scene. **Figure 8.5** is the same scene, but this time I used Manual mode, and instead of letting the camera pick the exposure settings, I picked the settings and purposely underexposed the image by three full stops.

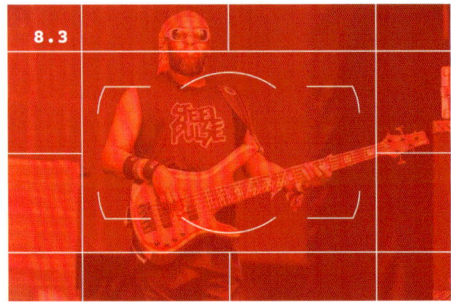

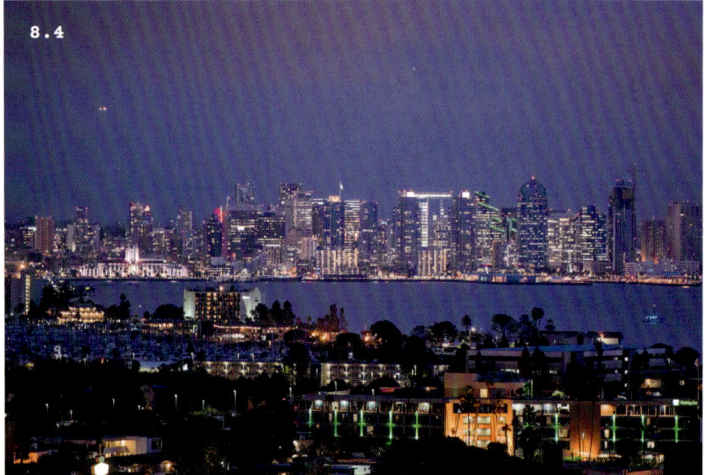

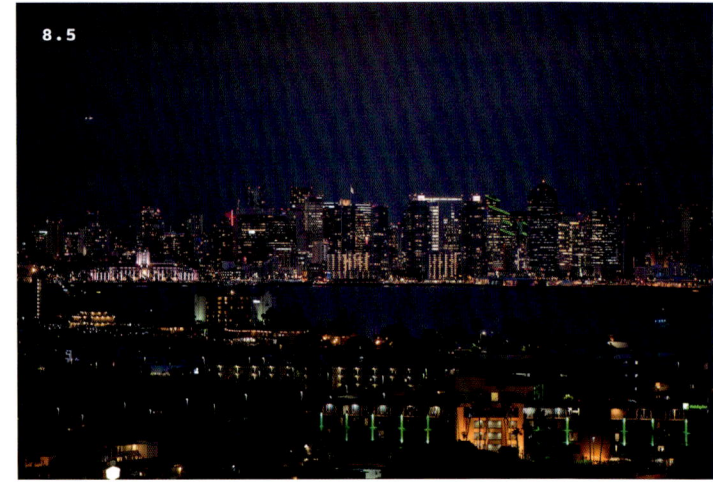

8.3 The red area is the portion of the scene that the Matrix or Evaluative meter looks at.

8.4 This image is overexposed because the camera saw all that dark sky and tried to make it an average gray.

8.5 I used Manual mode to photograph the same scene and adjusted the exposure settings to make the image look more like the scene in front of the camera.

9. HOW TO FOCUS IN LOW LIGHT

ONE OF THE MOST DIFFICULT things to master when photographing in low light is achieving proper focus. For autofocus to work properly, there needs to be enough light for the camera to "see" the subject, and there needs to be contrast in the scene so the focusing system has something to work with. The good news is that there are ways to help the autofocus system, and you can always use Manual focus for situations that are too difficult for the autofocus system.

The first and easiest solution is to use a separate light to help the focus work. Many cameras have a focus assist lamp that illuminates the subject when you press the shutter release button halfway down (**Figure 9.1**). This provides enough light for the autofocus system to establish focus before you take the photo. This works great for static subjects that are close to the camera and in situations where the light isn't going to disrupt anyone else, like when you're shooting portraits or still life subjects. This does not work for subjects like sports, concerts, weddings, and the like. Check your user's manual to see if your camera has this feature and how to turn it on or off.

If the built-in assist light doesn't do the job, you can always use a flashlight to help illuminate the subject so you can focus before taking the photo. If you use a flashlight, you need to make sure that you turn the flashlight off before you take the photo because the color of the light produced by the flashlight can adversely affect the image color. You also need to make sure that neither the subject nor the camera moves before taking the photo, since this will cause the focus to be off and will result in a blurry image. This last tip is the most important: you need to turn the autofocus off after you have adjusted the focus so that the camera doesn't try to refocus when you take the image. I used a flashlight to focus on the model in **Figure 9.2**, which turned out blurry because the camera hadn't locked focus before I took the image. You can see the light from the flashlight on her face. Once I had achieved focus, I switched to Manual focus mode and shot **Figure 9.3**.

The second method for getting better autofocus results in low light is to know which of the autofocus sensors are the cross-type sensors and to use those, if possible. Check your user's manual for information on the autofocus sensors in your camera. If you are having issues figuring out which ones are the cross-type sensors, use the ones in the middle of the frame; chances are, they will be the more accurate type. In **Figure 9.4**, you can see which of the autofocus points in the Nikon D4 are cross-type sensors (more accurate).

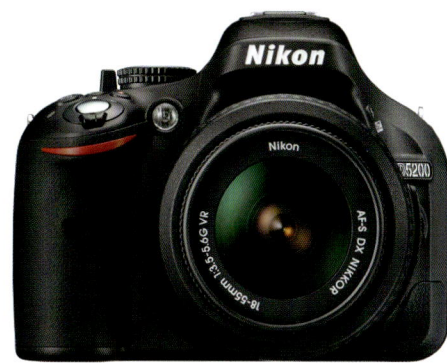

9.1 The focus assist lamp on the Nikon D5200 can be turned on or off in the Custom Setting Menu (A9).

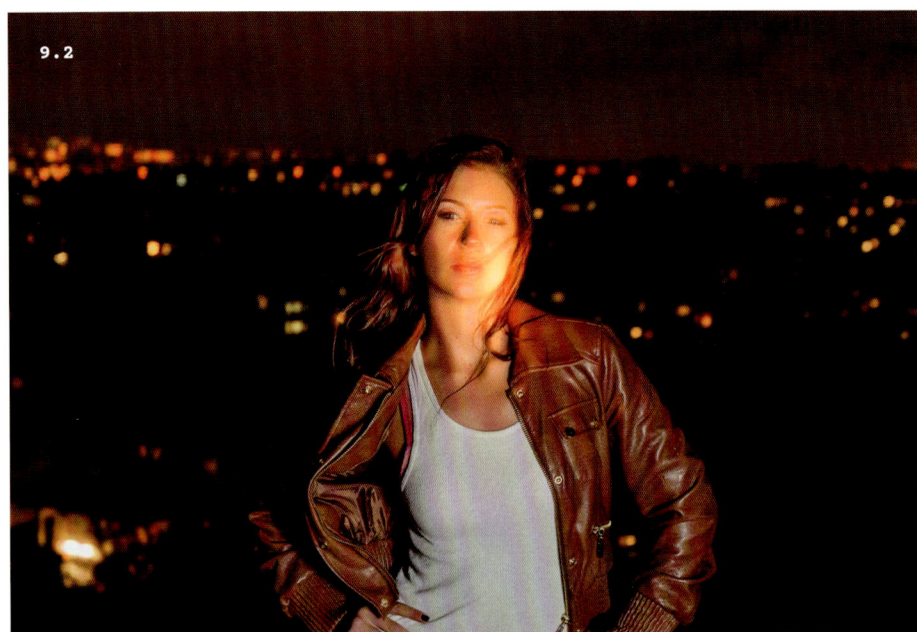

9.2

9.2 I illuminated the model with a flashlight so the autofocus could work. This photo was taken while the flashlight was still on, so you can see the brighter light right on her face.
ISO 200; 1/4 sec.; f/5.0; 50mm

9.3 For this photo, I used an off-camera flash to freeze the model in place and a slower shutter speed so that the background lights could be seen.
ISO 200; 1/4 sec.; f/5.0; 50mm

9.4 The cross-type autofocus points in the Nikon D4 are shown in red.

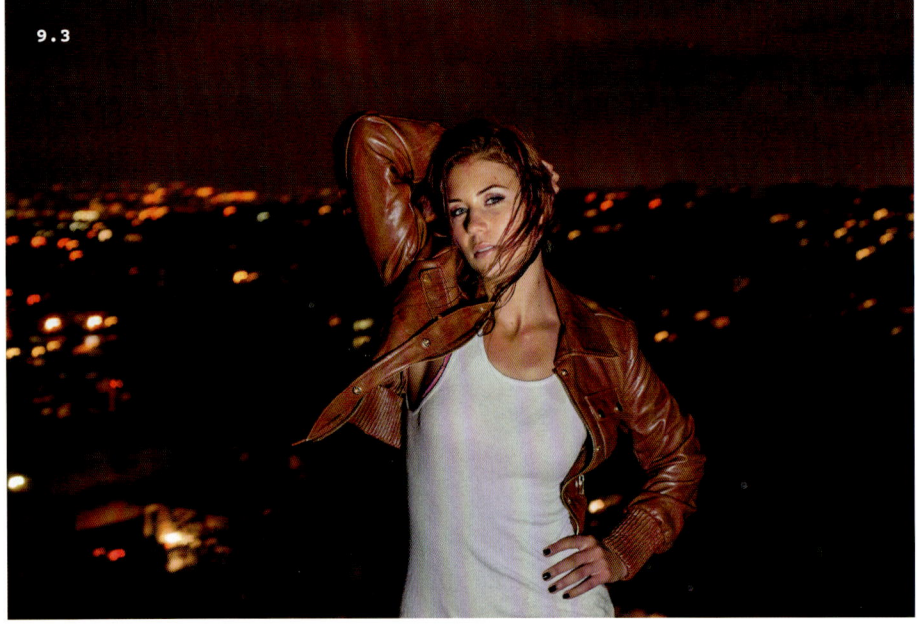

9.3

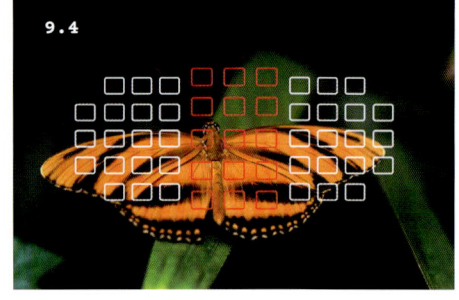

9.4

10. MULTIPLE EXPOSURES CAN SAVE YOUR SHOOT

THERE ARE SITUATIONS where shooting multiple images of the same subject can be really helpful. Many night scenes make great subjects for high dynamic range (HDR) images. You can also reduce noise by stacking images, a technique I'll discuss in chapter 5. These techniques work only with subjects that are not moving because you need to capture multiple images in which the subject is in the same spot.

To create an HDR image, you need to take multiple images of the same subject with different exposures, and then use specialized software to combine the images. **Figures 10.1–10.3** show the three images I used to create the final HDR image in **Figure 10.4**. The first image is underexposed by three stops, the second image is correctly exposed, and the third image is overexposed by two stops. I used Aurora HDR software to combine the three images.

If you want to learn more about multiple exposure photography, I suggest picking up a copy of *The Enthusiast's Guide to Multi-Shot Techniques* (Rocky Nook, 2016).

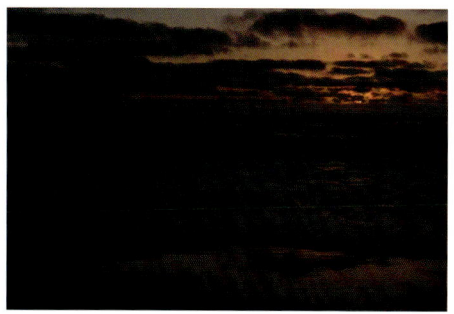

10.1 The underexposed image shows detail in the brightest areas.
ISO 800; 1/4000 sec.; f/8.0; 20mm

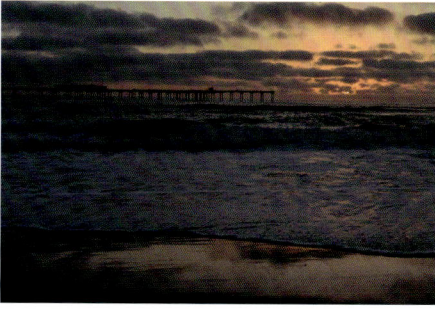

10.2 This is a normal exposure of the same scene.
ISO 800; 1/500 sec.; f/8.0; 20mm

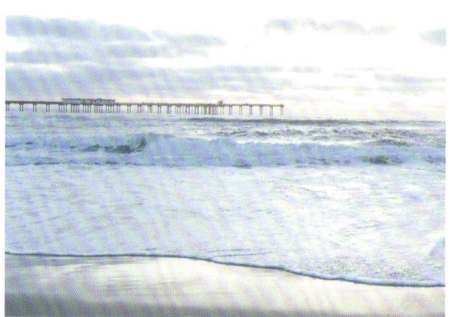

10.3 The overexposed image allowed me to capture detail in the darkest areas.
ISO 400; 1/125 sec.; f/8.0; 20mm

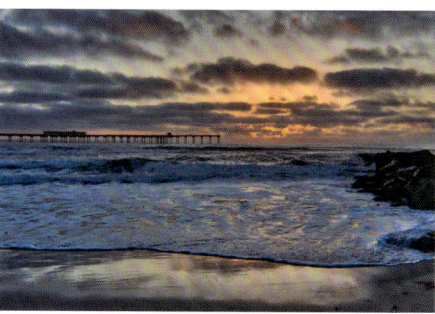

10.4 I combined the three exposures in Aurora HDR to create an image with a larger tonal range.

2

ALL THE GEAR YOU WILL WANT AND NEED

CHAPTER 2

I love cameras, lenses, and all the extra photography gear
that goes along with them, but I am also frugal, so I try
to get the best deal possible. This chapter is all about
the gear you need to shoot both types of low-light images—
the type where you need to freeze the action by using a
high ISO, wide open aperture, and fast shutter speed; and
the type where you capture the scene with a long shutter
speed, lower ISO, and smaller aperture. These two types of
photography require different cameras and lenses. You will
also need tools that allow you to keep the camera steady
during long exposures and trigger the shutter remotely.
This means investing in a tripod or monopod and a remote
trigger or cable release.

11. BASIC CAMERA NEEDS

YOU CAN SHOOT LOW-LIGHT images and get great results with just about any camera on the market today. When it comes to low-light photography, there are a few things that I look for in a camera. Each of these is covered in detail in this chapter, but in terms of a quick overview, you will need a camera that has a Bulb shutter speed mode, an acceptable (to you) level of noise at higher ISOs, and the ability to use a remote trigger or cable release. Some cameras have extra features that can be really fun to use, like in-camera time-lapse and double exposures, but these features are not critical.

If you have not purchased a camera yet, or are considering purchasing a new camera, the biggest choices you are going to face will be whether to get a full-frame or crop-sensor camera and how many megapixels to get.

Full-Frame vs. Crop-Sensor Cameras

Both crop-sensor and full-frame cameras have advantages and disadvantages depending on what you are photographing.

The sensor on a full-frame camera is the same size as a 35mm piece of film, whereas a crop sensor is anything smaller than a 35mm piece of film. In **Figure 11.1**, you can see the difference between the area captured by a full-frame sensor and that captured by a crop sensor when looking at the same scene.

As you can see, the crop-sensor camera records a smaller amount of the scene in front of the camera than the full-frame sensor. Fortunately, we can easily calculate the equivalent focal length by using the lens multiplier of 1.5 × focal length. For example, if you use a 50mm lens on a crop sensor, you would multiply 50 by 1.5, which equals 75. So a 50mm lens on a crop sensor captures the equivalent of a 75mm lens on a full-frame sensor. This works in your favor when you're shooting things that are far away and you need some extra reach. If you use a 70–200mm lens on a crop sensor, you end up with the equivalent of a 105–300mm lens. In **Figures 11.2** and **11.3**, you can see the same scene shot with a full-frame camera and a

crop-sensor camera, respectively. A crop sensor is a huge help when you're shooting subjects that are far away.

The downside to a crop sensor is that when you shoot wide scenic photos, you need to use very wide angle lenses to make up for the crop factor. Camera and lens manufacturers have created lenses specifically for crop-sensor cameras, which are covered in section 16.

Another important factor to consider when discussing the different sensors and their ability to capture images in low light is that full-frame sensors have more physical space for the photo-receptors, allowing for more space in between them, which can result in less digital noise. This means that cameras with full-frame sensors may do better in low light, especially when you're taking action shots and need to use high ISOs. This is not as true now as it once was, especially with newer cameras like the Nikon D500, but the image quality you get from full-frame sensors is still considered better than that of crop sensors.

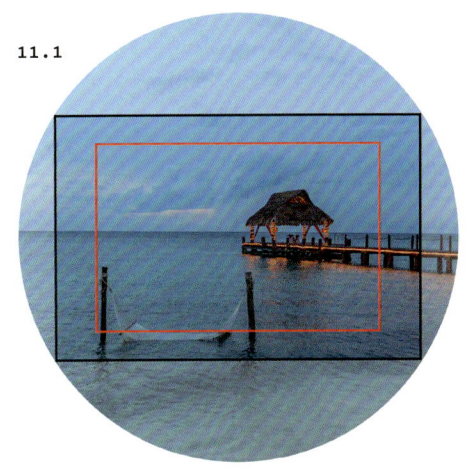

11.1

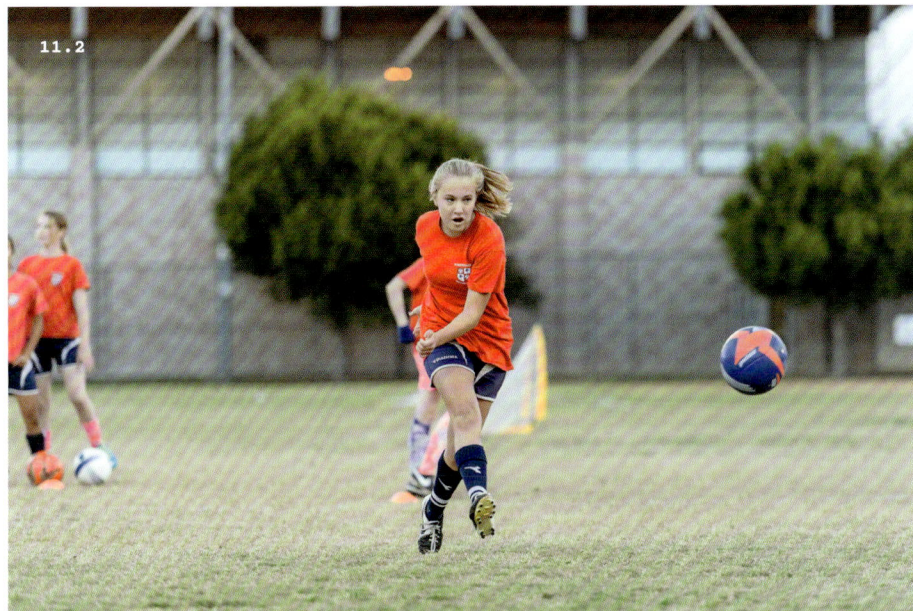

11.2

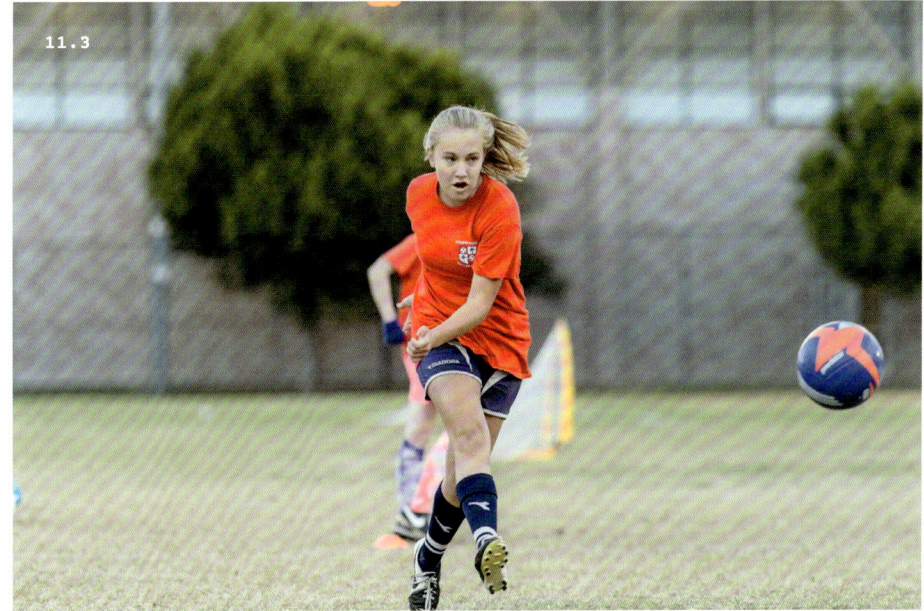

11.3

11.1 The black rectangle represents the area captured by a full-frame sensor. The red rectangle shows the area captured by a crop sensor.

11.2 Photographing soccer is tough because even if you can get on the sidelines, the action can still happen quite far away. I took this image with my full-frame Nikon D750 and 70-200mm f/2.8 lens at 200mm. **ISO 3200; 1/2500 sec.; f/2.8; 200mm**

11.3 The same scene shot with a crop-sensor camera like the Nikon D500 would result in this image. An effective focal length of 300mm gets you closer to the action.

There is one final difference between full-frame and crop-sensor cameras and that is the price. Full-frame cameras cost more than crop-sensor cameras. For example, the top-end crop sensor in the Nikon line right now is the D500 and it retails for roughly $2,000, whereas the top-end full-frame camera, the D5, retails for $6,500. At the time of writing, you can get a full-frame camera like the Nikon D750 for less than $2,000, and the consumer-level crop-sensor camera is well under $1,000.

What Are Megapixels How Many Do You (Really) Need?

A megapixel is 1,048,576 pixels, or roughly 1 million pixels. The maximum image size a camera sensor can capture is described in megapixels. If you know the height and width in pixels of your camera and multiply them together, then you know how many megapixels your camera can capture (or you can just read the marketing materials). Megapixels are great for marketing cameras because they can be compared easily—for example, this camera is a 12-megapixel camera whereas this other camera is a 24-megapixel camera, so the second one must be better, right? Not so fast.

When digital cameras first became widely available, they didn't have the resolution that is readily available today. It wasn't odd to see professional digital cameras with less resolution than current smartphones. For example, the Nikon D2H DSLR was a 4.1-megapixel camera. The iPhone 7 has a 12-megapixel camera and a 7-megapixel camera.

For many years, it seemed like camera manufacturers just kept increasing the number of megapixels in cameras, but it isn't the number of megapixels that matters, rather it is the quality of those pixels. Many of those cameras just crammed megapixels onto the sensor, which actually lowered the image quality even as it increased the number of megapixels. This increase directly affected images taken in low light, especially those shot at high ISOs, because when individual sensor pixels are packed in close to one another more noise is captured.

Now you can get cameras that range from 16 megapixels to more than 50 megapixels and they all produce files that can be blown up to epic proportions. In **Figure 11.4**, you can see me standing in front of one of my concert images that was printed 22 feet wide by 12 feet tall. The original image was taken with a Nikon D4, which has a 16.2-megapixel sensor.

When it comes to deciding how many megapixels you need, you need to look at how many photos you plan on taking and what you are planning to do with them. I photograph a lot of events and take a huge number of images. For example, I photographed a live music event that resulted in over 5,000 images. I use two cameras, one that has 24.3-megapixel sensor and another that has a 16.2-megapixel sensor, which gives me enough information to create huge prints and also allows me to crop images when I need to. If you shoot landscapes or portraits and only take a few hundred images at a time, then using a camera with more megapixels might be great for you.

When you're looking for a camera, I suggest you skip the high-megapixel hype and instead look at the marketing images that show the camera's ability to shoot sports or weddings in low light.

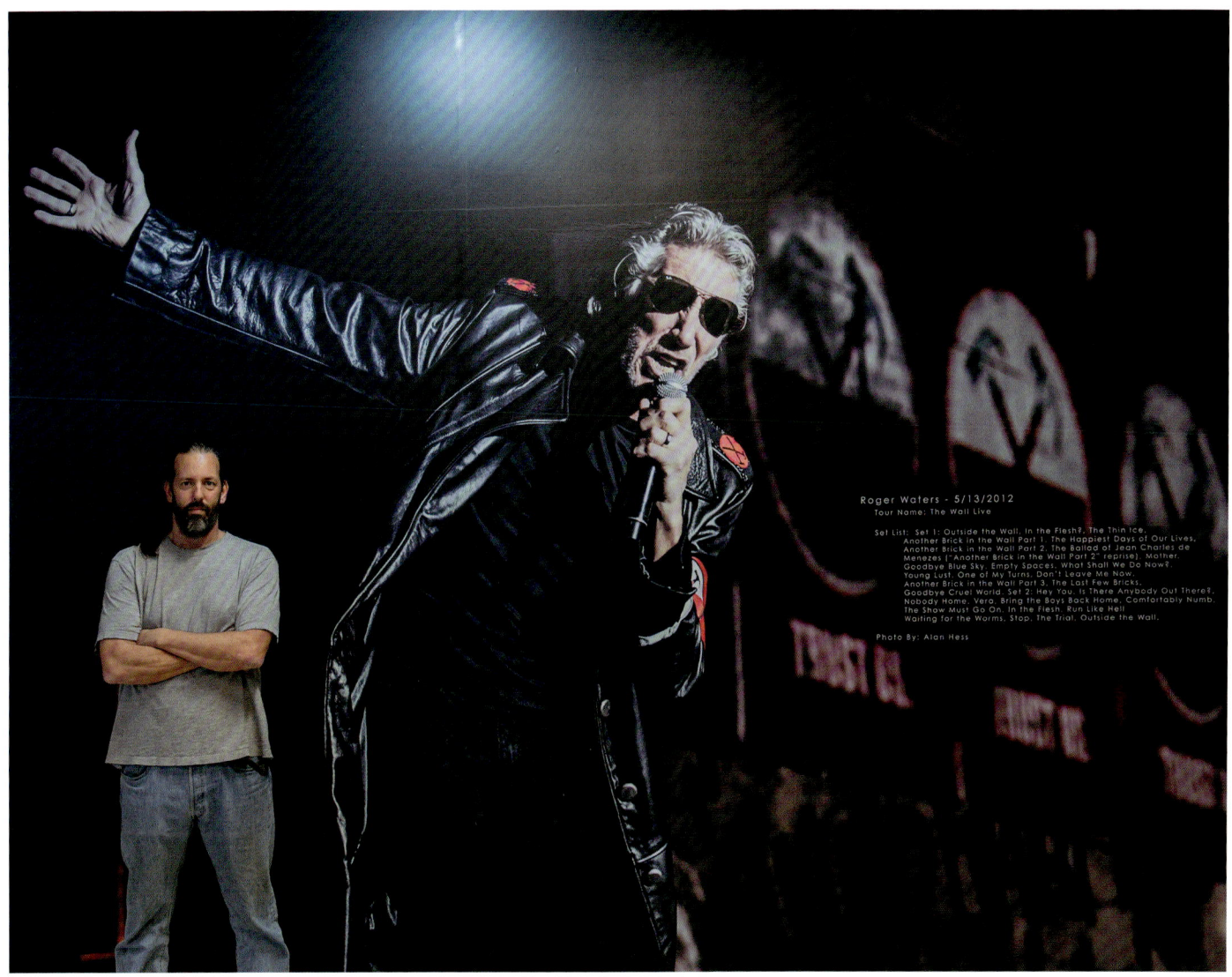

11.4 The 16.2-megapixel sensor in the Nikon D4 provided enough resolution to print this image 22 feet wide by 12 feet tall.

Frames per Second and Autofocus Points

There are some other camera features that you should at least know and understand because they can affect how you use your camera. If you're shooting sports and action, the camera's frame rate (frames per second, or FPS) and buffer size can have a large impact on how you shoot. The higher the frame rate, the more images you can take in a row. This can be especially important when you're shooting action in low light because the light can change in a second. A higher FPS allows you to take more shots in a row, increasing your odds of capturing just the right moment. In **Figures 11.5**, you can see a sequence of images I shot within a 1-second timeframe. I usually shoot in sequences of 3–6 frames, which makes capturing the height of the action easier. This allows me to capture the action and pick the best image later.

You can find the frame rate in the marketing materials for each camera, but the buffer size is much harder to find because camera manufacturers don't usually disclose this information.

The buffer is the internal memory space where the camera stores information until it is written to the memory card. The bigger the buffer, the more images you can take in a row. I have two suggestions regarding buffer size. If you're planning on buying a new camera, I suggest renting each camera you're considering and trying it out before you buy it to see how it works for you. I also suggest using memory cards with the fastest possible write speeds so that the camera can empty its buffer as quickly as possible.

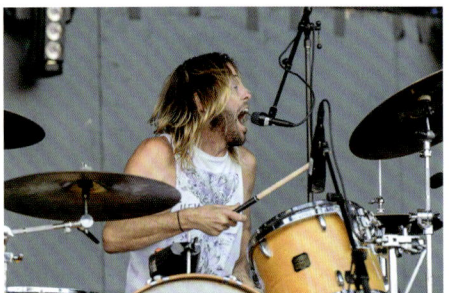
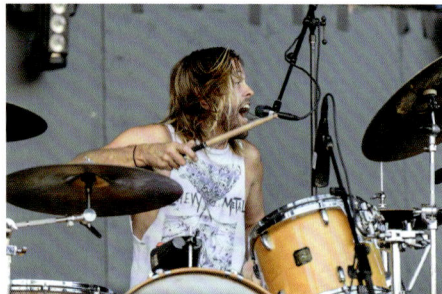
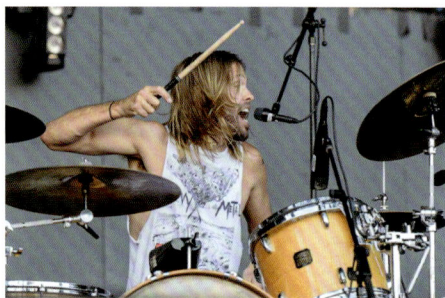
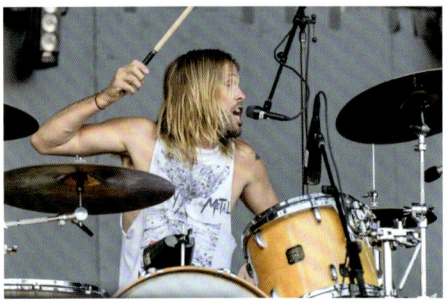
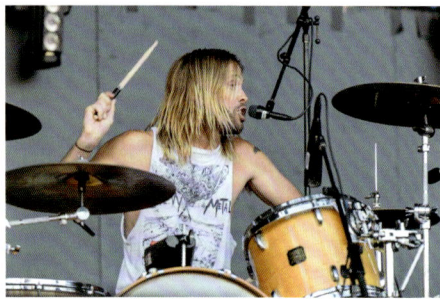
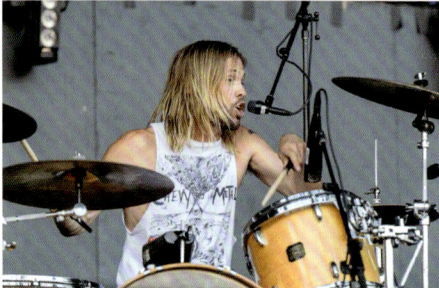

11.5 Drummer Taylor Hawkins performs during a Chevy Metal concert.
ISO 1600; 1/500 sec.; f/2.8; 200mm

Another factor to look at is the number, location, and type of autofocus points in the camera. Many cameras now have a large number of focus points—some have over 100—allowing you to fine-tune the spot in the frame where you want to focus. You can see how the focus points are spread out on the Nikon D500 and the Canon 5D Mark IV in **Figures 11.6** and **11.7**.

The focus points can also help you achieve better focus in low light. There are two different types of focus points: regular points that use either a horizontal or vertical sensor, and cross-type points that use both. Cross-type points are more sensitive and allow you to focus in lower light. Some cameras have a focus assist lamp that temporarily illuminates the scene before the image is taken to help the camera focus. This works well for portraits and static subjects that are close to the camera, but it won't work when you're shooting sports or fast-moving subjects.

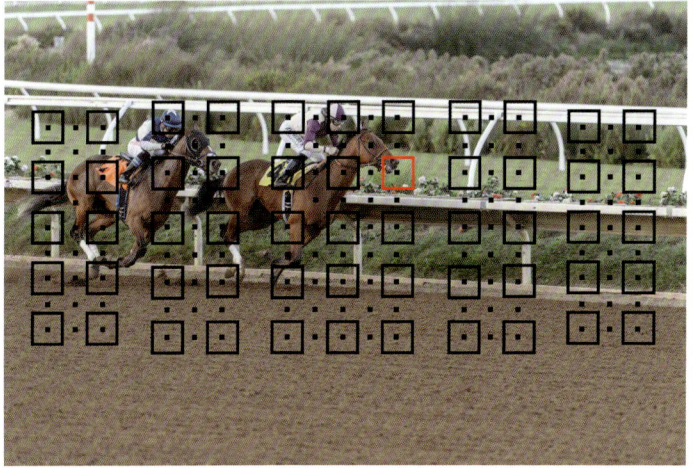

11.6 The focus points in the Nikon D500

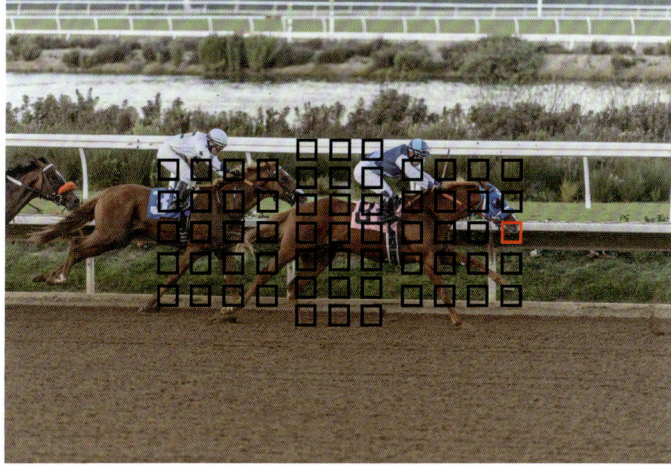

11.7 The focus points in the Canon 5D Mark IV

12. WHY YOU NEED BULB MODE

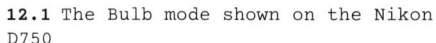

CAMERAS ALLOW YOU TO USE a wide range of shutter speeds from 1/8000 of a second all the way to 30 seconds. But what if you want to use a really long shutter speed, like 10 minutes or longer? This is where the Bulb shutter speed setting comes into play. This mode allows you to keep the shutter open for as long as you want. This isn't just a useful setting—it is imperative for those really long exposures (anything over 30 seconds).

You can only access the Bulb mode when the camera is in Manual exposure mode. The other exposure modes either require you to set the shutter speed before taking the picture (Shutter Speed Priority mode) or allow the camera to set the shutter speed (Program Auto and Aperture Priority mode). In the Bulb mode, the camera doesn't know how long you will keep the shutter open because you can close it at any time during the exposure, so it only works in Manual mode.

To get to the Bulb shutter speed setting, you need to go past the 30 second shutter speed until the display shows a B or Bulb, as seen in **Figure 12.1** on the Nikon D750.

In the past, you had to physically hold down the shutter release button for the length of the exposure. As you can imagine, this can really take a toll since sometimes the exposure lasts hours, not seconds, and holding your finger on the shutter release button the entire time is not feasible. This is one reason camera releases are an important piece of equipment.

I still remember my first camera release. It screwed into the top of the shutter release button and when you pressed the plunger on the end of the release, a metal rod extended down and pushed the shutter release. You could lock the release in this position to keep the shutter open as long as you wanted. The more modern releases also allow you to lock the shutter open until you decide to release it. In **Figure 12.2**, you can see the Nikon MC-36 with the lock feature that allows you to keep the shutter open as long as you want when you're using Bulb mode.

The downside to using the Bulb mode is that it can drain the camera battery pretty quickly compared to normal photography. Make sure that your battery is fully charged before going out to shoot long exposures. I always recommend having a second (or even third) fully charged battery with you.

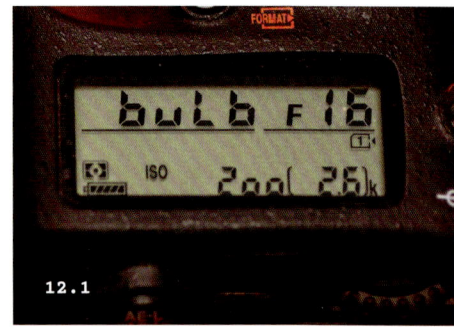

12.1

12.1 The Bulb mode shown on the Nikon D750

12.2 When the lock function on this Nikon MC-36 Multi-Function Remote Cord is engaged, you can see the red area under the remote shutter release button.

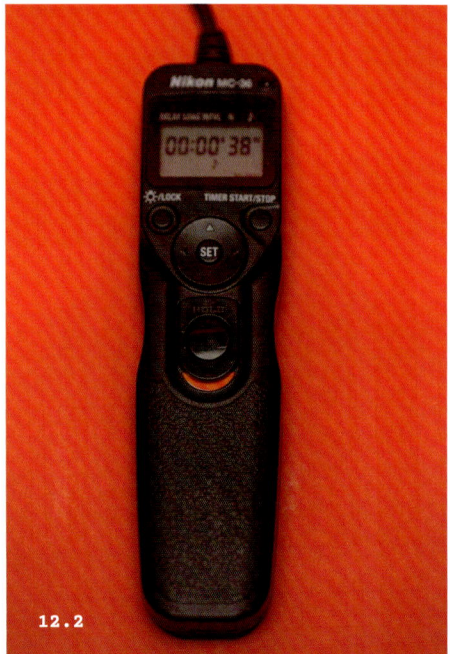

12.2

13. WHAT IS DIGITAL NOISE AND HOW NOISY IS YOUR CAMERA?

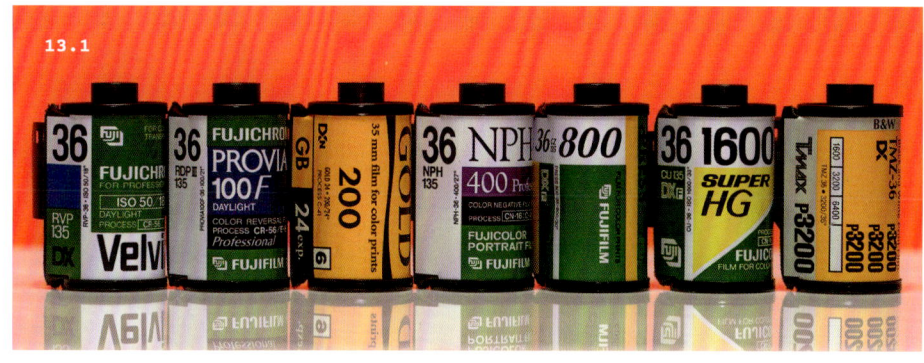

WHEN YOU USE FILM for photography, it's important to know how sensitive the film is to light. The more sensitive the film, the less light needed to create a proper exposure. Photographic film is made up of light-sensitive silver halide particles. The larger the particles, the less light needed and the higher the sensitivity (ISO). The downside to films that have a higher sensitivity is that the larger silver halide particles are visible in the prints created. This is called film grain and it becomes more noticeable in the images as the film sensitivity increases. Each roll of film is labeled with the ISO (**Figure 13.1**), making it easy to pick the appropriate film for any light condition. The problem is you have to shoot the entire roll at the same ISO; you can't change the ISO for each image like you can with digital cameras.

Since digital cameras use a digital sensor to record light, you can't change the actual sensitivity of the sensor, but you can amplify the information that is captured by the sensor. This is how digital cameras mimic the ISO of film. Similar to how higher-sensitivity film produces grain, when the information is amplified by the sensor, digital noise can be introduced into the image. The noise shows up as unwanted spots of color that are especially noticeable in the darker tones of the image. There is visible noise in **Figure 13.2**, for example, because the image was taken at an extremely high ISO of 12800.

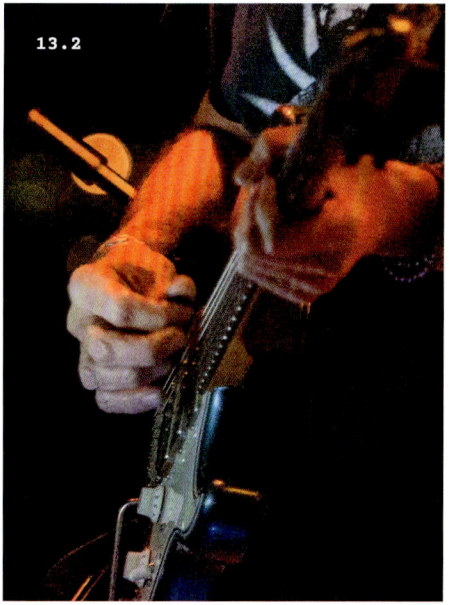

13.1 The light sensitivity of film is described by an ISO number. Each of these rolls of film is twice as sensitive as the film to its left.

13.2 Shooting a concert outdoors under very low light meant using a very high ISO—in this case, ISO 12800—just to get the proper exposure. Most of the light in this image was from the iPad screen and the few LED lights used to illuminate the stage.
ISO 12800; 1/125 sec.; f/2.8; 200mm

The good news is that camera manufacturers have worked really hard to expand the range of ISOs and reduce the noise created at higher settings. I routinely shoot sports and concerts at ISO settings that I never would have attempted just a few years ago. I shot **Figure 13.3** at ISO 1600 and there is practically no noise, especially compared to files I shot at similar ISOs just a few years ago.

It is always a good idea to know how noisy your camera is and how much noise you find acceptable in your images. You can perform the following test to determine how high you can push your camera's ISO.

Start with a fairly dark scene and mount your camera on a tripod so that each image will be the same, allowing for a proper comparison. You also want to make sure that there are some different size objects in the image so that you can look at the detail and how your camera captures it.

Then set the camera to Aperture Priority mode and pick a small aperture like f/8.0 or f/1.6. Set the ISO to 200 and take a photo, then double the ISO and shoot again. Continue shooting at each ISO setting until you reach the highest one. You will now have a set of images like those shown in **Figures 13.4–13.6** where you can see the images taken at ISO 3200, ISO 6400, and ISO 12800.

Chapter 5 covers a variety of different techniques to reduce the noise in your images if needed.

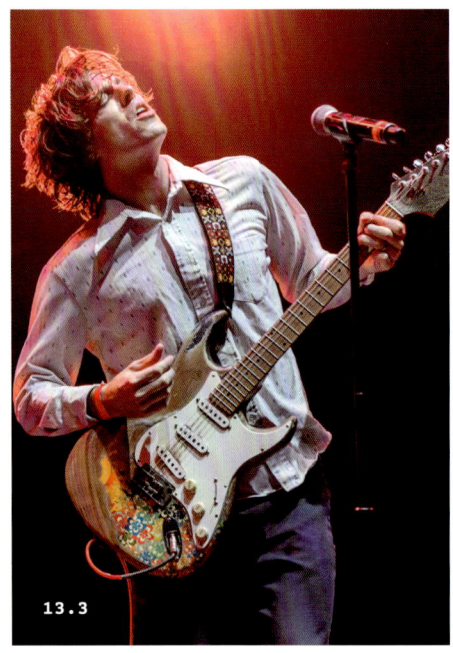

13.3

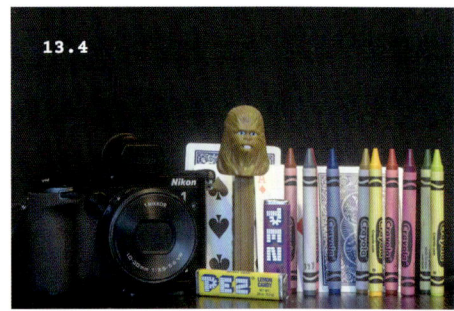

13.4

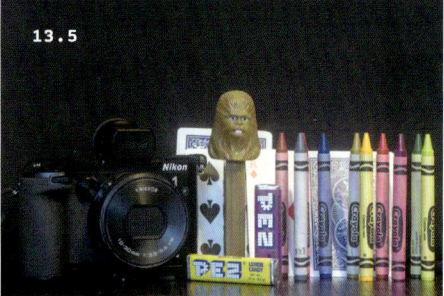

13.5

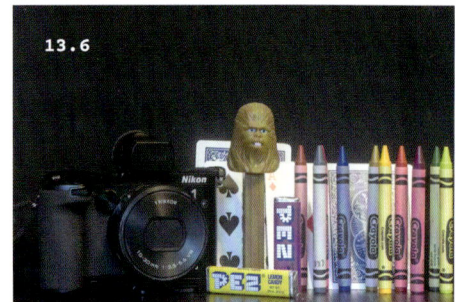

13.6

13.3 Shooting concerts at ISO 1600 is now commonplace, and there is very little noise in this image. Even a high-resolution print like the one in this book won't show any noise. **ISO 1600; 1/250 sec.; f/2.8; 200mm**

13.4 Shooting **ISO 3200; 1/10 sec.; f/16; 105mm**

13.5 Shooting **ISO 6400; 1/20 sec.; f/16; 105mm**

13.6 Shooting **ISO 12800; 1/40 sec.; f/16; 105mm**

14. THE OFTEN-IGNORED SELF-TIMER MODES

YOUR CAMERA HAS a built-in timer designed to allow you to delay the image being taken so that you can run around and get into the photo. Think of it as the first way to take a selfie, but this function can do a lot more for you than just give you time to hop into the picture. By using the self-timer, you give the camera time to settle down after the shutter release button is pressed.

When you use a tripod and a very long shutter speed, it is imperative that the camera does not move at all during an exposure since any movement can cause blurring in the resulting image. Pressing the shutter release button on the camera can cause slight vibrations in the camera at the beginning of the exposure. This can turn a great image into one that is just so-so. The best solution is to use a remote or cable release (as discussed later in this chapter), but you can also use the self-timer mode to reduce the camera movement.

This works for subjects that are not moving because the image is taken a few seconds after you press the shutter release button. The time between when you press the shutter release button and when the shutter is actually moved out of the way allows for any vibrations caused by pushing the button to dissipate.

Figure 14.1 shows the self-timer mode settings on the Nikon D750. You can select a delay of just a couple seconds to the longer 20 seconds. The longer the camera sits and waits after you press the shutter release, the less chance there will be for any camera shake to cause

blurring in your image. In **Figure 14.2**, you can see that the camera was absolutely still during the exposure, making for a razor-sharp image.

14.1 The Nikon D750 self-timer menu allows you to choose from four delay settings.

14.2 I took this photo of the San Diego skyline after dark and used the self-timer mode to make sure the camera was really steady during the exposure.
ISO 200; 8 sec.; f/10; 200mm

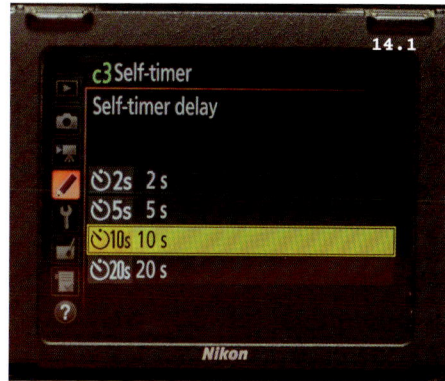

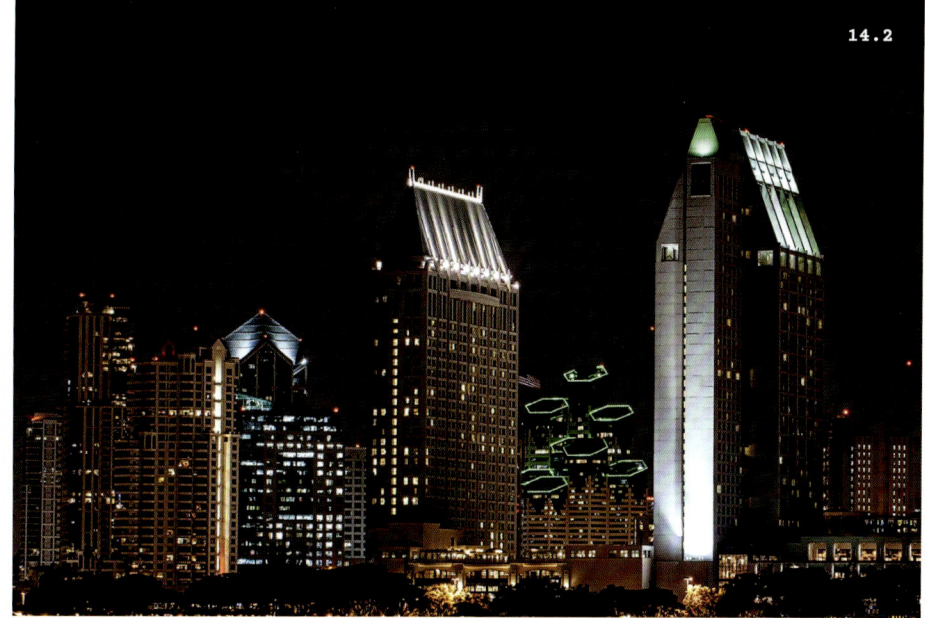

15. IN-CAMERA TIME-LAPSE

CREATING A TIME-LAPSE used to take a lot of work. You had to shoot many individual frames and later combine them all into a movie with special software. Many cameras now allow you to create a time-lapse right in the camera. This makes it a lot easer to experiment with time-lapse photography, especially if you're shooting in low light.

The in-camera time-lapse feature allows you to put in the variables, and then creates the time-lapse movie after the last frame is shot (**Figure 15.1**). For example, if you use a frame rate of 30 FPS and you want to create a 30-second movie, you will have to take 900 frames (30 × 30 = 900). The next step is to figure out how long the event is so you can calculate the interval between frames. If the event you are trying to capture lasts hours, then the interval between each frame will be much longer than if you were shooting an event that only lasted an hour.

Start by converting the length of your event to seconds (e.g., a one-hour event is 3,600 seconds and a four-hour event is 14,400 seconds). To create a 30-second video at 30 FPS documenting a four-hour event, you will need to take 900 frames over a period of 14,400 seconds. That means that you need to take a single frame every 16 seconds. The basic equation for this is:

Length of Event in Seconds ÷ Length of Movie in Frames = Interval Between Frames.

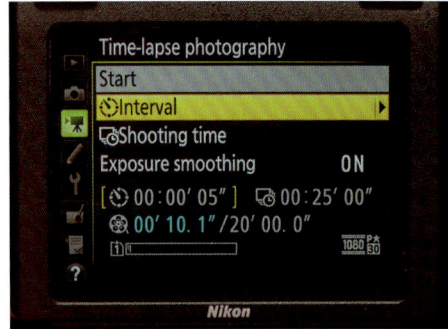

15.1 The Time-lapse photography menu on the Nikon D750 allows you to enter the interval between frames and total shooting time, and then it uses this information to create an in-camera time-lapse movie.

16. LENS CHOICES, OR WHAT'S YOUR FAVORITE FOCAL LENGTH?

MANY CAMERAS come as a single piece with the lens and camera body as one unit. Your smartphone has a built-in lens, or in some cases, two. The real power of DSLR and mirrorless cameras is their ability to utilize different lenses. You can decide if you want to shoot a scene ultra wide or just capture a tiny sliver of it by choosing a specific lens.

The first compositional choice you make, before you even lift the camera to your eye, is what lens you attach to the camera. I have a favorite focal length and I know a lot of other photographers who do, too, but that doesn't mean I don't use any other focal lengths or never change my mind. What it does mean is that I see the world a certain way and want to capture it that way. Your choice might be very different from mine.

The focal length of a lens is the distance (usually measured in mm) between the camera sensor and the lens when the image is in focus. The angle of view is the amount of the area in front of the lens that is captured by the sensor. A lens with a short focal length gives you a wide angle of view and a lens with a long focal length gives you a narrow angle of view. For example, you can see in **Figures 16.1–16.4** that the shorter the focal length (24mm), the more of the scene is captured.

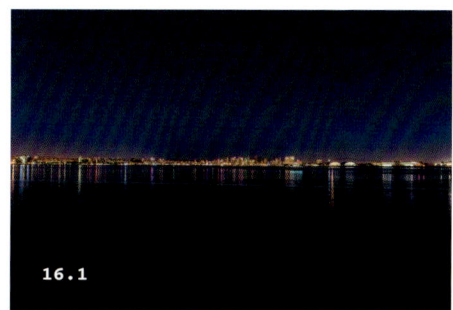

16.1

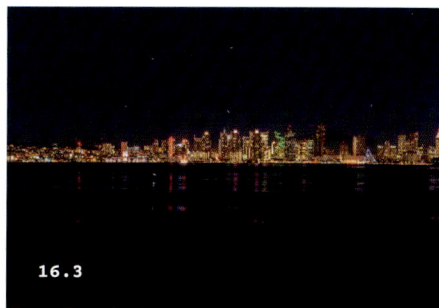

16.3

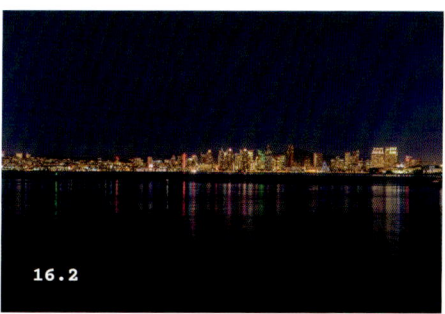

16.2

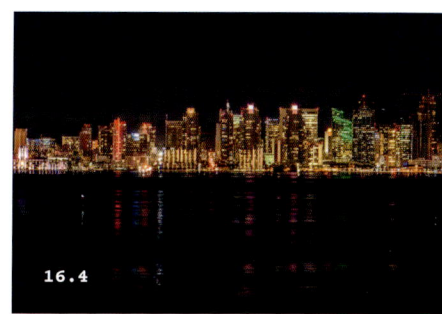

16.4

16.1 The San Diego skyline photographed from Shelter Island at 24mm. **ISO 400; 1/250 sec.; f/5.6; 24mm**

16.2 The San Diego skyline photographed from Shelter Island at 70mm. **ISO 400; 1/250 sec.; f/5.6; 70mm**

16.3 The San Diego skyline photographed from Shelter Island at 100mm. **ISO 400; 1/250 sec.; f/5.6; 100mm**

16.4 The San Diego skyline photographed from Shelter Island at 200mm. **ISO 400; 1/250 sec.; f/5.6; 200mm**

If all your lens choice did was determine how much of the scene is captured, then the choice would be really easy. But the focal length also makes a big difference in how people look in your photos and how much of the background is shown. The longer the focal length, the more the image is compressed, meaning the items in the foreground and background appear closer. Take a look at **Figures 16.5–16.8** and you can see how much of a difference the focal length makes in a portrait. The size of the person stayed the same as I moved further back for each frame, but the way she looks changes drastically.

When you are shooting in low light, the focal length isn't going to make a huge difference, especially if you're using a tripod. But it can make a difference if you are shooting handheld and trying to capture a low-light scene. The rule many photographers follow to get a sharp image without any camera shake is to use a shutter speed that is 1/focal length of the lens. So if you use a 200mm lens, you need a shutter speed of 1/200 second. If you use a 50mm lens, your shutter speed should be 1/50 second. This could change which lens you reach for when you are looking at the scene you want to photograph. If you need to use a slower shutter speed to let in enough light, you'll want to use a shorter focal length.

Earlier in this chapter I talked about the difference between full-frame and crop-sensor cameras. There are also two different types of lenses—one that is designed to be used on all cameras (FX) and the other to be used on crop-sensor cameras only (DX). The lenses that are made for crop sensors are generally lighter, cheaper, and most importantly, cannot be used on full-frame sensor cameras without cropping. As you can see in **Figure 16.9**, DX lenses are designed to only capture the area of the crop sensors. The black rectangle represents the area covered by a full-frame sensor, whereas the red rectangle is the area covered by a crop sensor.

One thing to consider when you're buying a lens is that while the DX lenses might be cheaper up front, if you are planning on getting an FX camera, the DX lenses will not capture the full scene. An FX lens will work on both DX and FX cameras.

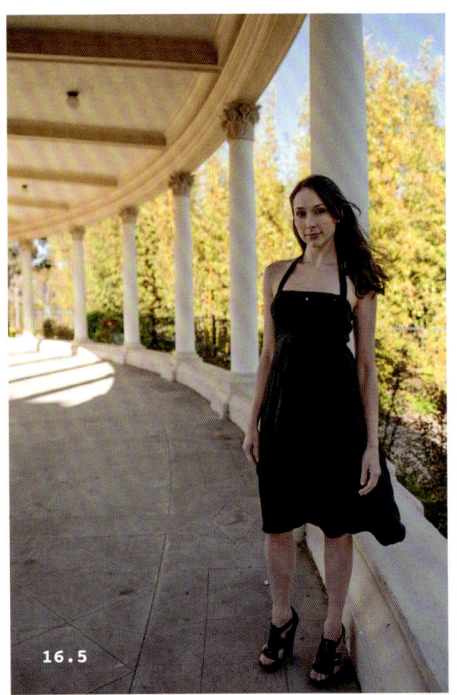

16.5

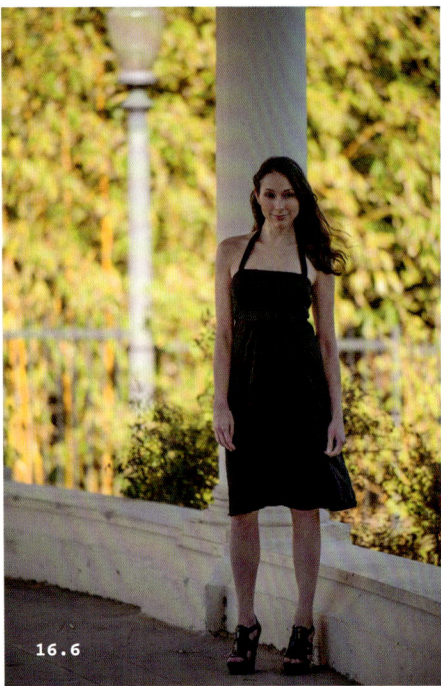

16.6

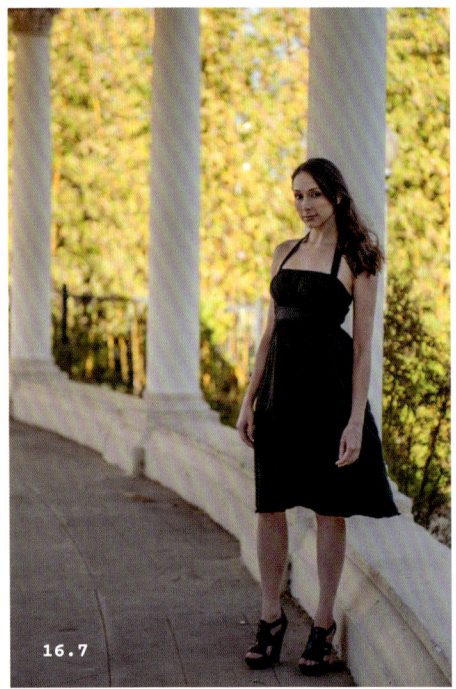

16.7

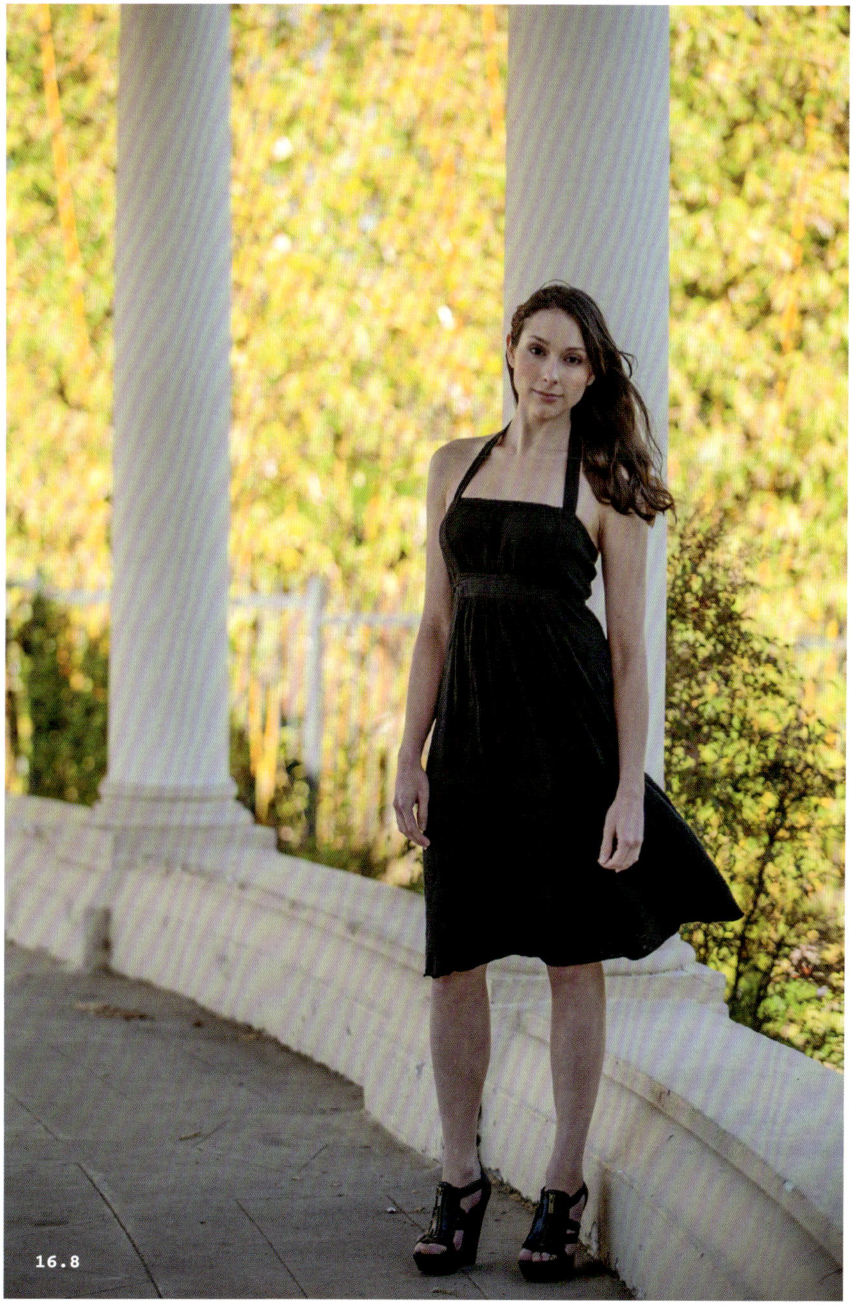

16.5 In this portrait shot at 24mm you can see a lot of the background.
ISO 400; 1/250 sec.; f/5.6; 24mm

16.6 At 70mm, you can see that the face looks a little more natural and is not as pinched and less of the background is visible.
ISO 400; 1/250 sec.; f/5.6; 70mm

16.7 At 100mm, the face looks the same as it did in the image shot at 70mm, but there is slightly less background.
ISO 400; 1/250 sec.; f/5.6; 100mm

16.8 At 200mm, the face looks very natural and there is very little background in the image.
ISO 400; 1/250 sec.; f/5.6; 200mm

16.9 This is same scene that is shown in Figure 11.1, but it was shot with a DX lens. The lens only captures the crop sensor area.

16.8

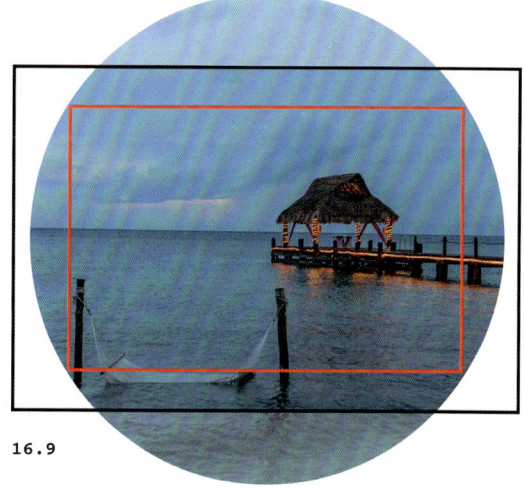

16.9

17. VARIABLE APERTURE VS. CONSTANT APERTURE LENSES

THE MAXIMUM APERTURE of a lens is the widest that the lens can open, and it is included in the name of the lens. For example, a 50mm f/1.8 lens has a 50mm focal length and can open to f/1.8, whereas an 85mm f/1.4 lens has an 85mm focal length and can open to f/1.4 (**Figure 17.1**). You can divide all lenses into two different classes: those that maintain the same maximum aperture regardless of the focal length (constant aperture) and those whose maximum aperture changes depending on the focal length (variable aperture).

A prime lens has a single focal length, while a zoom lens has a range of focal lengths. The advantages that prime lenses have over zoom lenses are that they can have a wider maximum aperture and they can be sharper than zoom lenses. All prime lenses have a single focal length and a single maximum aperture.

This is not the case for zoom lenses. Some zoom lenses have a constant maximum aperture no matter which focal length you use, but others change the maximum aperture as you change the focal length. My favorite lens is the 70–200mm f/2.8, which has a constant maximum aperture of f/2.8. This means that the exposure won't change as I zoom in and out. The Nikkor 80–400mm f/4.5–5.6 has a maximum aperture of f/4.5 when it's at a focal length of 80mm and a maximum aperture of f/5.6 at a focal length of 400mm. This means that as you zoom in and out, the maximum aperture changes, which could make your exposure settings change.

For example, let's say you have a proper exposure at ISO 1600, 1/250 sec, and f/4.5 at 80mm, and you decide to zoom to 400mm. When you do so, the aperture will automatically change from f/4.5 to f/5.6, letting in less light. You will have to either increase the ISO or decrease the shutter speed to get a proper exposure.

This won't make a big difference when you're shooting low-light scenic photos because you can use a slower shutter speed to allow enough light to reach the sensor if the aperture is decreased. But it can have a huge impact when you're shooting low-light sports and action images since you need to use a fast shutter speed to freeze the action and a wide aperture to let in as much light as possible.

The downside to constant aperture zoom lenses is that they are usually bigger, weigh more, and can be much more expensive than variable aperture zoom lenses.

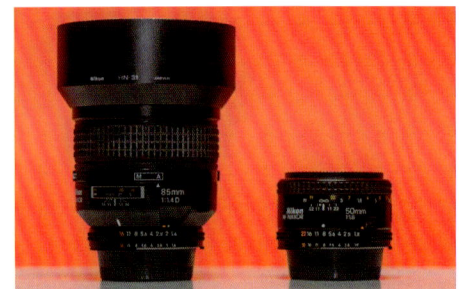

17.1 Nikon 50mm f/1.8 and 85mm f/1.4 lens

18. KEEPING THE CAMERA STABLE AND LENS TECHNOLOGY THAT HELPS

CAMERA STABILITY IS key when you're shooting any type of photograph. It is especially important when you are using slow shutter speeds, as is often the case in night and low-light photography. The next sections cover all the different tools you can use to hold your camera steady—tripods, monopods, or any number of clamps and mounts—but in this section we are going to look at the best way to handhold the camera.

Many photographers follow the rule (mentioned in section 16) that says when you're shooting handheld, you should not use a shutter speed slower than the reciprocal of the focal length of the lens. For example, if you're using a focal length of 200mm, the shutter speed should be 1/200 sec or faster.

Many years ago I saw Joe McNally demonstrate the proper way to handhold a camera and it changed the way I photograph. It has allowed me to use slower shutter speeds when shooting handheld without causing blurring or camera shake. His technique is to turn your body sideways and use part of your shoulder to make a stable place for your camera, then use your hands to support the camera and lens. This technique can be seen on Joe's YouTube channel: https://www.youtube.com/watch?v=EDsx3-FWfwk

I suggest that you practice holding your camera until it you find a position that is very comfortable and feels like second nature.

Some cameras and lenses have special technology that measures camera shake and then counteracts it when the shutter release button is pressed, allowing you to use slower shutter speeds and produce sharper images when shooting handheld. This is called Vibration Reduction in Nikon lenses, Image Stabilization in Canon lenses, and Steady Shot in Sony cameras. In the older generations of this technology, there was a very slight delay as the vibration reduction technology kicked in to counteract the camera shake, making it only useful for stationary and slow-moving subjects. However, the technology keeps getting better, and the lag time between when you press the shutter button and when the photo is taken has been reduced, which means it can be useful even when you're photographing fast-moving subjects.

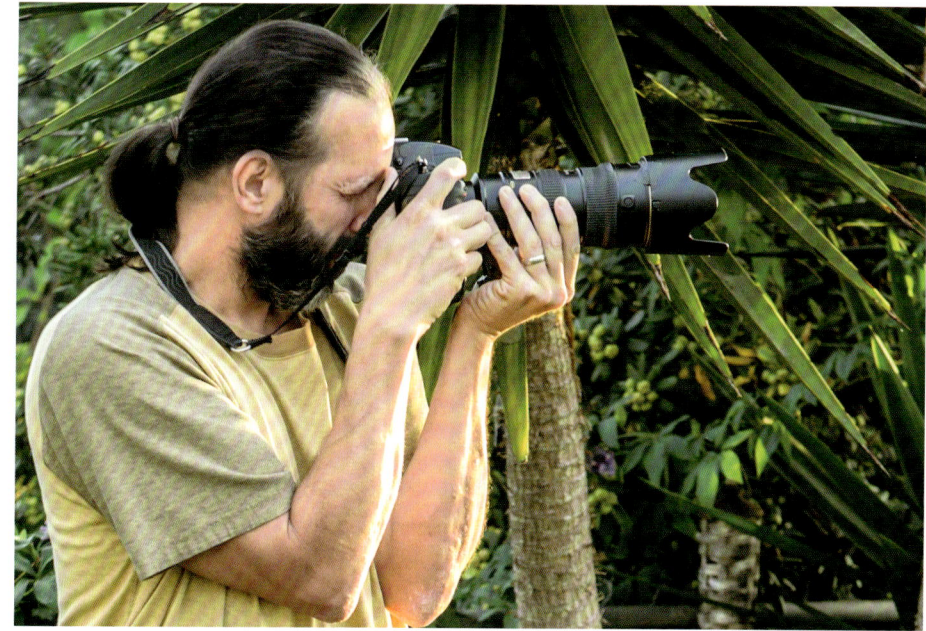

18.1 Holding the camera steady is really important, especially when shooting at slower shutter speeds.

19. TRIPODS

A TRIPOD IS probably the most essential piece of photography gear for low-light photography. There are thousands of different tripods available for purchase, so how do you pick the right one? I can't tell you which tripod to buy, but I can give you some information so you can make an informed decision. Let's look at the different parts that make up a tripod and the choices you get to make.

Tripod Legs

A tripod has three telescoping legs made of a sturdy, lightweight material that create a solid platform for the camera. Tripod legs come in a huge variety of sizes, materials, and price.

Materials: The four main materials used for tripod legs are carbon fiber, basalt, aluminum, and wood. Carbon fiber legs are the lightest and most rigid, have great vibration reduction, and cost the most. Basalt legs are just a tad heavier than the carbon fiber legs and can be slightly cheaper. Aluminum legs are heavier and cheaper, and they do not dampen vibration as well as legs made of other materials. Wood legs can be really heavy, but they are good when it comes to vibration dampening. The cost of wood legs can range from inexpensive to very expensive. For me, it is always a matter of sturdiness compared to price. I have a few tripods, but the one I use the most is made of basalt fiber and it gives me the best of all worlds.

Locking mechanism: There are two main types of leg-locking mechanisms: a twist lock and a lever lock. I prefer lever locks (**Figure 19.1**) because I can instantly tell if they are closed tight, but I know many photographers who swear by twist locks (**Figure 19.2**). My advice is to check out both types for yourself in a good camera store and see which you like better. Remember that you will be using the tripod in very low light, so being able to tell if the legs are locked just by touch is handy.

Height: The legs of the tripod determine the height of the tripod. Tripods come in all heights, ranging from about a foot high to those that tower overhead. The proper height of the tripod depends on your height—you want something that holds the camera steady at a height that is comfortable for you. I do not include the height of the center column when determining the height of the tripod because it can make the tripod less stable than if you just use the legs without the center column extended.

Tripod Head

Most tripods allow you to mix and match the legs and head so you can get a combination that suits your photography needs. There are three basic tripod heads: a ball head, a pan and tilt head, and a video head.

Ball head: A ball head allows you to position the camera quickly and easily by just using one locking screw or lever in a wide variety of positions. These tripod heads can also be used very successfully on a plate or clamp, which we'll discuss a little later in this chapter. The downside is that it is very difficult to fine-tune just one axis by itself. As you can see in **Figure 19.3** the ball head can hold the camera at just about any angle.

Pan and tilt head: These are the more traditional tripod heads that allow separate adjustments for each axis (**Figure 19.4**). The real advantage to this type of head is the ability to fine-tune the camera placement and angle. This is the type of head I use the most when I'm shooting at night with a tripod.

Video head: Video heads are created to allow smooth movement when the camera is locked in place. These heads use a fluid technology so that when the camera is moved during filming, the motion is smooth and not jerky. These can be used for regular photography, but you are going to pay a premium for the smooth movement.

Other Factors

There are a few more important factors to take into consideration before settling on a tripod.

Weight: You need to carefully consider the weight of the tripod and head, especially if you plan on carrying the tripod around a lot. I photograph most of my images pretty close to where I can park my car, so having the lightest tripod is not that important. I also have a very heavy studio tripod that I would never take with me when I'm out scouting locations or on a trip.

Load weight: You need to make sure the tripod can handle the weight of your camera and lens combination, and any camera and lens combination you plan on using in the future. Many inexpensive tripods work great until you put a full-size DSLR with a big, heavy lens on it; then the tripod becomes unsteady and your images won't be tack sharp. One of the real advantages of the newer mirrorless cameras is that they are much lighter than their DSLR equivalents, meaning you can use a lighter tripod.

Cost: No one wants to waste money or feel like they paid too much for something, but you do have to pay for quality. While a good tripod can be expensive, with the proper care, it will last for a very long time.

L-plate: One of the best things I ever bought was an L-plate for my camera. You can see the plate by itself in **Figure 19.5**, and attached to my Nikon D4 in **Figure 19.6**. The plate allows me to easily switch the orientation of my camera from landscape to portrait (or vice versa) without having to adjust the tripod head. This L-plate fits all of the Arca-Swiss heads and is a very secure fit.

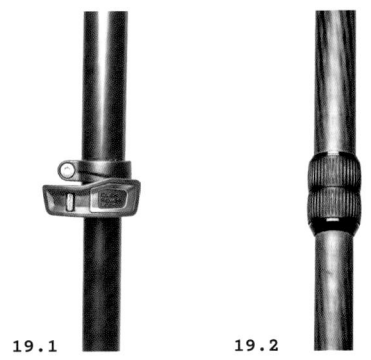

19.1   19.2

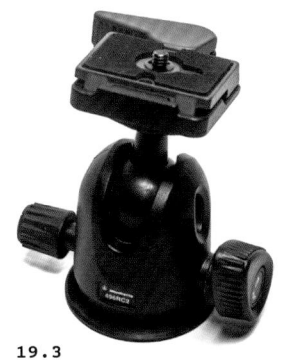

19.3

19.1 The lever lock on my tripod legs makes it easy for me to tell if it is open or closed, even in the dark.

19.2 Many photographers prefer the twist locks.

19.3 Manfrotto 495RC2 Compact Ball Head

19.4 A pan and tilt head allows you to adjust each axis independently, giving you a lot of control and the ability to fine-tune the position of the camera so you can get the exact scene you want in front of the camera.

19.5 A Really Right Stuff L-plate for my Nikon D4

19.6 L-plate attached to my Nikon D4

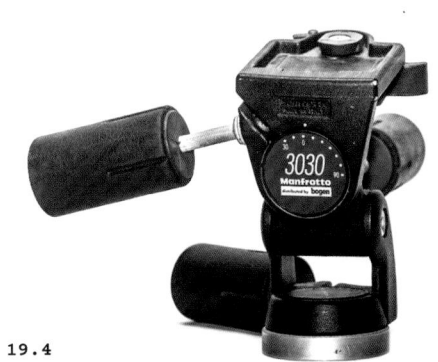

19.4

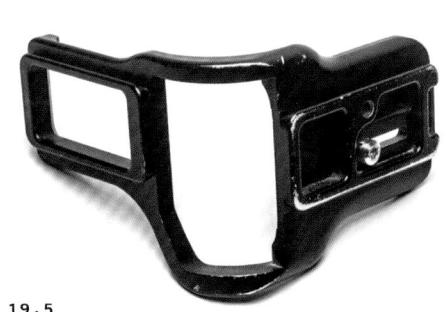

19.5

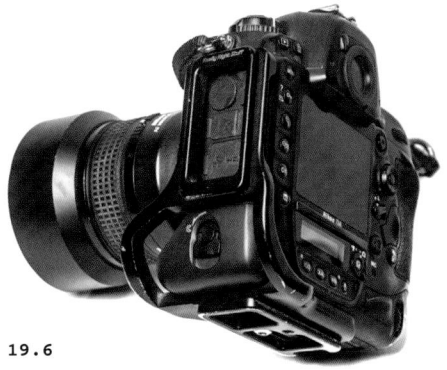

19.6

20. MONOPODS

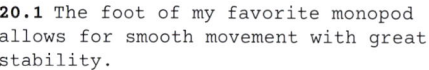

A MONOPOD IS basically a stick used to help support a camera and lens. They make it easier to hold heavier lenses and keep them stable. While monopods are not nearly as stable as tripods and can't be used for long exposures, they are very helpful when you're shooting sports and action. Check out the sidelines of any professional sporting event and you will see the photographers with those huge lenses all supported by monopods. The weight of those lenses makes it difficult to handhold them for long periods of time.

In my experience, any time you are using a lens with a focal length of 300mm or more, it is a good idea to use a monopod. The monopod is usually attached to the lens because lenses often weigh much more than the camera, and the placement gives you more stability when holding the lens.

My favorite monopod is actually one that is designed for shooting video. It is the older Manfrotto 562B-1 Fluid Video aluminum monopod, which has been replaced with the Manfrotto MVM500A video monopod and 500 series head. This monopod has a very cool foot that allows the photographer (or videographer) to smoothly move the camera around without moving the foot (**Figure 20.1**). The foot stays stable while the supporting leg tilts. I typically use this monopod with the video head removed so that it attaches directly to the lens (**Figure 20.2**).

When looking at monopods, you can use the same criteria as are used for for selecting a tripod. The weight, height, cost, materials, and locking mechanisms should all be taken into account.

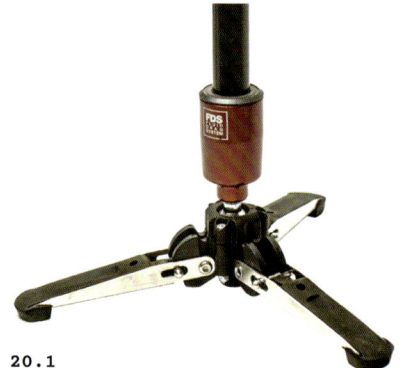

20.1

20.1 The foot of my favorite monopod allows for smooth movement with great stability.

20.2 The monopod attaches directly to the tripod hole in the bottom of the camera, or more likely, in the tripod hole of the long lens.

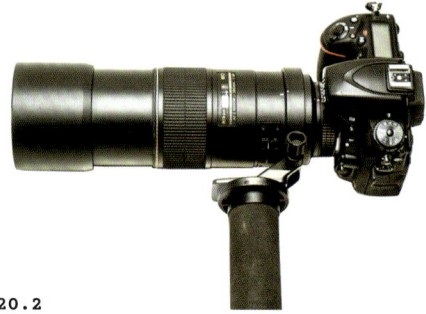

20.2

21. CLAMPS AND PLATES

THERE ARE OTHER OPTIONS out there to secure your camera in place. One of my favorites is the Manfrotto Super Clamp and a ball head (**Figures 21.1** and **21.2**). The Super Clamp is a heavy-duty clamp that is designed for clamping lights to bars, but it can also be used to secure your camera. The best part is that it costs about $30 and it is much smaller than a tripod. You can easily put it in a camera bag or take it on vacation without taking up much space. The downside is that you need to attach it to something for it to be useful, and it is only as stable as whatever you attach it to.

Another great product is the Platypod, which is heavy metal base to which you can attach a ball head. It acts as a very stable support for your camera and lens. There are a variety of Platypod products for different size cameras and lenses. The Max can support up to 300 pounds of gear, which is plenty for any photographer. The device comes with spiked feet to help it stay stable and keep the camera secure in place.

To really take advantage of the Platypod base, you need to use a ball head. As you can see in **Figure 21.3**, I have attached a small ball head to the base and secured a camera onto the ball head. This setup allows me to get the camera as stable as possible.

If none of these tools are available to you, there is one more option; it is not the best, but it can work in a pinch. Simply place the camera on a flat surface and put a piece of clothing under the lens to keep it from moving. Hey, I did say this was a last-ditch kinda thing. This works best if you have a cable release or remote.

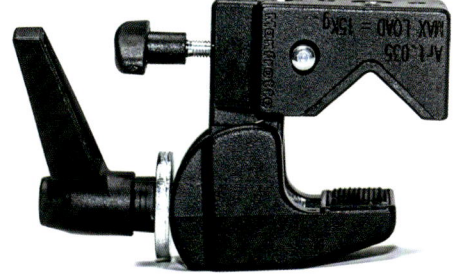

21.1 The Manfrotto Super Clamp

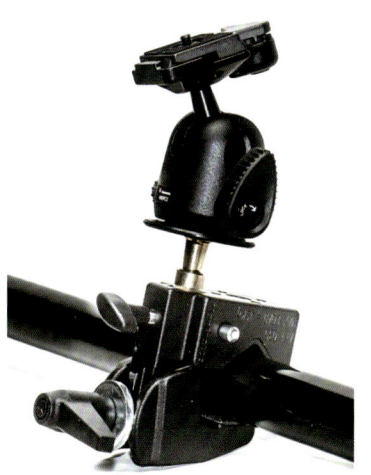

21.2 The Super Clamp attached to a ball head

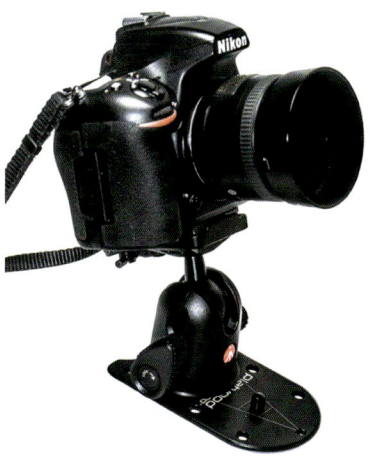

21.3 The Platypod Pro setup with a compact ball head and Nikon D750

22. REMOTES, RELEASES, AND TIMERS ARE ESSENTIAL

LET'S SAY YOUR CAMERA is mounted on a tripod and it is as stable as possible, and then you press down on the shutter release button to take the photo. After the image is taken, you check to see how it looks and notice there is a slight blur. The physical act of pressing the shutter release button can cause small vibrations to travel through the camera, resulting in a slightly blurry image. Being able to trigger the camera without actually touching it reduces the chance of any camera shake and enables you to capture a sharper image.

There are numerous tools you can use to trigger the camera remotely, from a simple, wired, one-button release to wireless remotes with a ton of functionality. Which remote you use will depend on what it is you want to do and how much you want to spend. I have four different remotes that range in price from less than $20 to more than $300, and each one does a different job.

For long-exposure low-light images, all you really need is a trigger that can open the shutter and keep it open for as long as you want. This requires you to use the Bulb shutter speed, which we discussed in section 12. The shutter stays open as long as you keep the button on the trigger depressed. All remotes can do this, but what differentiates the more expensive units is the ability to set an amount of time to keep the shutter open, automatically take multiple images, and auto bracket for long-exposure HDR images. In **Figure 22.1**, you can see all the remotes I have for my current cameras: the Nikon MC-36, a simple off-brand release, the Phottix Aion, and the Nikon ML-L3 Wireless Remote.

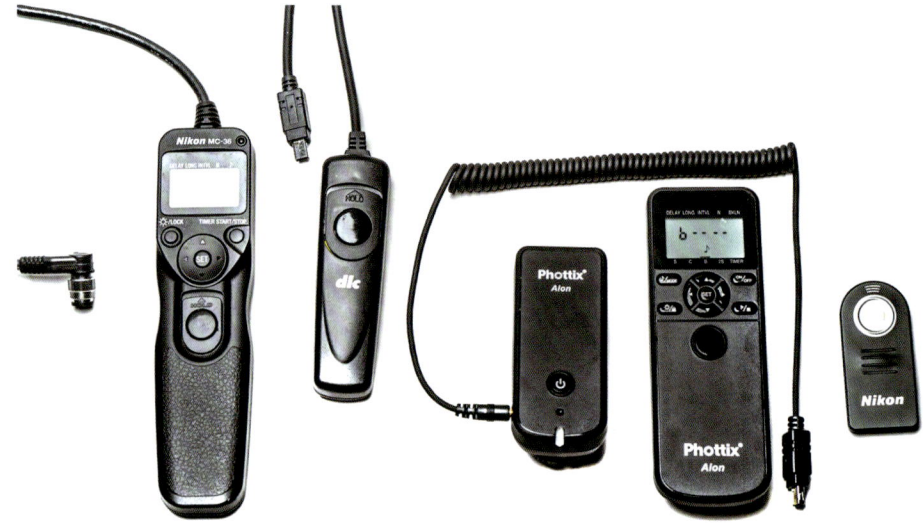

22.1 My collection of remotes and releases for the Nikon cameras I use

23. USING A CABLE RELEASE

THERE ARE TWO TYPES of cable releases. The first simply allows you to trigger the camera's shutter, and the second not only allows you to trigger the shutter, but also has a set of more advanced features. These features include the ability to set the length of the exposure, shoot time-lapse movies, shoot multiple timed exposures, and more.

These releases are attached to the camera via a cable. It's important to get a cable release that works with your camera. Each brand uses a different plug, and sometimes there are even differences in the ports on different camera models from the same manufacturer.

I still use the older Nikon MC-36 release I purchased years ago, which was designed to be used with cameras that had the Nikon 10-pin port. There is a newer version of this release called the MC-36a. This cable release allows you to lock the shutter open for long exposures and it has a slew of other features that were very useful before we had the ability to create in-camera time-lapses. You can set the length of time the shutter will stay open, and the release can also act as an intervalometer for doing time-lapse photography. It does come with a pretty hefty price tag at about $230, but it offers a great build and serious functionality.

Another alternative for a cable release is a generic-brand wired release that attaches to the camera and allows you to press and lock the shutter release (**Figure 23.1**). These are simple, inexpensive (about $20), and work perfectly for long exposures. I purchased one of these when I got a Nikon D750 because the camera does not have a 10-pin port, so my MC-36 release would not work with it. On the plus side, a lot of the functions of the MC-36 are actually built into the camera now, so a simple cable release works wonders.

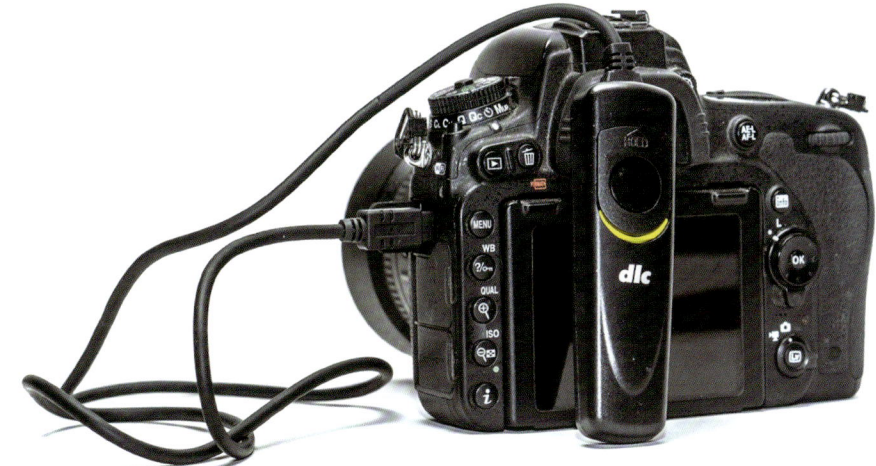

23.1 A simple cable release plugged into the Nikon D750. You can see that the button on the release can be locked to keep the shutter open for as long as necessary.

24. GOING WIRELESS WITH REMOTES

WIRELESS REMOTES ARE just cool. They allow you to trigger the shutter release on your camera from a distance without anything touching the camera. I have two different wireless remotes that I use regularly. The first is the Nikon ML-L3, a very simple single-button remote that costs less than $20 and works with a variety of Nikon cameras. It uses an infrared line of sight to control the camera shutter. You press the button once to open the shutter and a second time to close it. Check the Nikon website for camera compatibility:

http://www.nikonusa.com/en/nikon-products/product/remote-cords/ml-l3-wireless-remote-control-(infrared).html

In order to use this, you need to activate the remote setting in your camera's menu system

(**Figure 24.1**). The only downside of this remote is that it is really small and pretty easy to misplace in a camera bag.

My other wireless release is the Phottix Aion, a two-piece system with a transmitter and a receiver that attaches to the camera. This wireless timer and remote comes in sets for Nikon, Canon, Sony, and Olympus. It costs less than $100 and works great. It is especially useful if you have multiple cameras with different ports because you can purchase the appropriate system with the all the necessary cables for each brand. The version I use is made for Nikon and it came with the proper cables for all my Nikon cameras. It has a lot of different functions, so I suggest you read the user's manual before trying to figure it out at a shoot.

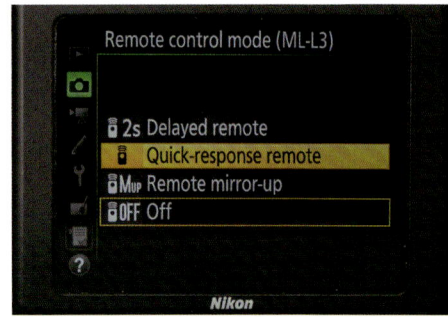

24.1 The menu system on the Nikon D750 showing the remote options.

THERE ARE MANY smartphone apps for photographers, a few of which I really like and use on a regular basis. However, it's important to keep in mind that apps change, get updated, or sometimes go away. This selection of apps was current at the time of writing (early 2017; **Figure 25.1**).

PhotoPills: This app has a huge amount of information in it that is useful for any photographer, but the one feature I love more than any other is that it provides details about the sun and moon for each day. You can find out the exact times of the sunset, golden hour, blue hour, nautical twilight and astronomical twilight, and when it is full nighttime. It also lists the moonrise and the amount of the moon that will be visible. These two functions alone make the app a must-have for those who photograph at night. The rest of the tools—like the exposure calculator, depth of field calculator, and photo planner—are just great bonuses.

ProCamera: This is another app that gives you more control over the smartphone camera, allowing you to take test shots with your smartphone instead of having to use your full DSLR setup. I like to use this app when I'm scouting new locations and trying to see if it is worth coming back with my tripod and all of my Nikon gear.

Slow Shutter Cam: This app allows you to experiment with night and low-light photography with your smartphone camera. You can capture images using the Low Light mode, Light Trail mode, or Motion Blur mode, each of which allows for more than just basic control over the camera settings. You can use a variety of shutter speeds and even control the ISO. I like to use this app to get a better idea of what the scene will look like without having to set up my DSLR and all of its associated gear.

LExp (Long Exposure Calculators): This app has all the calculators you could ever want. It provides the information in a very clear and concise format, and includes things like moon photography, a star trails calculator, and even Aurora Borealis photography. It also has solid information on shooting fireworks and how to photograph flowing water.

Sadly, the company who created one of my favorite apps, Triggertrap, is shutting down. Triggertrap is a great app and hardware combination that allows you to use your smartphone as a remote for your DSLR. If you already have the app and connection cables, hold on to it!

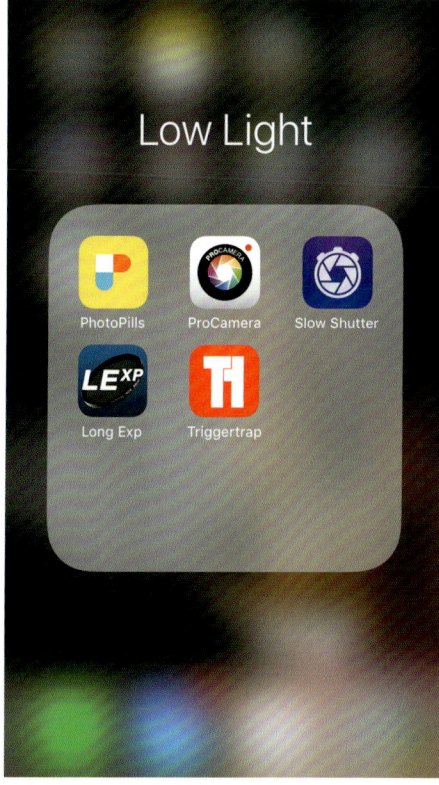

25.1 My Low Light apps folder on my iPhone

3

CAPTURING ACTION
IN LOW LIGHT

CHAPTER 3

In this chapter, we'll cover how to shoot moving subjects in low-light situations. You may want to capture fast-moving athletes under the Friday night lights or musicians rocking out on stage. Or you could be photographing a bride and groom in a church or temple, or actors on a stage. In these situations, you cannot just mount your camera on a tripod and use a long shutter speed because the subjects are moving and you will end up with a blurred image. I really love this type of photography, and it is what I am best known for. Capturing the energy of a live performance is one of the most satisfying types of photography to me. In the following pages, I share my thought process and how I go about achieving proper exposure, including what settings I use and why. The information in this chapter can help you get better images at everything from a wedding to a child's birthday party.

26. HOW HIGH CAN YOU PUSH THE ISO?

ISO IS THE (not so) secret weapon when it comes to capturing action in low light. If you are keeping track, this is the third section on ISO in this book. There is a really good reason for that. Pushing the ISO higher and higher allows you to shoot in lower and lower light.

As we've discussed previously, there are three settings that work together to create the exposure—aperture, shutter speed, and ISO. You can't magically increase the opening in the lens wider than it can go, and you have to use a shutter speed fast enough to freeze the action, so your only solutions are to either add more light or increase the ISO. If you tested the noise level of your camera as I suggested in chapter 2, section 16, you know exactly how high you can set the ISO and still get images that you are comfortable with.

There is something inherently scary about pushing the ISO really high, and I try to keep it as low as possible, but I've gotten more comfortable with pushing it a little over the years. As a photographer, I am very aware of digital noise (or grain when I use film), but most of the people looking at my images are not, and if the noise or grain is the focus of the image,

then chances are the subject wasn't worth photographing. **Figures 26.1** and **26.2** are from the same show and both were shot at ISO 6400 with a slower shutter speed (the performer wasn't moving very fast) and the widest aperture available. The noise really isn't notable because the images are more about the moments captured than the noise in the image.

Despite the fact that both images were taken at the same high ISO, there is a difference in the amount of noise visible, which is due to the overall tone of the images. Noise tends to be more noticeable in the dark areas, so you will see less noise when the image is lighter overall.

In the past, I would have stopped at ISO 6400 because I would have been afraid of what the noise would look like at anything higher. But the truth is that newer cameras can shoot at even higher ISOs and still produce really great images. **Figure 26.3** was shot at ISO 25600, and yes, it is noisy and there are color issues. However, in **Figure 26.4**, you can see that I was able to fix the color issues and reduce the noise when I edited the image in Adobe Camera Raw. We'll go over how to do this in chapter 5.

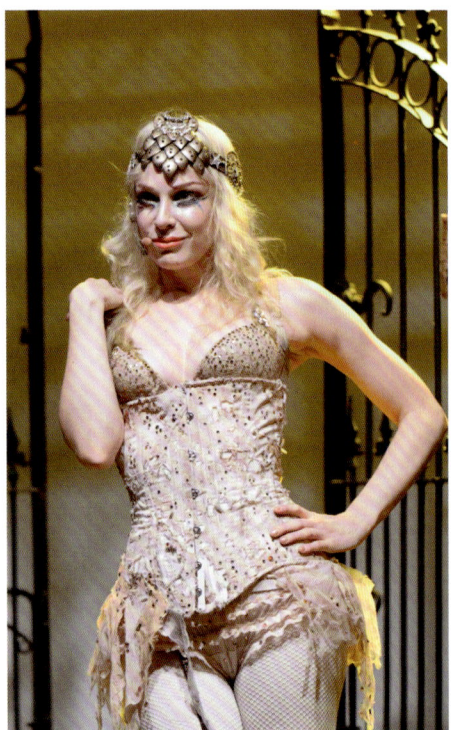

26.1 There was very low light in the venue during this performance.
ISO 6400; 1/80 sec.; f/2.8; 140mm

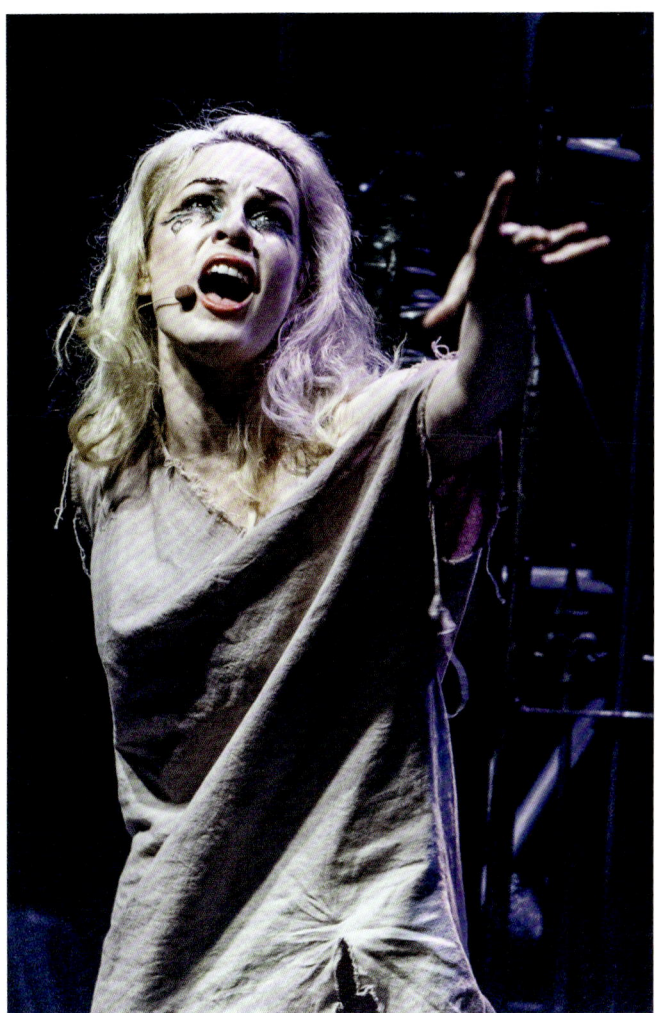

26.2 The darker background makes it easier to see the digital noise in this image.
ISO 6400; 1/80 sec.; f/2.8; 140mm

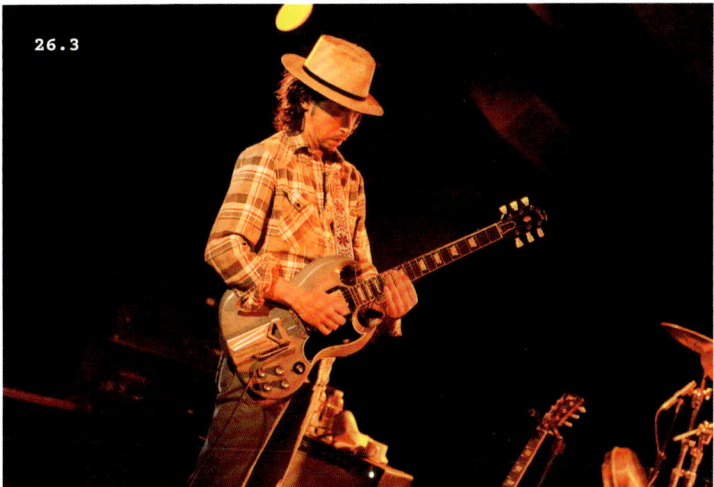

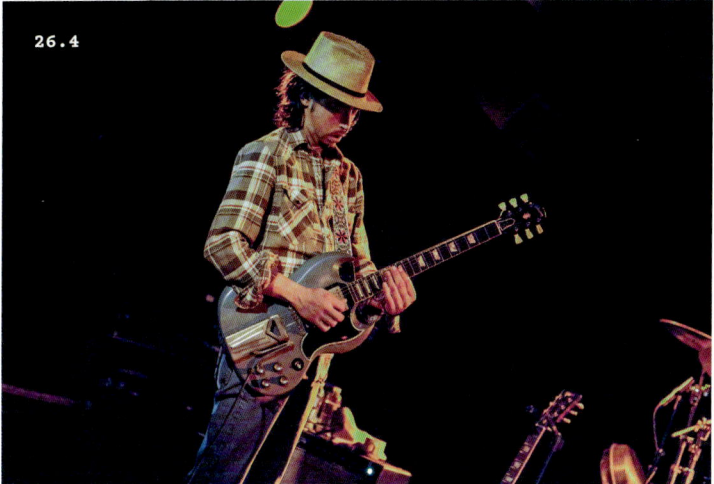

26.3 I shot this photograph of Jackie Greene in a very dark club where I needed to use an extremely high ISO to get a proper exposure.
ISO 25600; 1/320 sec.; f/2.8; 60mm

26.4 I processed the image in Adobe Camera Raw and was able to fix the color issues and reduce the noise.
ISO 25600; 1/320 sec.; f/2.8; 60mm

27. FREEZING THE ACTION

IT'S IMPORTANT TO be able to freeze the action in a photo, especially when you're shooting events like sports, concerts, and weddings. There are actually two ways to freeze moving subjects: you can use a fast shutter speed or you can use a flash. Let's look at both of these methods and when you can use them.

Shutter Speeds for Action

The shutter speed freezes the action by causing the camera to open and close the shutter quicker than the subject moves. So the faster the subject moves, the faster the shutter speed needs to be. To freeze the action in low light, you need to know how much light there is in the scene and how fast the subject is moving. The lower the light and the faster the movement, the more difficult it is to freeze the action.

There is one more piece to the puzzle, which is the direction the subject is moving in the frame. You can use slower shutter speeds if the subject is moving toward or away from you, but you need faster shutter speeds if the subject is moving across the frame.

In **Table 1**, I've listed some moving subjects and the minimum shutter speeds needed to freeze them in place. These are just guidelines, so check your images to make sure you are actually freezing the action.

The following images were all taken with action-stopping shutter speeds. This varied from 1/30 second to 1/1600 second, all depending on the speed of the subject.

Using a Flash to Freeze Time

There are times when you can use a flash to freeze the action. The first thing that you need is a situation in which you can use a flash. You can't use this technique to photograph concerts because flash is not allowed in most venues, and you can't use it for a lot of sports because the action is too far away and, again, you are often not allowed to use a flash at sporting events. However, you can use this technique when you're photographing portraits and other subjects where you have control over the shoot.

Flash can freeze action because the duration of the flash is very, very short. For example, the flash duration of the Nikon SB-910 Speedlight at 1/128 power is 1/38,500 second. If you use a high-end professional flash system like the Pro-10 from Profoto, you can get a flash duration of 1/80,000 second. This means that even if you use a slower shutter speed, the flash freezes the action when it fires. You do need to tell the camera when to fire the flash, either at the beginning of the exposure when the shutter first moves out of the way of the sensor, or at the end of the exposure right before the shutter closes.

Table 1

Action	Min. shutter speed to freeze action
Person standing or sitting still	1/15 sec. – 1/60 sec.
Person walking toward you	1/60 sec.
Person walking across frame	1/125 sec.
Person jogging toward you	1/80 sec.
Person jogging across frame	1/250 sec.
Person running toward you	1/125 sec.
Person running across frame	1/500 sec. – 1/1000 sec.
Person sprinting across frame	1/1000 sec. – 1/2000 sec.
Person kicking a soccer ball across frame	1/500 sec.
Car driving across frame	1/500 sec. – 1/1000 sec.

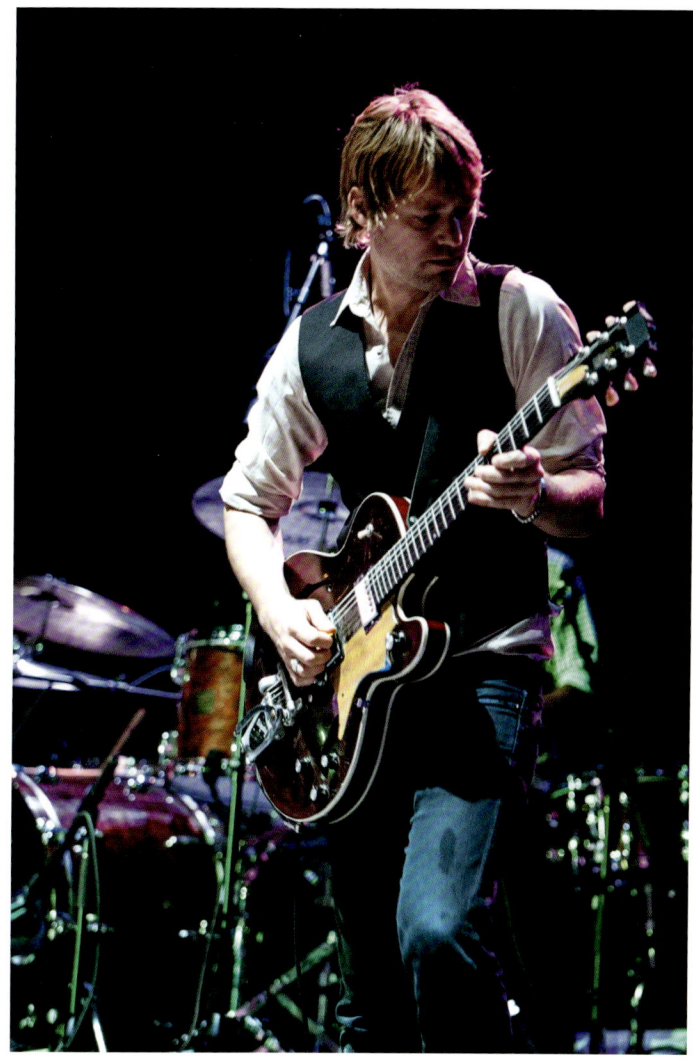

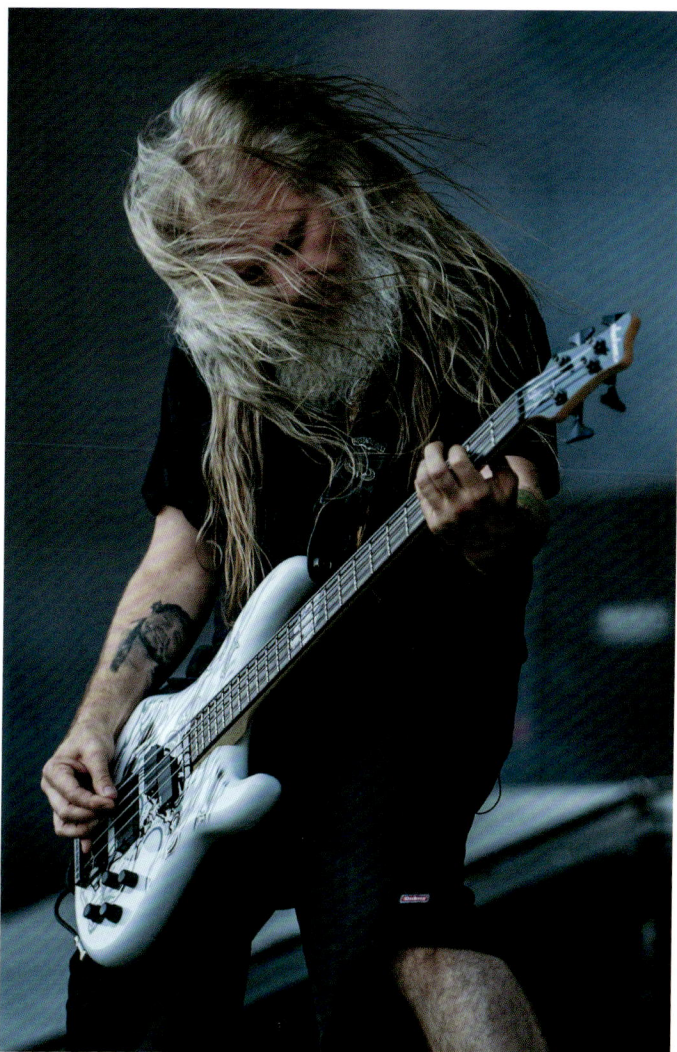

27.1 Some musicians just don't move around a lot so a slower shutter speed works great.
ISO 800; 1/125 sec.; f/2.8; 200mm

27.2 Heavy metal shows can include fast action and crazy head banging, so a much faster shutter speed is needed. For this image I used 1/500 second to freeze the wild hair.
ISO 1600; 1/500 sec.; f/2.8; 200mm

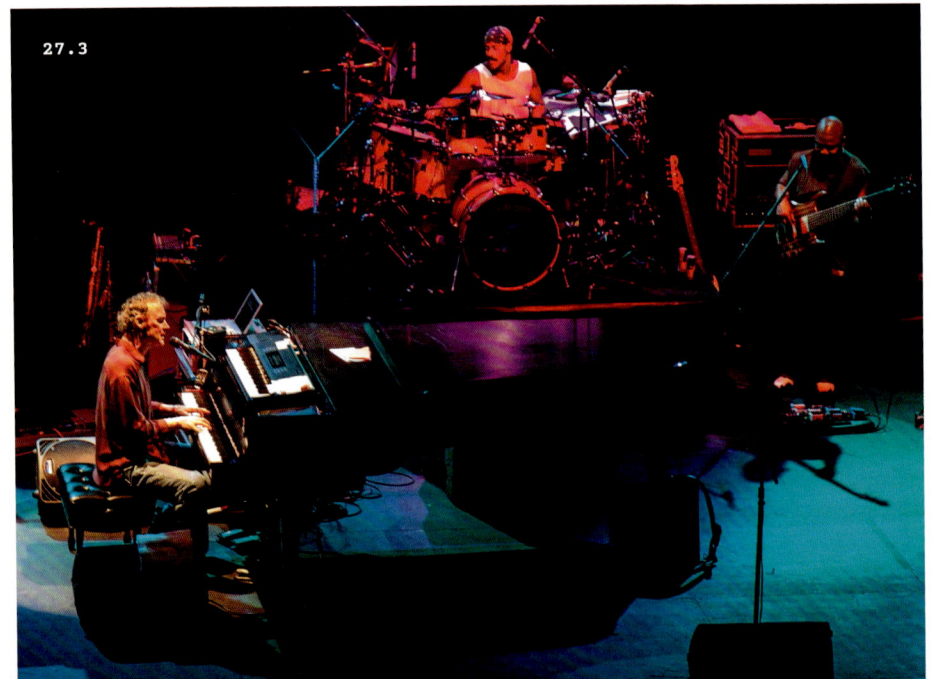

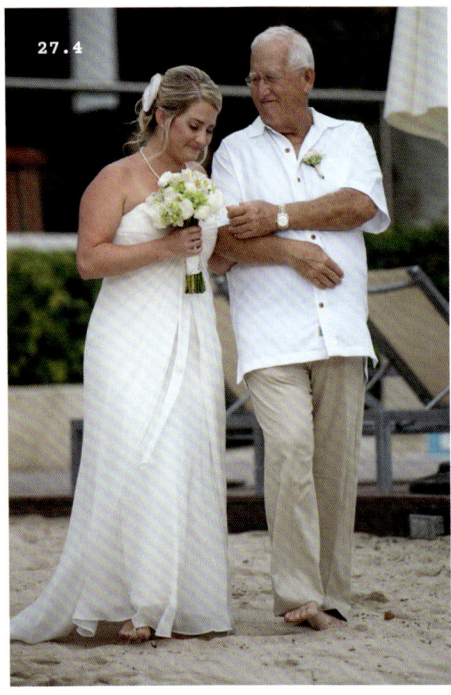

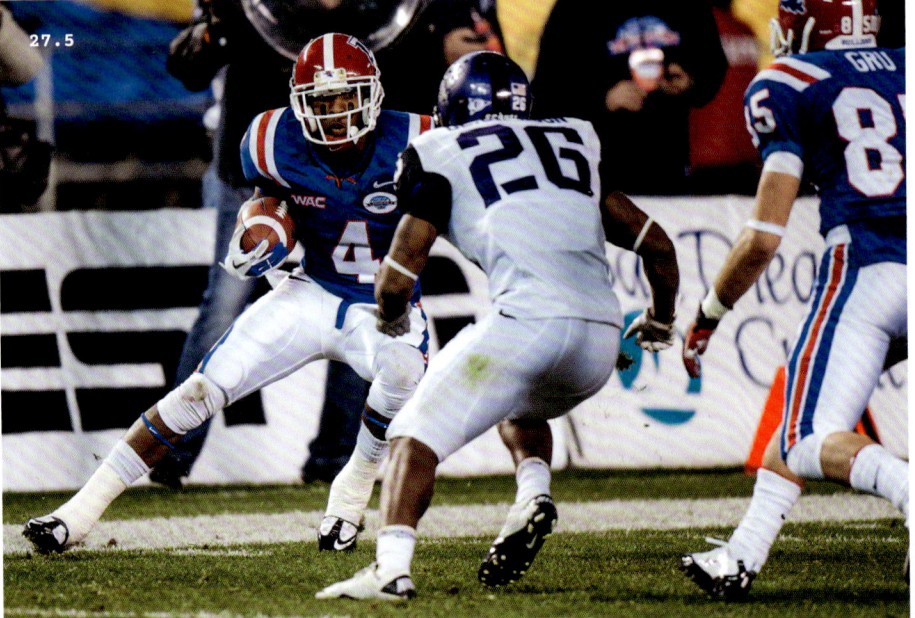

27.3 When the subject is sitting down and not moving much, you can use a slower shutter speed. For this shot of Bruce Hornsby, I used a shutter speed of 1/30 second.
ISO 1600; 1/30 sec.; f/2.8; 200mm

27.4 The father walking his daughter down the aisle at her wedding can be shot at a pretty slow shutter speed since they are not usually running and they are moving toward the camera, not across the frame.
ISO 800; 1/60 sec.; f/2.8; 200mm

27.5 American football moves fast, so I needed a fast shutter speed to freeze the action.
ISO 3200; 1/1600 sec.; f/2.8; 400mm

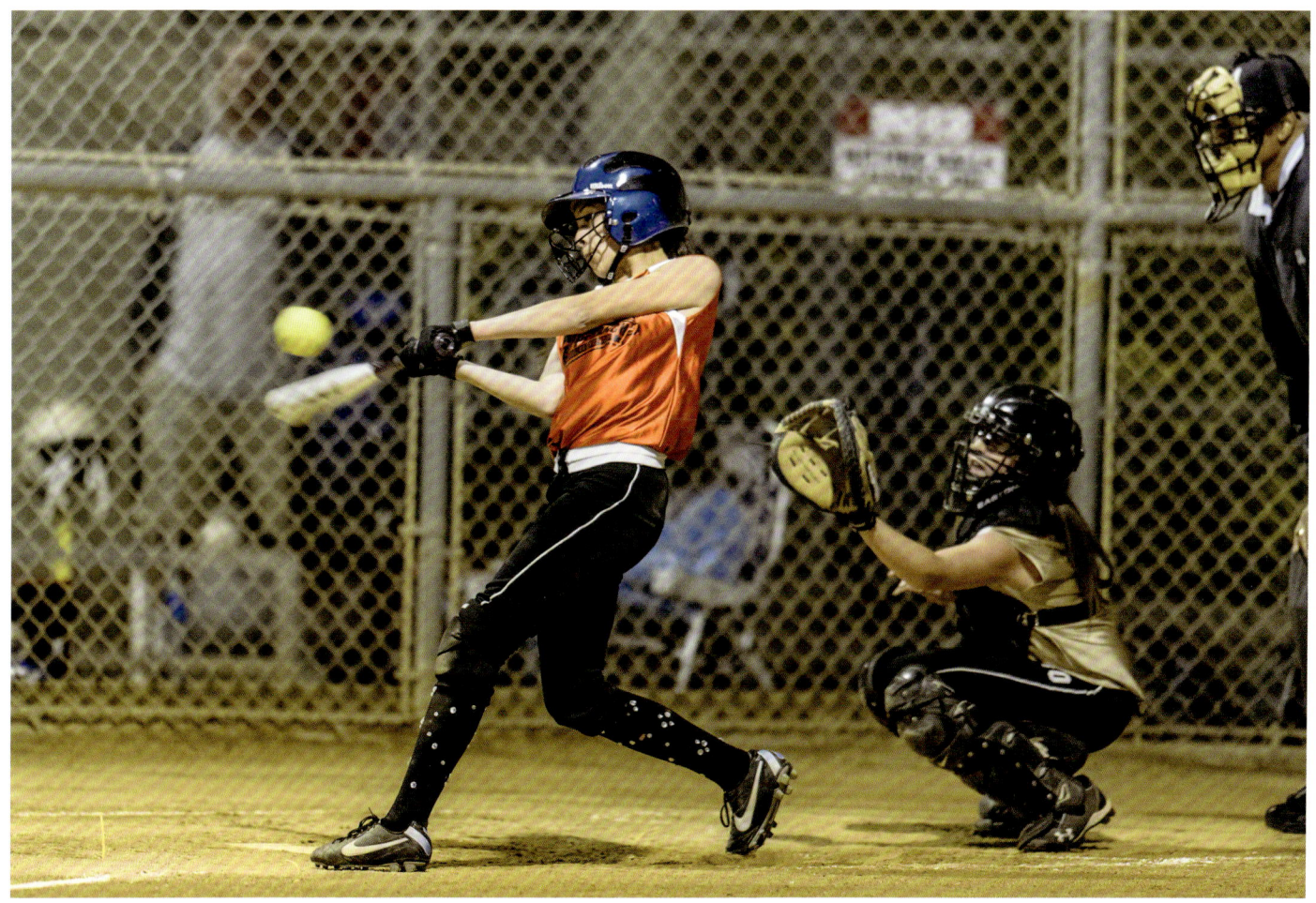

27.6 Photographing softball at night requires a very high ISO to get an action-freezing shutter speed. Even at 1/800 second, the softball and bat are still blurred, but the player is frozen in place.
ISO 6400; 1/800 sec.; f/2.8; 400mm

Share Your Best Low-Light Action Photo!

Once you've captured your best low-light action photo, share it with the Enthusiast's Guide community! Follow *@EnthusiastsGuides* and post your image to Instagram with the hashtag *#EGLowLightAction.* Don't forget that you can also search that same hashtag to view all the posts and be inspired by what others are shooting.

28. CAPTURING MOTION

THE SHUTTER SPEED controls how motion looks in your images. Up to this point we have talked about freezing action, but there are times when you might want to show motion in your images. To do this successfully, it needs to look like you captured the motion on purpose and didn't just shoot a slightly blurry image by mistake. There are a couple of ways to do this and both take practice. The first method is to use a shutter speed that is fast enough to freeze some action but slow enough to allow some movement (**Figure 28.1**). This adds a dynamic feel to the image.

This method works best when the subject isn't moving very much, but is doing something that makes and arm or leg move faster than the rest of their body. For example, when I photograph drummers, I try to get a few shots in which the drumsticks are blurry but the drummer is frozen in place. This lets the viewer know that the drummer was actually playing the drums and was not just sitting there behind the drum kit (**Figure 28.2**).

The second method you can use to show motion is called panning. This works for a subject that is traveling across the frame. Using a slower shutter speed, you track the subject with your camera as it moves from left to right (or right to left). With practice, you can keep the subject in focus by matching the speed at which you pan the camera to the speed of the subject. This will also blur the background. To get a successful panning photo, the shutter speed needs to be long enough to allow the subject to move enough for the background to be blurred. The slower the subject is moving, the longer the shutter needs to stay open.

These images are a lot of fun to take and you can get some really great results. In **Figure 28.3,** I tracked a yellow cab as it went through an intersection. The resulting image shows the motion of the cab and the bright lights of the restaurant behind the car.

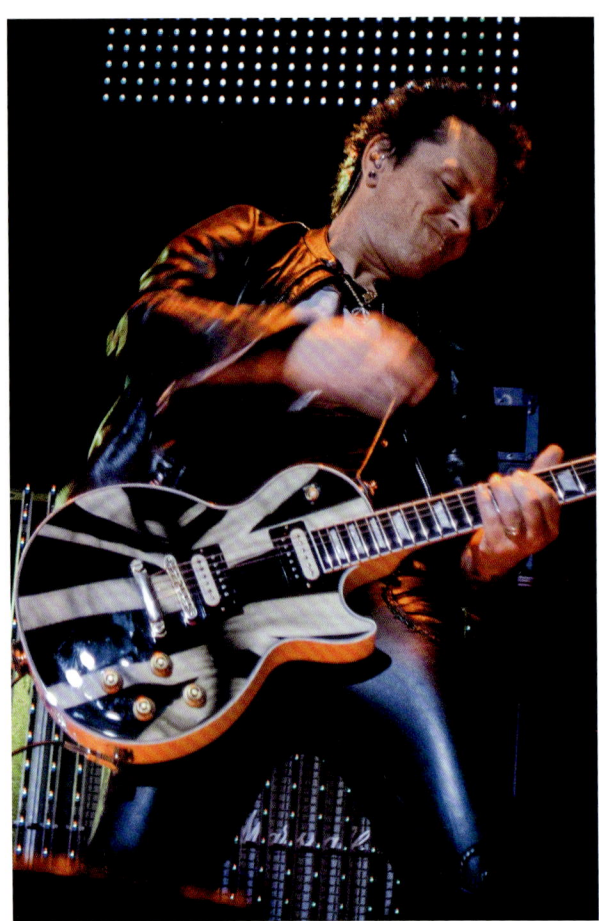

28.1 I used a shutter speed of 1/100 second to freeze Billy in place, but you can still see the motion in his right arm, making the photo more dynamic.
ISO 800; 1/100 sec.; f/2.8; 200mm

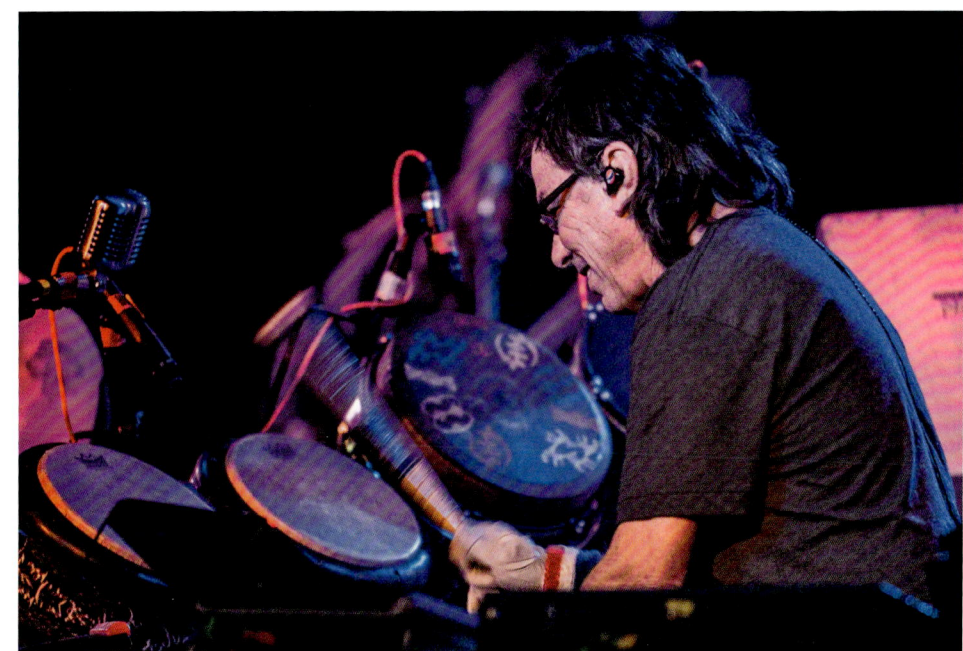

28.2 The drummer is frozen in place, but you can see that the drumsticks are in motion.
ISO 2500; 1/125 sec.; f/2.8; 200mm

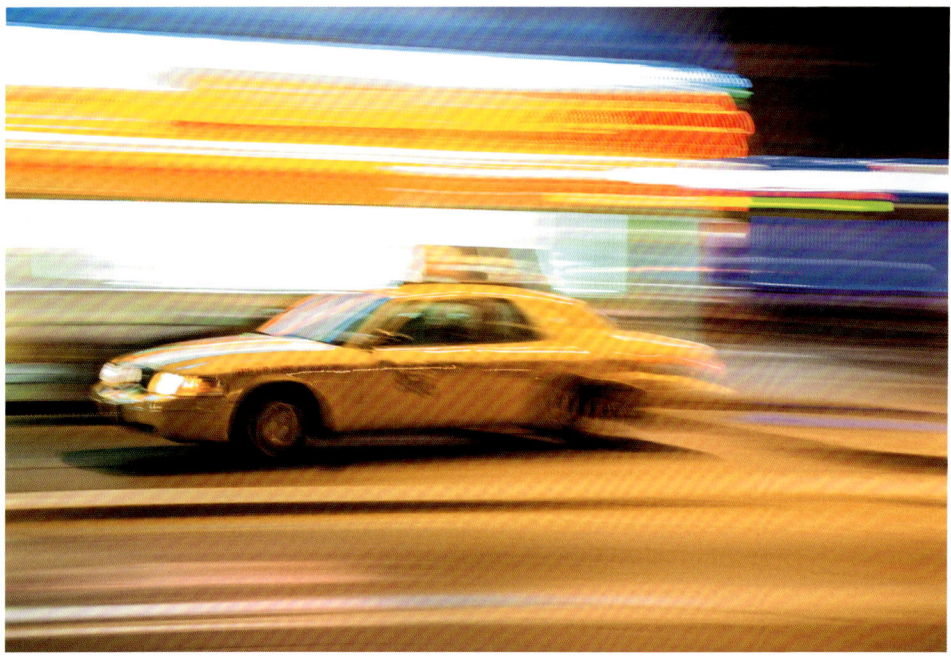

28.3 I used a shutter speed of 1/2 second to photograph this cab, which allowed it to move enough to show motion in the image.
ISO 200; 1/2 sec.; f/2.8; 70mm

29. AN EASY WAY TO GET PROPER EXPOSURE

I USE A VERY SIMPLE method to get the proper exposure for low-light action shots. This works both when the light is changing and when it is constant. I came up with this method after looking at a huge selection of my concert images. When I examined the metadata for the images, I found that a large number of them were taken with the same settings. I now use these settings as the starting point when I'm photographing a concert or just about any low-light performance. While you may not need to change the settings, it will all depend on the light in which you are photographing.

Start with the following settings:

- **ISO:** 1600
- **Aperture:** f/2.8
- **Shutter Speed:** 1/250 second

Since this is just a starting point, you still need to evaluate the lighting and adjust the settings depending on the show. First, take a photo and check it on the LCD on the back of the camera. There are three possible outcomes:

- If the image is too light, increase the shutter speed.
- If the image is too dark, reduce the shutter speed until the exposure is right. If the shutter speed becomes too slow to freeze the action, raise both the ISO and shutter speed and start the testing process over.
- If the image is blurry at 1/250 second, increase both the shutter speed and the ISO.

This sounds much more complicated than it really is. I can usually get the proper exposure within two or three frames, and that only takes a second or two.

The next step depends on what type of lighting you are shooting under. If you are shooting an event that has constant light, like an indoor sporting event, you are now set to shoot away without really having to adjust the exposure. I shot **Figures 29.1–29.3** at indoor sporting events where the light didn't change. To capture **Figure 29.1,** I needed a very fast shutter speed to freeze the tennis ball in place, so I upped the ISO from 1600 to 3200, and then to 6400 so I could get a 1/1250 second shutter speed.

The more difficult situation is when you're photographing a play, dance, concert, or other event where the lights are changing. Once you have your initial settings dialed in, you just need to adjust the shutter speed depending on how the light changes. If the lights get brighter, increase the shutter speed. If the lights get dimmer, decrease the shutter speed. If the lights get really low, you may need to increase the ISO. This does take some practice, but remember that you don't have to worry about all the light in the scene, just the light that is illuminating your subject. For example, in **Figure 29.4,** it doesn't matter how bright the smoke behind the guitarist is; it only matters how much light is falling on his hands and face.

29.1 I needed a shutter speed of 1/1250 second to freeze the tennis ball in flight. This meant I had to use ISO 6400 and an aperture of f/2.8. Once I had these settings dialed in, I was able to concentrate on the action and not the exposure.
ISO 6400; 1/1250 sec.; f/2.8; 400mm

29.2 Photographing indoor soccer is not easy because the action moves across the field at a fast rate. But it doesn't move as fast as tennis, so a shutter speed of 1/500 second was enough to freeze the action, which allowed me to use ISO 3200.
ISO 3200; 1/500 sec.; f/2.8; 200mm

29.3 Boxing and the mixed martial arts take place in a small area that is usually evenly lit, but you need a fast shutter speed to freeze the action, which can be pretty quick when a pro fighter is throwing a punch or kick.
ISO 2500; 1/1000; f/2.8; 70mm

29.4 Kerry King
ISO 1600; 1/800 sec.; f/2.8; 200mm

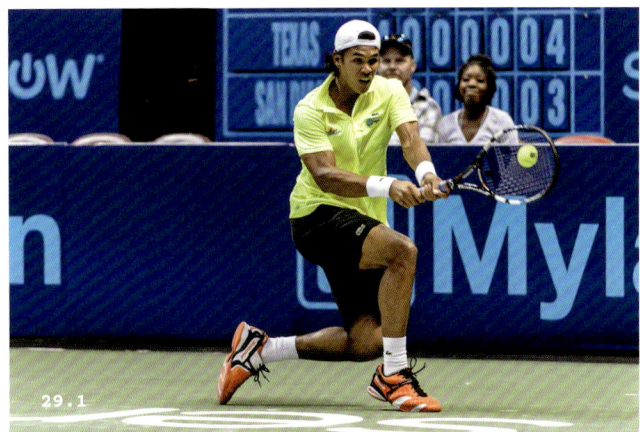

29.1

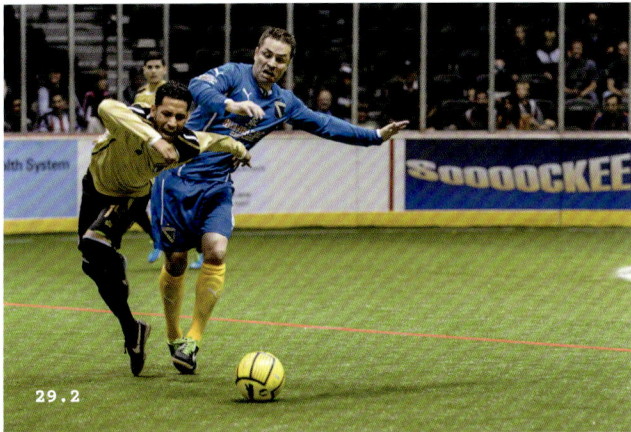

29.2

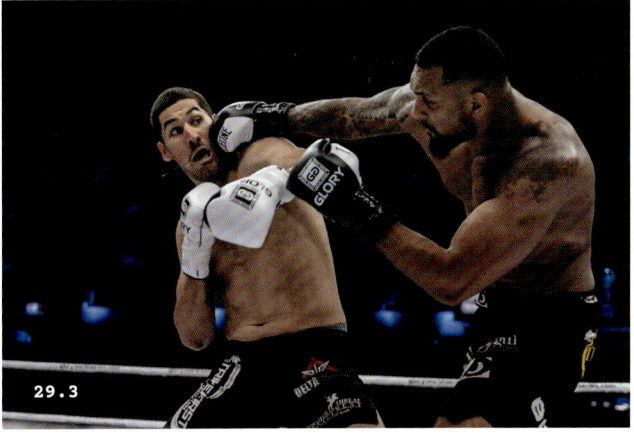

29.3

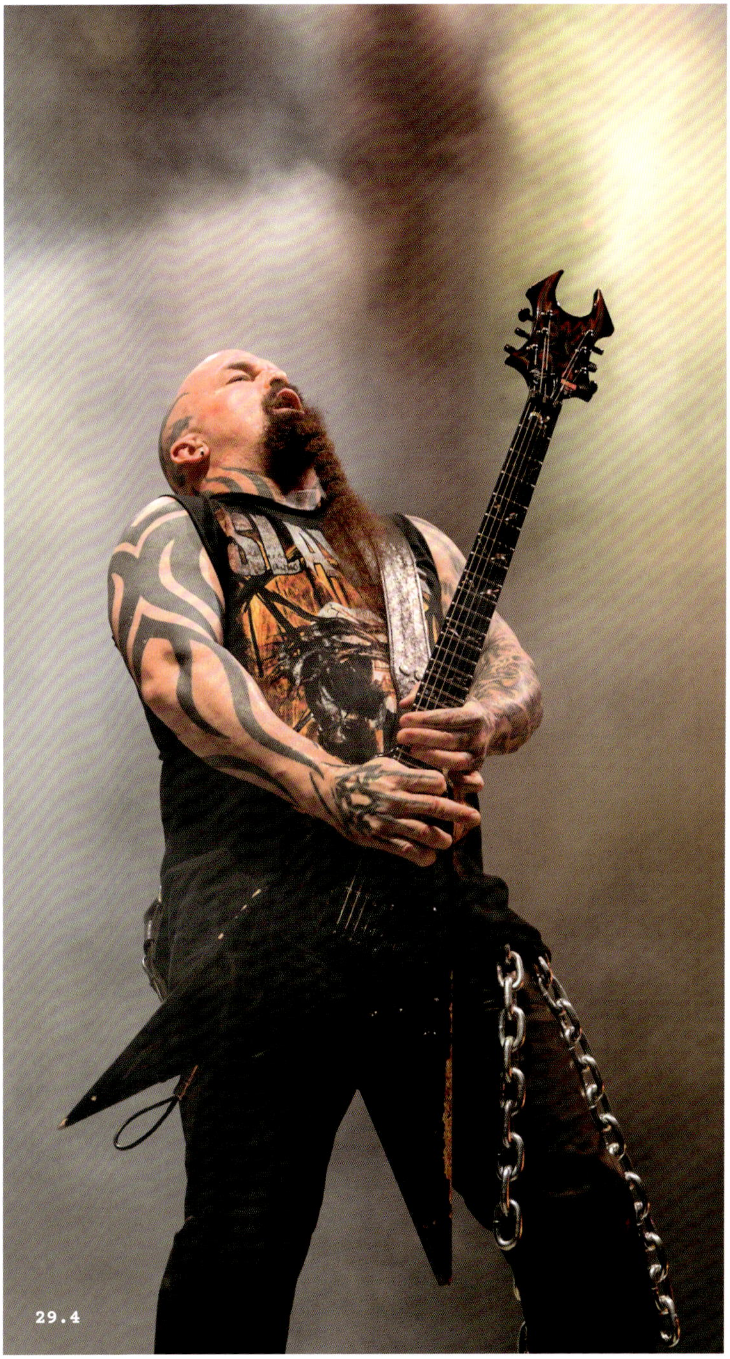

29.4

30. THE OTHER SETTINGS

IN THE PREVIOUS SECTION I talked about the exposure settings, but there are other settings that can make a huge difference in your images. These are the settings that control the color of your images, the number of photos taken, the file type, and the image size.

- **White Balance:** The white balance setting on digital cameras lets the sensor know what type of light is illuminating the scene so that the colors can be rendered properly. Each type of light has a different color cast. For concerts and other events where the lights are changing colors all the time, I use the Auto white balance setting, which allows the camera to adjust the color depending on what it thinks is correct. This works best for concert images because it tends to show the colors that are present during the performance.

  If the lights are constant, the easiest way to pick the correct white balance is to look at the scene on your camera's LCD screen and just cycle through the white balance settings until you see the one that looks the best to you. It is easy to adjust the white balance of an image during post-processing (covered in chapter 5). In **Figures 30.1** and **30.2** you can see the difference the white balance can make in an image.

- **Drive Mode:** The drive mode controls how many images are taken when you press and hold the shutter release button. The main settings are single frame advance and continuous advance. (Some cameras call these settings low-speed advance and high-speed advance, but the general concept is the same.) The camera either takes a single frame when you press the shutter release button, or it keeps taking photos until you release the button or the buffer in the camera (or the memory card) is full. For sports and action photography, you'll want to use continuous advance, and for portraits and scenic shots it's best to use single frame advance.

- **File Type:** Your camera can save images in two main formats: RAW or JPEG. Some cameras allow you to save images in both formats at the same time. A RAW file includes all of the information collected by the sensor and must be processed later. A JPEG file is processed in-camera and has all of the camera settings applied. It can be taken directly from the camera and emailed, posted to a website or social media channels, or printed without any additional editing. JPEG files are also smaller than RAW files. All of these qualities make the JPEG file format really desirable for photographers under deadlines, like those who shoot sporting events and need to deliver the images as soon as possible.

  In the past, I used the JPEG file type when my images needed to be turned around quickly, such as at an event like the San Diego Comic Con, where the client was actually going to be sorting and editing my images. Now that many cameras (including the two I work with all the time) have multiple memory card slots and the memory cards are bigger and faster than ever before, I often shoot in both formats, sending RAW images to one card and JPEG images to another. This gives me speedy access to the JPEG images, but if I need to go back and really edit an image, I have the RAW file with all the data collected by the sensor. In **Figure 30.3** you can see all the file type options available on the Nikon D750.

- **Image Quality and Size:** When you shoot in JPEG mode, you can also change the image quality and size. Check your camera manual for the options available to you. I recommend using the highest quality and biggest size. You can always reduce the quality and size of an image later, but you will have a difficult time increasing it. There is nothing worse than wanting to make a big print, or a client wanting to use the images in a large format, and not having enough data to do it.

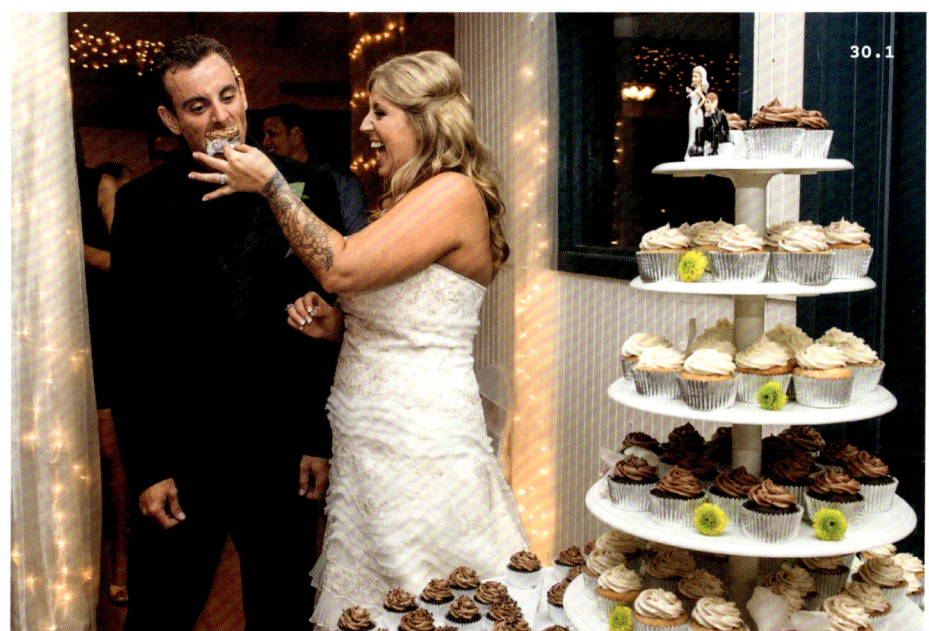

30.1

30.1 The white balance in this image is correct and the wedding dress is the proper color.
ISO 500; 1/30 sec.; f/6.3; 70mm

30.2 In this image the white balance is not correct and the image has an overall blue tone.
ISO 500; 1/30 sec.; f/6.3; 70mm

30.3 The Nikon D750 gives you seven different options for file type.

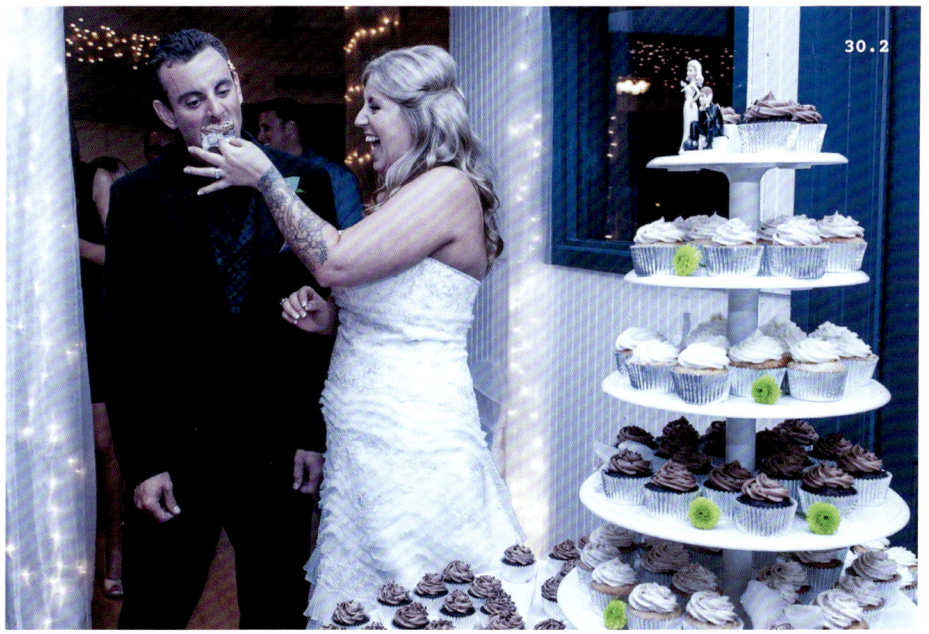

30.2

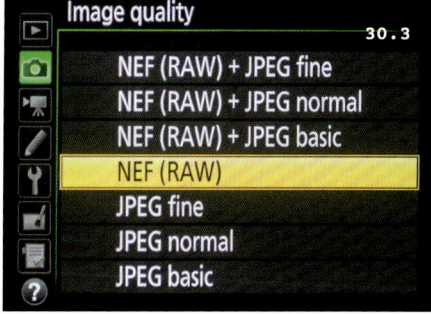

30.3

Image quality

- NEF (RAW) + JPEG fine
- NEF (RAW) + JPEG normal
- NEF (RAW) + JPEG basic
- NEF (RAW)
- JPEG fine
- JPEG normal
- JPEG basic

31. FOCUS ON THE RIGHT THING

EACH PHOTOGRAPH TELLS a story, and the area that is in focus becomes the focus of the story. This is critical when you are shooting action in low light because you have to use wide apertures, which creates very shallow depth of field. You can use this to your advantage because the viewer's eyes will always be drawn to whatever is in focus in your image. For example, I photographed musician Mark Karan playing guitar with a very wide aperture (**Figure 31.3**). The hand closest to the camera is in sharp focus, but the focus drops off really quickly, keeping the viewer's attention where I want it.

This also works when you're photographing things that are further away, like sports and weddings, and is the reason those great action shots seem to leap right off the page (or screen). A shallow depth of field combined with some space between the subject and the background allows the subject to really pop (**Figure 31.2**).

A shallow depth of field also works well for portraits. When I photographed Elina in the park during sunset (**Figure 31.3**), I kept the aperture wide and added some fill light from an off-camera flash to balance out the light. The shallow depth of field keeps the attention on the model while creating a beautiful out-of-focus background.

To ensure that your focus is on the right area, you need to understand how your camera focuses and know how to pick the right focus point. Most cameras have different focus modes for different subjects. The two main focus modes are continuous autofocus and single subject autofocus. In continuous autofocus mode, the camera starts to establish focus when you press the shutter release button halfway down and continues to focus until you take the photograph. In single subject autofocus mode, the camera starts to focus when you press the shutter release button halfway down and stops focusing once focus is achieved, even if the subject or camera moves. The focus will remain locked as long as you keep the shutter release button pressed halfway down. This allows you to lock the focus and then adjust the composition, which is really useful when you're shooting static subjects and want to make sure the focus is on one specific thing. When you are shooting subjects that are moving, it's better to use continuous autofocus so the camera will keep adjusting the focus until the image is taken.

Cameras also have multiple focus points that you can use to direct the focus. You can choose whether to use a single focus point or multiple focus points. The more focus points you use, the easier it is for the camera to lock onto a subject. However, it might lock onto the wrong thing. When I'm shooting concerts and events, I use a single focus point to make sure the camera focuses on exactly what I want it to. When I'm shooting sports, I will use a small group of focus points because this tends to work better with fast-moving subjects. At no time do I give the focus control over to the camera because it will usually just focus on whatever is closest to the lens.

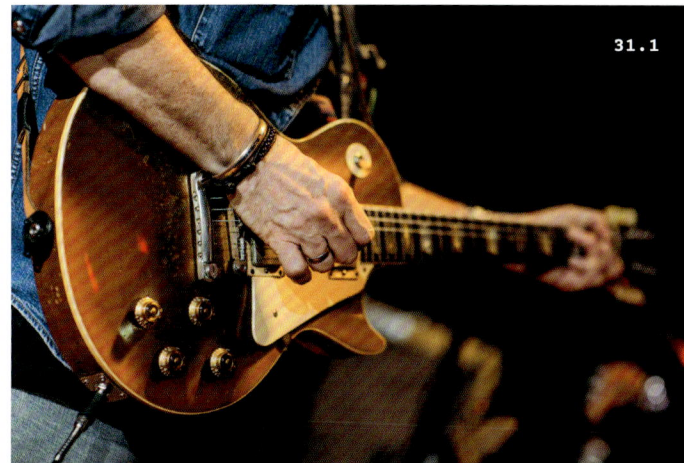

31.1

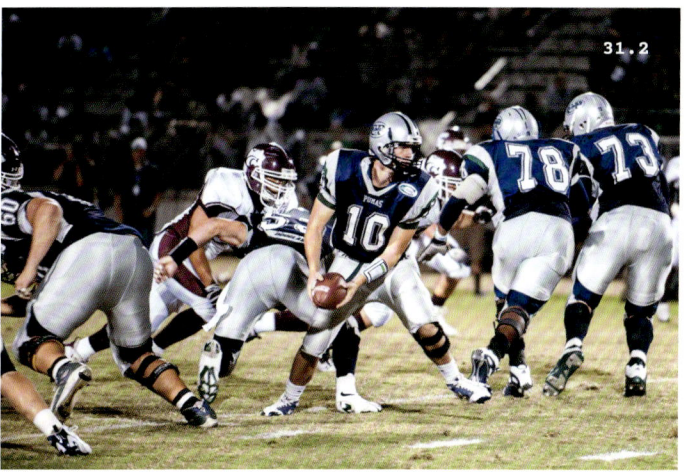

31.2

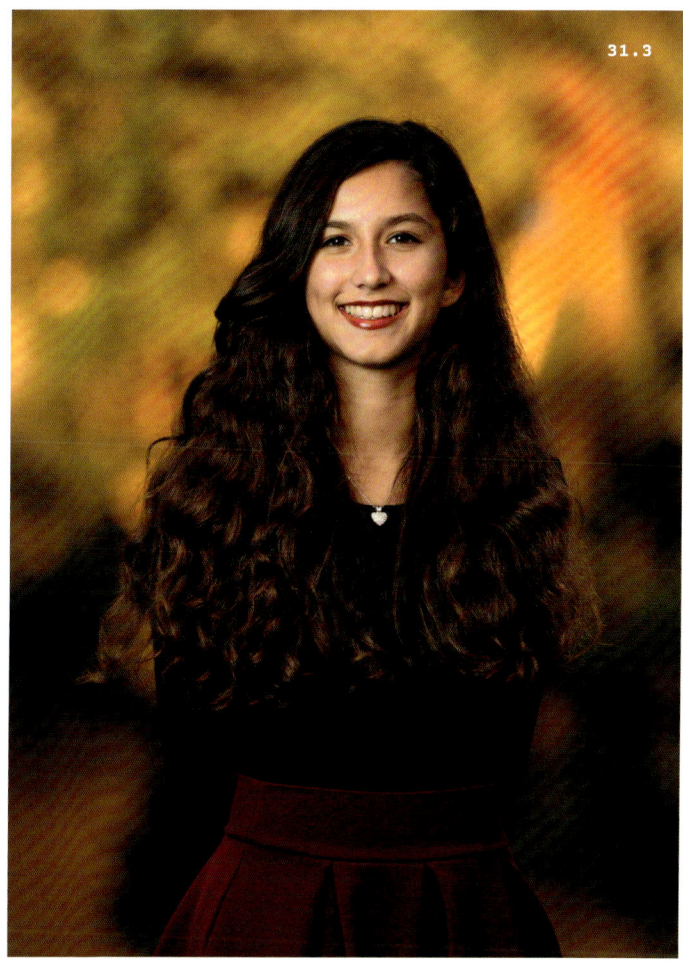

31.3

31.1 A shallow depth of field draws the viewer's attention directly to Mark's right hand.
ISO 1600; 1/320 sec.; f/2.2; 85mm

31.2 For this photo of a high school football game, I used a wide aperture to blur the stands in the background and keep the focus on the players.
ISO 2500; 1/320 sec.; f/2.8; 300mm

31.3 The wide aperture and longer focal length created a blurred background, and the addition of a fill flash produced nice, even lighting, allowing Elina to stand out from the background.
ISO 1600; 1/250 sec.; f/3.5; 200mm

32. PLAN AHEAD

PLANNING AHEAD greatly increases the chances that you will capture better images. When it comes to photographing sports, weddings, concerts, and other events of this kind, there are some things you can do ahead of time that will help.

- **Watch the lights:** When you shoot concerts, plays, recitals, and other low-light events, the lights can change drastically during the shoot. Watch how they move and what they illuminate. For example, if there are spotlights, there will be a lot more illumination on the main performer, making him or her easier to shoot and a lot brighter than the surrounding areas. You can use higher shutter speeds and lower ISOs when you're photographing the performers that are under the spotlight.

- At concerts, spotlights are usually directed toward the performer who is singing or a band member who is performing a solo. For example, when I shot **Figure 32.1**, I knew the spotlight was going to be on Billy during the vocal parts of the song, so it was easy for me to get the proper exposure. If the lights are moving, they usually move in a noticeable pattern, which allows you to determine when will be the best time to take the photo. For weddings and sports, the lights are usually the same for the entire event, so you can set the exposure for each area before the action begins, and then focus on composition during the event.

- **Know where the action is and where it will be:** This might seem simple, but it can really help you to capture the peak of the action. Determine where the main action will happen and keep your attention on those areas. For example, when I'm photographing a hockey game, I pay attention to the goal areas at the ends of the rink because capturing the puck flying past the goalie is more important than a random play in the middle of the rink. At a concert, you can figure out the basic locations of the performers before they even take the stage just by looking at where the microphones and musical equipment are placed. Understanding the event you are shooting makes it possible to know where and when the action will take place, allowing you to be in the right spot with the right gear at the right time.

- **Know your shooting positions:** Life would be great if we were allowed to shoot from wherever we wanted during an event, but that is usually not the case. Most venues have rules and regulations that restrict where we are allowed to shoot from. For example, at a concert, photographers are either in the photo pit at the front of the stage or back at the soundboard. Knowing which area you are allowed to shoot from before the show allows you to bring and use the right lens. The same is true for weddings, sports, plays, and other events. Check beforehand to find out where you will be shooting from and what gear you will need.

32.1 When Billy Idol is singing, the spotlight is usually right on him, making it easy to know when he will be brightly lit.
ISO 1600; 1/250 sec.; f/2.8; 200mm

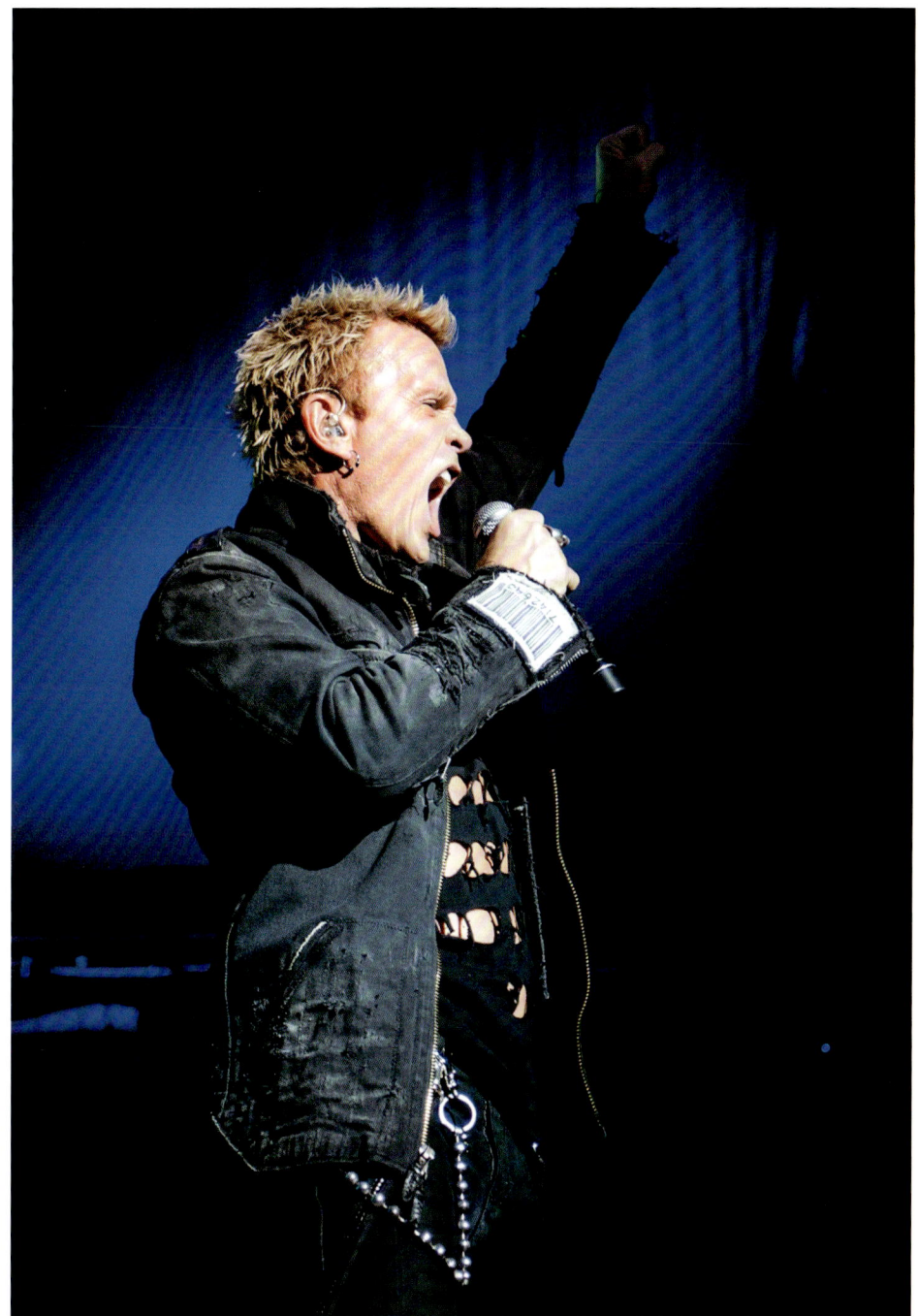

- **Know the schedule of the event:** This is particularly important when shooting dance performances, plays, recitals, weddings, and any event with a specific schedule. You need to know who is going to be performing when so you can be ready to capture the height of the action or any specific portion of the event. I usually try to make sure that I have spoken to the performers so I know the order of the show, or at the very least, I study the program so I am prepared for each part of the performance (**Figure 32.3**).

- **Make sure your lens and camera are ready:** Make sure that your camera has a charged battery, a freshly formatted memory card, and the right lens attached before the event even starts. Then make sure you know what the current camera settings are so you can easily adjust them as you start shooting. For example, I know that when I am photographing a concert, my camera is set to Manual exposure mode, ISO 1600, 1/250 second, and f/2.8 with high speed advance turned on, Auto white balance, Spot metering, and continuous autofocus with a single focus point. I am ready to go when the action starts, and since I know the current settings, I can easily adjust them when I need to.

- **Set the exposure quickly:** The quicker you can get the exposure settings nailed down, the more time you get to work on the composition. Know which buttons do what on your camera and learn to locate them by touch so you don't have to bring the camera down away from your eye to look at the buttons and dials when shooting. You want to be able to adjust the aperture, shutter speed, and ISO without looking at the camera. This is particularly helpful when you're photographing in low light and it's more difficult to see. Sit on the couch and practice this until it's muscle memory—then when you are at the event, it's natural.

When a sports team takes the playing field, they have a plan, and they have a backup plan, and they have plans to counteract what the other team throws at them. As a photographer, you need to have a plan, a backup plan, and ideas about what to do when things go wrong. Many times being a successful photographer is less about pressing the shutter release button and more about quickly solving problems.

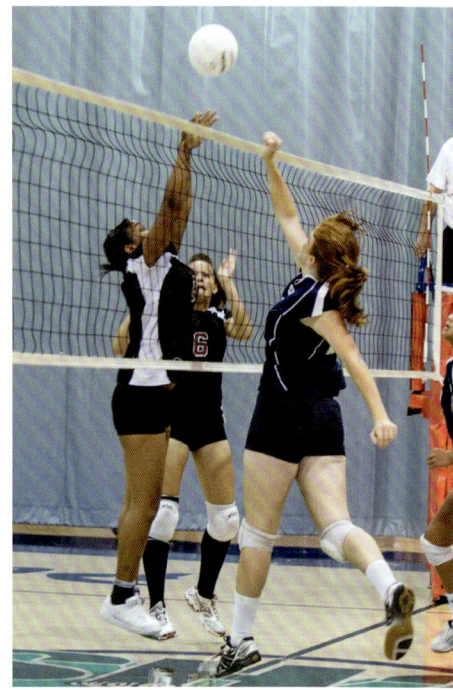

32.2 I knew that the action at this volleyball game was going to take place right above the net, so that's where I focused.
ISO 3200; 1/250 sec.; f/2.8; 70mm

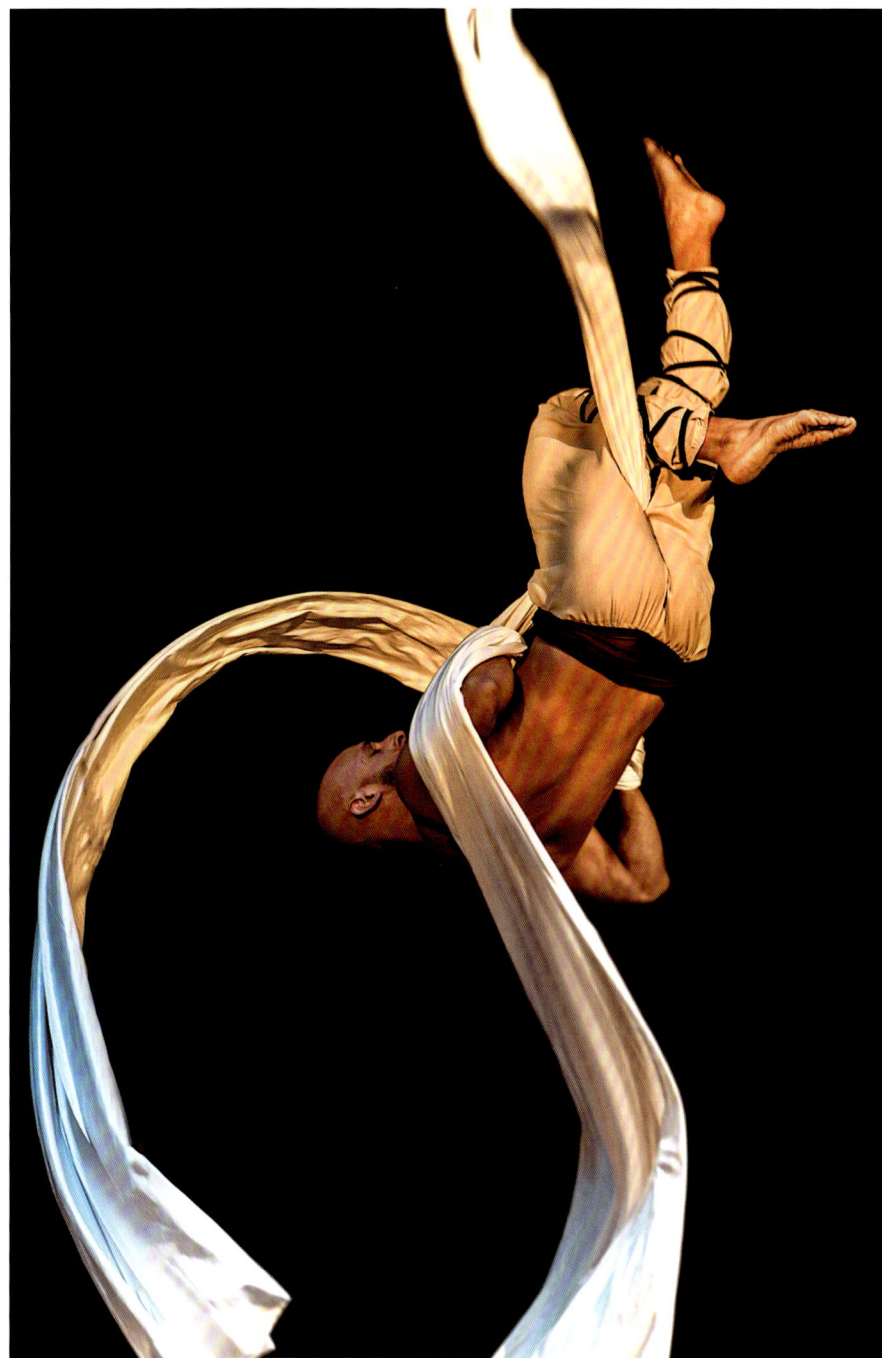

32.3 I was ready to capture Armando during the Astraeus Aerial Dance Theatre performance of Mythos at the San Diego Fringe Festival because I knew the order of the show, including who would be performing when and where.
ISO 1600; 1/400 sec.; f/2.8; 200mm

4

LOW-LIGHT PORTRAIT AND SCENIC PHOTOGRAPHY

CHAPTER 4

There is a world filled with wonderful photographic opportunities after the sun starts to go down. A drab and boring city street takes on a whole new appearance when the city lights come on. That bland, cloudless sky turns into an expanse of beautiful hues as the sun sets and the moon rises. Photographing at night is not easy. It takes planning and some know-how, but the results can be fantastic. This chapter begins with some low-light portrait solutions, and then covers photographing the scenes that appear only when the sun has set—city lights, the night sky, and fireworks. You'll also learn how to paint with light and capture light trails.

33. LOW-LIGHT PORTRAITS

THIS SECTION IS ABOUT creating a portrait in low light by using the existing light or by adding some light of your own. This could mean using natural light that is coming in through a big window, a slower shutter speed, a wide-open aperture, a high ISO, or any combination of these to get a proper exposure. For **Figure 33.1**, I used a slow shutter speed and a wide aperture to take advantage of the existing dawn light. The most difficult part of the shoot was getting the riders to stand still.

Using existing light can be simple when you mount your camera on a tripod and set it to Aperture Priority mode so that the camera sets the shutter speed. You just have to get the subject to hold still during the exposure.

A more difficult scenario is when there is no light and you need to add some of your own. I am a huge fan of the small, powerful, dedicated flash units that are made for digital cameras. These flash units can be mounted directly on the camera and controlled from the camera. Many of them are capable of automatically adjusting the amount of light they put out depending on the scene in front of the lens. These flashes are pretty great, but they do have a few limitations:

- **Size:** The same small footprint that makes these flash units easy to take with you also means that they produce a small, hard light.
- **Sync Speed:** Most of these flashes can only sync to a shutter speed of 1/250 second or lower. Many of the more advanced cameras and flashes have a high-speed sync mode that allows for much higher sync speeds, but these only work when the flash is mounted on the camera or is being controlled by the built-in triggering system. They will not work with radio triggers, such as those made by Pocket Wizard.
- **Battery Life:** These flash units use AA batteries, which won't last long. I suggest using rechargeable batteries because the cost of disposable batteries can start to add up if you have to buy new ones every time you need the flash.

In **Figure 33.2**, you can see the Nikon D4 with the SB-900 Speedlight attached. You can rotate the flash head and change its angle, which gives you some control over the light while it is attached to the camera. The real advantages of these flashes become apparent when they are used off camera and have some light modifiers attached.

Share Your Best Low-Light Portrait!

Once you've captured your best low-light portrait, share it with the Enthusiast's Guide community! Follow *@EnthusiastsGuides* and post your image to Instagram with the hashtag *#EGLowLightPortrait*. Don't forget that you can also search that same hashtag to view all the posts and be inspired by what others are shooting.

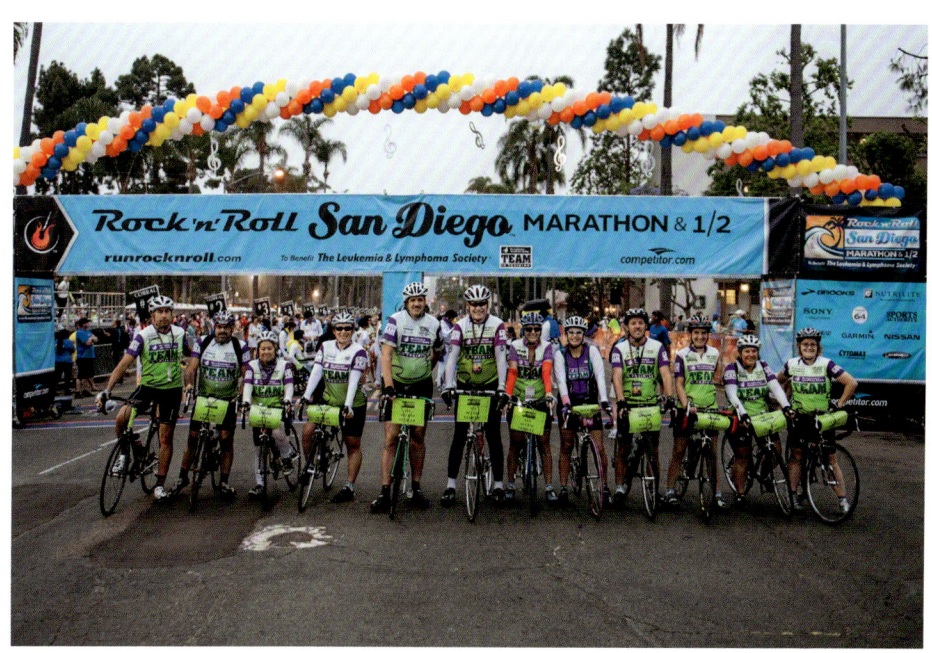

33.1 A shutter speed of 1/20 second was slow enough to allow the available light to illuminate this scene.
ISO 400; 1/20 sec.; f/2.8; 24mm

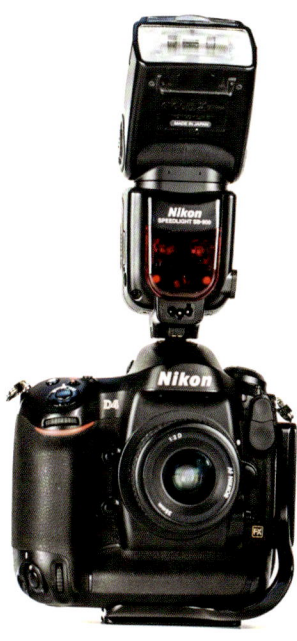

33.2 The Nikon D4 with the SB-900 on the camera.

There are different methods for using the flash off camera. You can use a TTL cord that attaches to the camera hot shoe on one end and to the flash on the other. When this type of cord is attached, the flash thinks it is still mounted directly on the camera and acts as if it is.

You can also use radio triggers, such as those from Pocket Wizard, by mounting a transmitter on the camera and a receiver on the flash. When you press the shutter release button on the transmitter, it sends a radio signal to the receiver. The downside to this method is that it is expensive because you have to buy a transmitter and a receiver for each individual flash.

In my opinion, the best method for using a flash off camera is the built-in trigger that is available on most high-end flashes, like those that are part of the Nikon Creative Lighting System. This allows off-camera flash triggering and control right from the camera. Once you have the flash off camera, you can control how the light interacts with your subject.

Figures 33.3–33.5 are examples of portraits I took using a small flash in dark areas, with the flash both on and off the camera. I shot **Figure 33.3** during a press event inside a small tent that had a white roof. I aimed the flash up at the ceiling to bounce the light down onto the actors, which gave me a soft, even light. For **Figure 33.4**, I set up the flash in a small softbox off camera and used Nikon Creative Lighting System (CLS) technology to trigger it with the camera's built-in flash. To capture **Figure 33.5**, I used an off-camera flash with a snoot, which I connected to the camera via a TTL cord, allowing the flash to fire as if it were attached to the camera. These images show what you can do in low light with just a single flash. If you want more information on portraiture, check out *The Enthusiast's Guide to Portraiture*, by Jerod Foster (Rocky Nook, 2016).

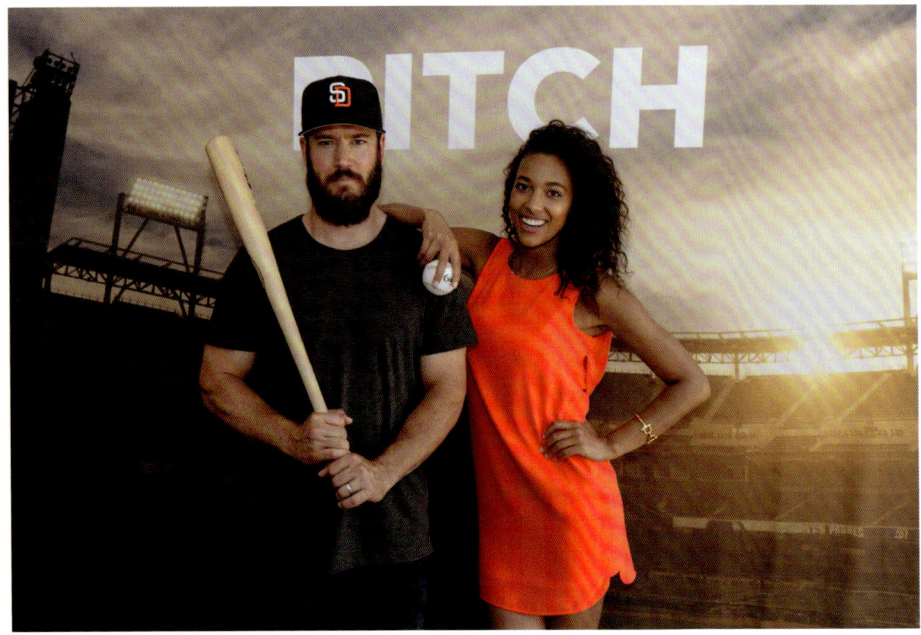

33.3 Photographing inside a dark tent was a challenge, but by aiming an on-camera flash up at the white ceiling, I was able to create a soft, even light. Since it was coming from above, it looks pretty natural.
ISO 400; 1/60 sec.; f/5.6; 36mm

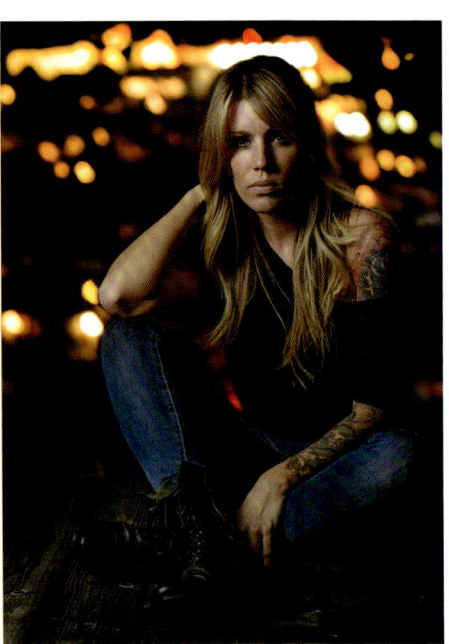

33.4 For this photo of Nicole, I used a single Nikon Speedlight, which I placed in a small softbox at camera left and triggered by using Nikon CLS technology. The slow shutter speed allowed for the lights behind her to bleed through.
ISO 800; 2.5 sec.; f/5.6; 70mm

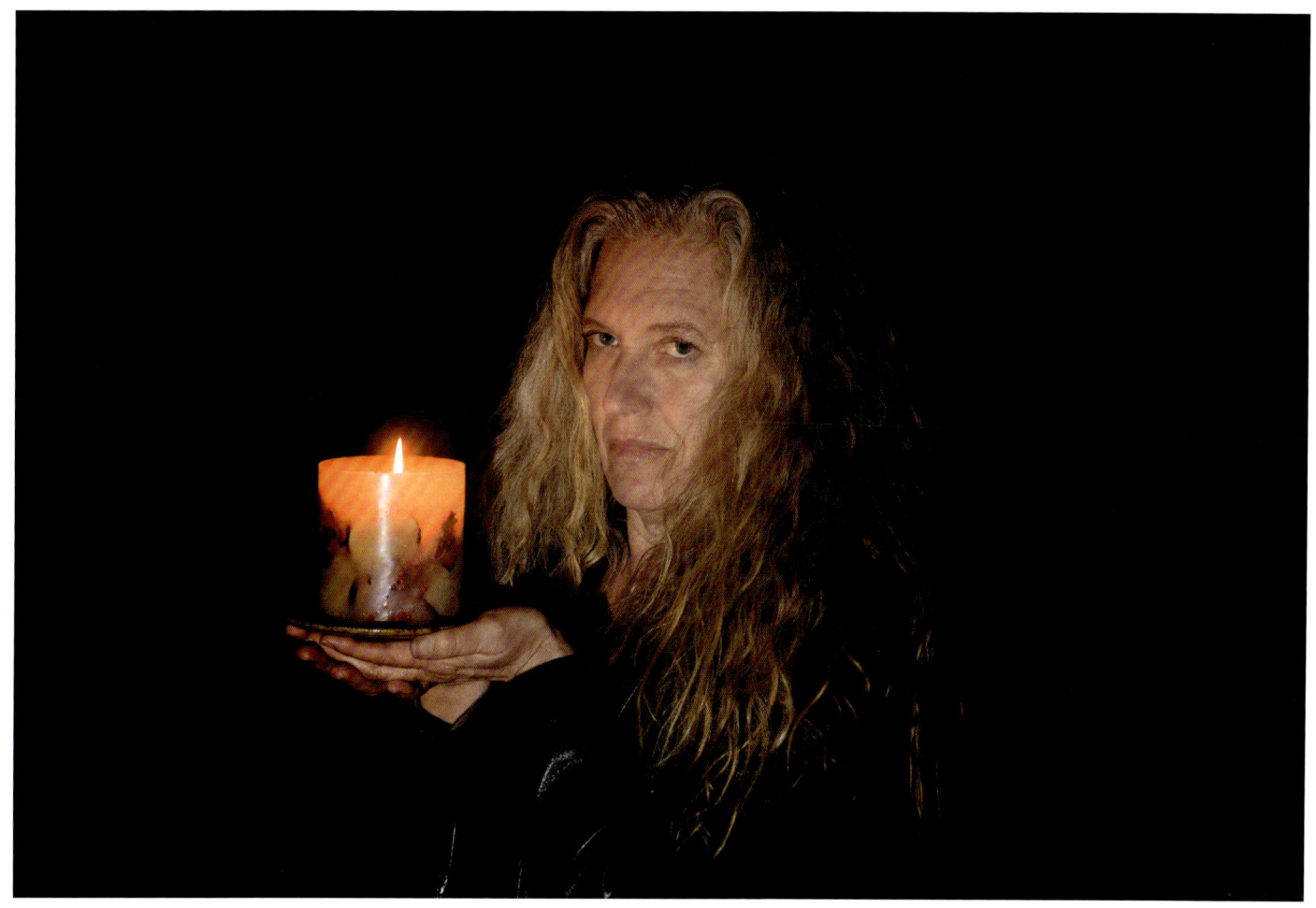

33.5 For this image, I used a single off-camera flash at low power with a snoot to keep the light right on the face, making it look like the subject was lit by the candle.
ISO 400; 1/15 sec.; f/2.8; 140mm

34. DRAGGING THE SHUTTER

DRAGGING THE SHUTTER is a technique whereby you use a slower shutter speed to allow the ambient light from a scene to illuminate the background, and then use a flash to add some fill light on the subject. The idea is to balance the ambient light with the fill light so you can maintain the atmosphere and mood of the background and surrounding areas.

This technique is not very difficult if you have a basic understanding of what is going on in the image and how much of the ambient light you want in the image. As you can see in **Figure 34.1**, the lights from the background are allowed to bleed into the frame, while the subject is still evenly lit.

The key here is to remember that the aperture controls the amount of light from the flash that is allowed through to the sensor, while the shutter speed controls how much of the ambient light influences the exposure.

In **Figures 34.2–34.4**, you can see the same scene photographed at three different shutter speeds. Even though the background becomes more visible in each successive frame, the woman in the foreground remains the same because she is lit by a flash.

You can create really stunning images with this technique, as long as you don't forget to balance the light from the flash so it looks more natural and doesn't draw too much attention to the subject.

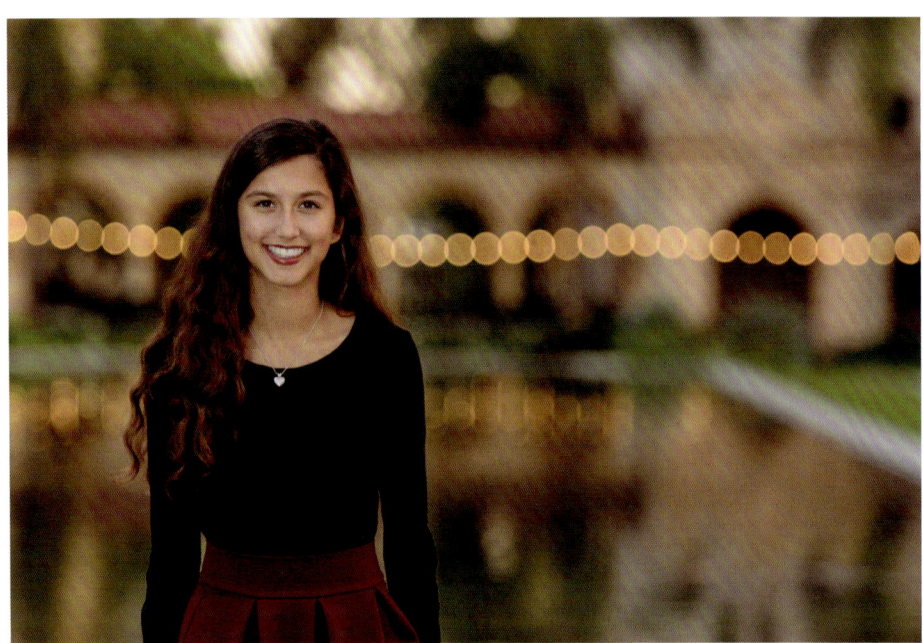

34.1 I took this photograph in Balboa Park in the evening. I used a slow shutter speed to capture the background lights and lit the subject with a flash.
ISO 400; 1/60 sec.; f/2.8; 140mm

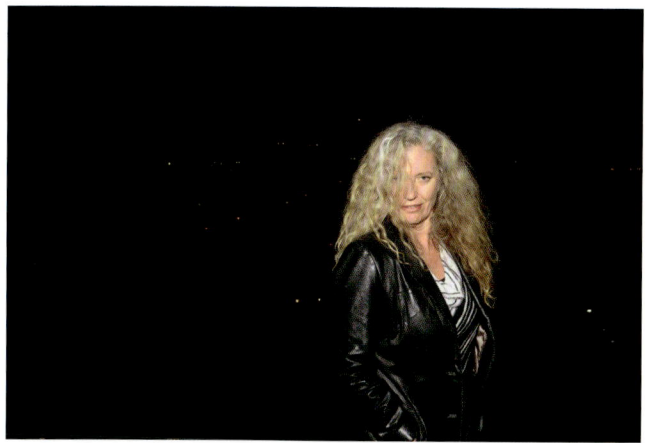

34.2 Having the city in the background makes for a fun photo, but at a shutter speed of 1/250 second, you can't really see much of it.
ISO 400; 1/250 sec.; f/4; 70mm

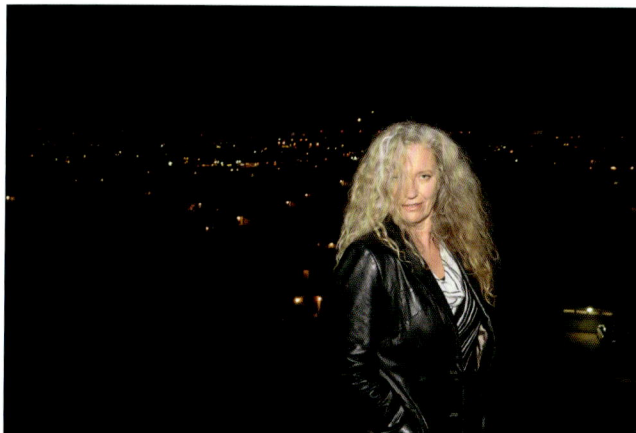

34.3 The city lights become more visible as the shutter speed drops to 1/60 second.
ISO 400; 1/60 sec.; f/2.8; 70mm

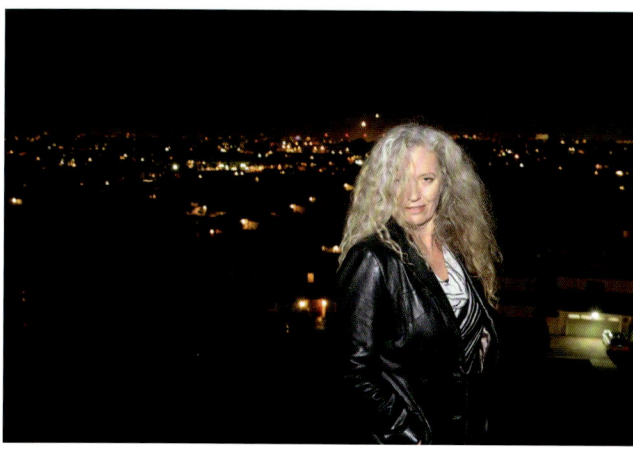

34.4 A much slower shutter speed allows more of the city lights to shine through. The tough part was having the subject not move for a full second.
ISO 400; 1 sec.; f/2.8; 70mm

35. THE IMPORTANCE OF LOCATION SCOUTING FOR NIGHTTIME PHOTOGRAPHY

PHOTOGRAPHING A SCENE at night means working in the dark, which is not the easiest thing to do. Because the color and quality of the light changes minute by minute after the sun drops below the horizon, you need to figure out what your subject is and where you will be photographing from so you can set up your camera and tripod before the sun starts to set. This involves going around earlier in the day to scout locations that you think will make the best images later.

Night photography begins before the sun sets and preparing for a shoot requires some imagination. You need to be able to visualize what the scene will look like when the sun goes down and the nighttime lights come on. As you can see in **Figures 35.1–35.4**, the scene can look very different during the daylight hours compared to how it looks after the sun sets.

Another really good reason to scout locations when it is still light out is that it's safer than trying to navigate an unfamiliar area in the dark. Some areas that are safe during daylight can become unsafe as the day ends. You need to be aware of your surroundings. Many times, you can get a sense of the safety of an area just by looking at it closely when there is light. You can also familiarize yourself with the terrain, which will come in handy when you're trying to move around in low light. You don't want to trip or step into a hole while you're setting up a shot or after you're done photographing for the night.

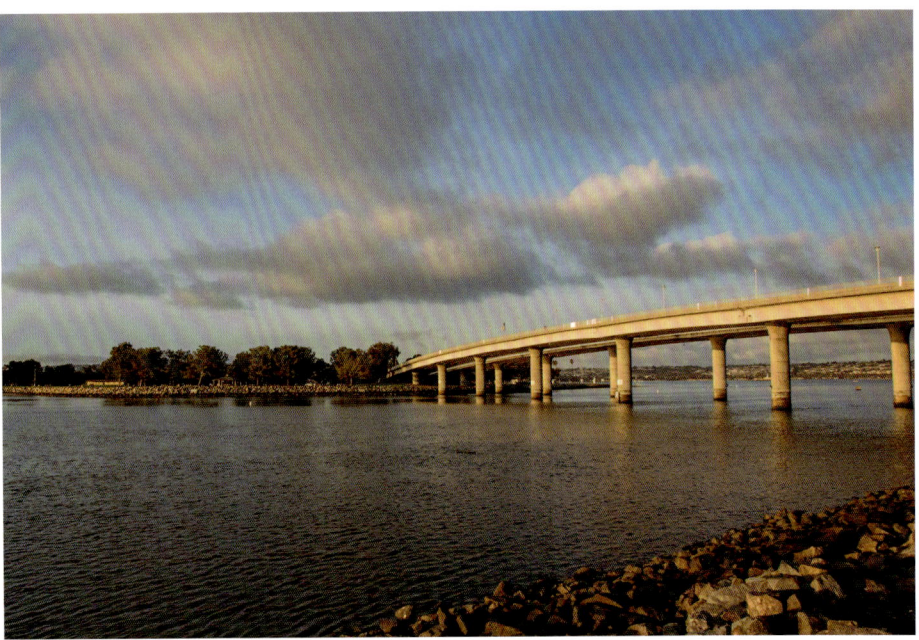

35.1 During the day, this bridge isn't all that interesting, but at night, the lights and reflections can make the scene look very different. **ISO 800; 1/1600 sec.; f/6.3; 20mm**

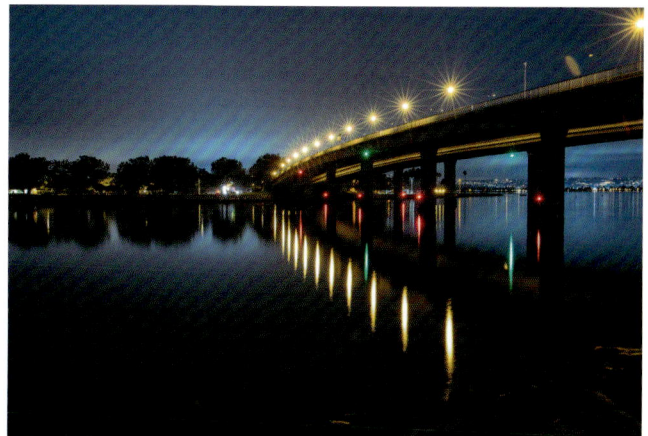

35.2 The lights on the bridge and the reflections in the water make for an interesting image that looks very different than the image shot in bright daylight.
ISO 200; 174 sec.; f/16; 35mm

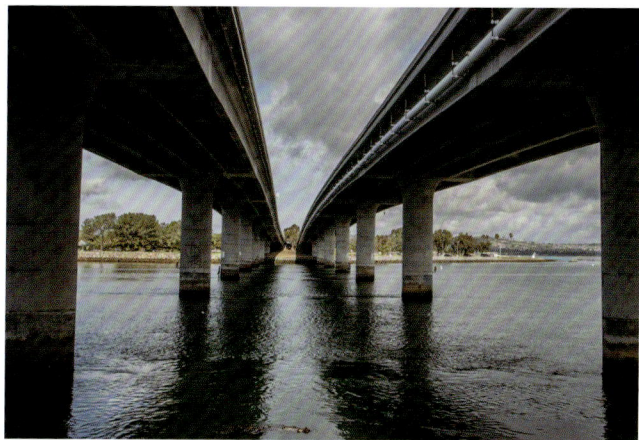

35.3 The area under the bridge is interesting during the day because of the way the graphic elements combine, but it looks even cooler at night.
ISO 400; 1/80 sec.; f/16; 35mm

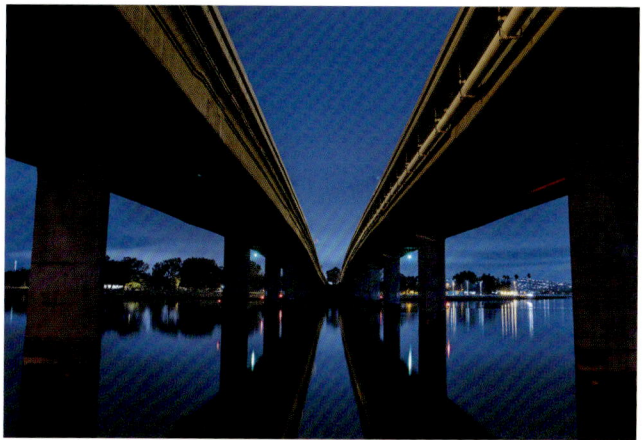

35.4 I used a long exposure to smooth out the water, which makes the reflection much more defined. The color of the sky also adds to the look of the image.
ISO 200; 120 seconds; f/11; 28mm

36. SLOW SHUTTER SPEEDS AND DEEP DEPTH OF FIELD

LOW-LIGHT SCENES require you to use long shutter speeds to allow enough light to enter the camera and reach the sensor. Many times, we use the widest aperture possible to allow the most light to reach the sensor, but with night photography, you can get really great results by using a very long shutter speed with a small aperture and a low ISO.

The idea here is to use a shutter speed that is long enough to really compress time, and in doing so, create a more interesting image. The long shutter speeds will allow any item that is moving in the frame to become just a blur and any lights that are moving (like car lights) to become streaks of light. To be able to use very long shutter speeds, you need to restrict the amount of light that reaches the sensor by using a very small aperture, like f/22, and the lowest ISO possible. The secondary effect of using such a small aperture is that the depth of field is greatly increased, bringing more of the scene into acceptable focus.

When you're taking photos like this, it is extremely important that the camera does not move at all during the exposure. You need to make sure that the tripod is set up correctly, the camera is mounted on the tripod properly,

and that you use a remote or cable release to trigger the camera. If your camera has a mirror up shooting mode, I suggest you use it for this type of photography (**Figure 36.1**).

On DSLR cameras, there is a mirror in front of the shutter that allows you to see exactly what the sensor will see when the photo is taken. This mirror is moved up and out of the way right before the shutter opens when you press the shutter release button. This causes small vibrations in the camera body, which can result in a blurry image. In the mirror up shooting mode, you press the shutter release button once to move the mirror up and lock it into position, and then you have to press it a second time to move the shutter out of the way and take the photo. This allows time for any small vibrations caused by the movement of the mirror to dissipate.

In **Figures 36.2** and **36.3**, you can see the effects of using very long exposures. The car lights blend to become lines of light and anything moving becomes a blur like the water in **Figure 36.3**. To determine the exposure for this type of image, you can use the equivalent exposure math covered in lesson 5, "Why Equivalent Exposures Are Important." Take a shot

with a high ISO and shallow depth of field (wide aperture) until you get the exposure dialed in, then adjust the aperture and ISO for the long exposure.

When I shot **Figures 36.2** and **36.3**, I started out with very different exposure settings, as you can see in **Figures 36.4** and **36.5**. Once I had the exposure I wanted, I translated the settings into small apertures, long shutter speeds, and low ISOs.

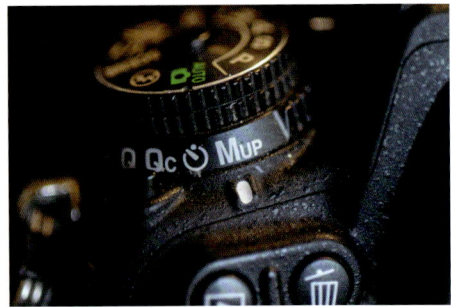

36.1 The mirror up (MUP) shooting mode on the Nikon D750 moves the mirror up and locks it into place before the image is shot, allowing time for vibrations to die down.

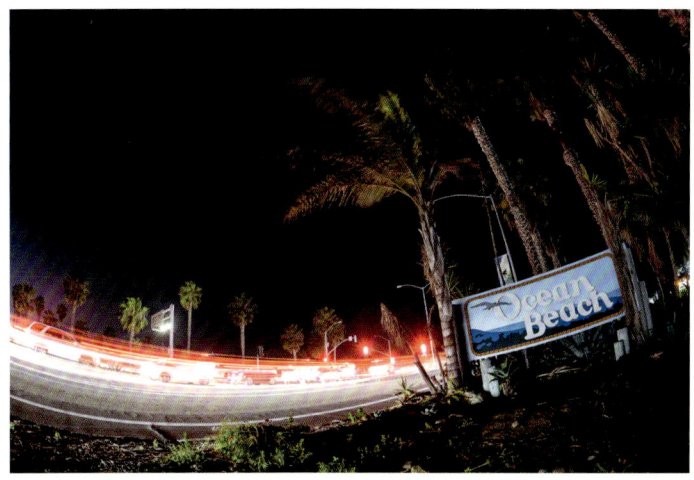

36.2 A long shutter speed turns car headlights and tail-lights into light trails.
ISO 200; 30 sec.; f/16; 35mm

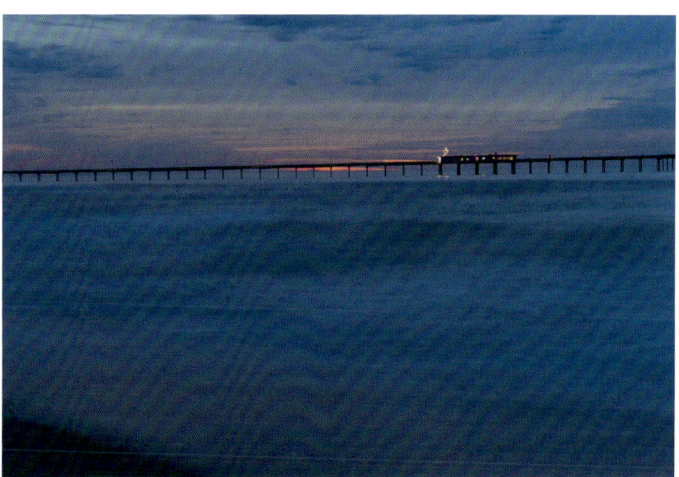

36.3 I used a 20-second exposure to smooth out the water.
ISO 100; 20 sec.; f/16; 70mm

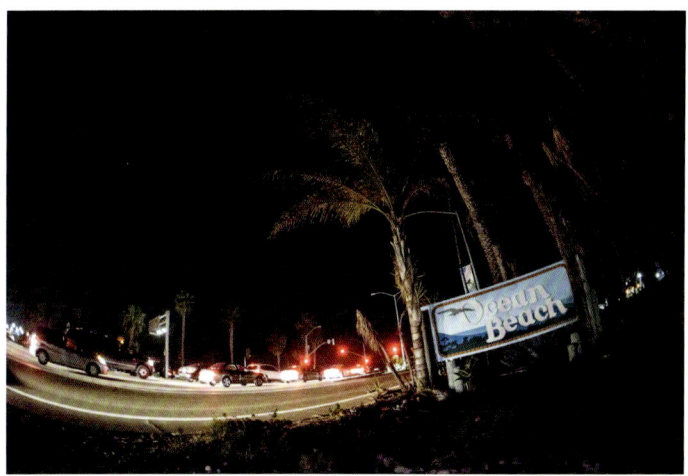

36.4 A fast shutter speed freezes the cars as they drive by—a pretty boring image.
ISO 12800; 1/400 sec.; f/2.8; 35mm

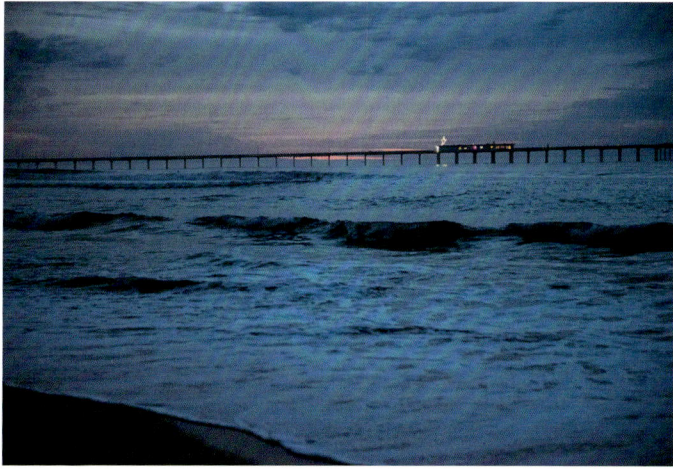

36.5 Fast shutter speeds freeze the waves as they roll to the shore.
ISO 12800; 1/200 sec.; f/2.8; 70mm

37. WHY I LOVE PHOTOGRAPHING BY WATER

I AM VERY LUCKY to live in Southern California. Not only is the weather great, but living close to the ocean gives me access to great scenery for night photography. Water is a fantastic foreground for night photography because it can be turned into a silky smooth surface that reflects any light, creating great images.

I have two tips for when you're shooting close to the water. The first is to use a long shutter speed so that the water looks smooth, and the second is to explore different shooting angles until you find the spot at which you can pick up the reflection of the light on the water.

Getting that ultra smooth water look is actually quite easy. You just need to use a 1 second or longer shutter speed and check out how the image looks on the back of the camera. The easiest way to get the proper exposure is to set the ISO to 400, the aperture to f/8.0, the exposure mode to Shutter Speed Priority, and the metering mode to Spot metering. Then press

the shutter release button halfway down and look at what the camera believes is the correct shutter speed. If that shutter speed is 1 second or greater, go ahead and take the photo, then check to see how it looks on the back of the camera. To get a longer shutter speed, you can use a lower ISO or a smaller aperture (or both). The longer the shutter speed, the smoother and more dreamlike the water will be. In **Figure 37.1**, the silky smooth water is a result of using a 30-second shutter speed.

When you're photographing long exposures on the beach, make sure you know which way the tide is going so you and your tripod and camera don't end up getting wet. I have been at the beach with my camera on a tripod when the water came in and washed away some of the sand under the tripod legs. Luckily, the tripod didn't fall and the camera stayed dry, but the tripod did move, which ruined the photo. Had I taken a minute to look at which way the tide

was going, I could have easily avoided the water.

To pick up the reflection of the light on the water, mount your camera on your tripod, turn on the Live View function, and while watching the screen on the camera, adjust the height and angle of the camera until you see the reflection. The longer the shutter speed, the smoother the water becomes and the blurrier the reflected light is. In **Figure 37.2**, the city lights are reflected in the smooth water between downtown San Diego and Shelter Island.

If you don't live near the ocean or a lake, you can still use water reflections in your nighttime images, but you will either have to add your own water or wait until just after a storm. After rain (or during if you have protective camera coverings), the streets actually reflect a lot of light, creating some great photographic opportunities. Look for areas where you can shoot down at the wet areas so they reflect the surroundings.

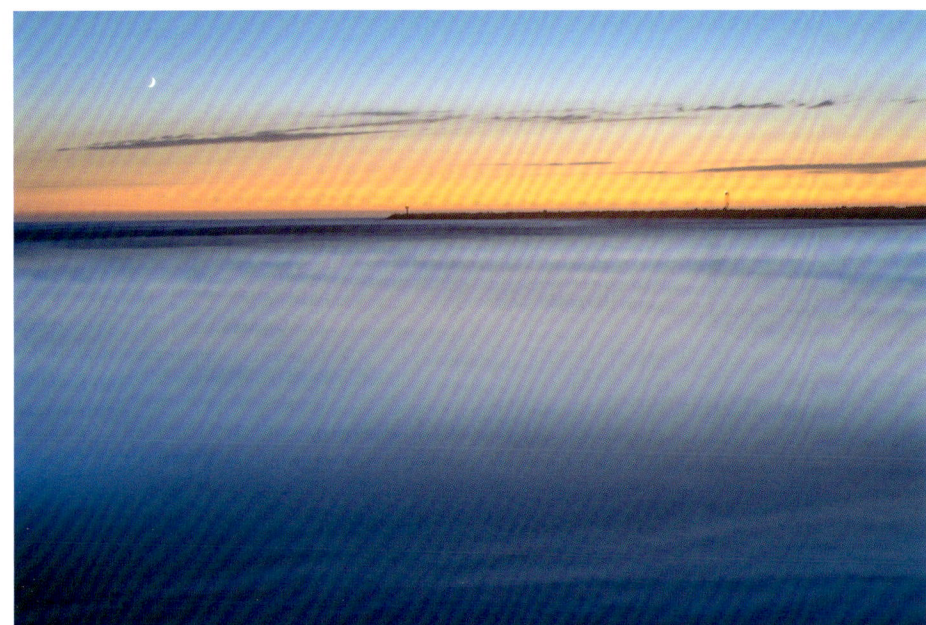

37.1 The long shutter speed creates smooth-looking water.
ISO 100; 30 sec.; f/16; 20mm

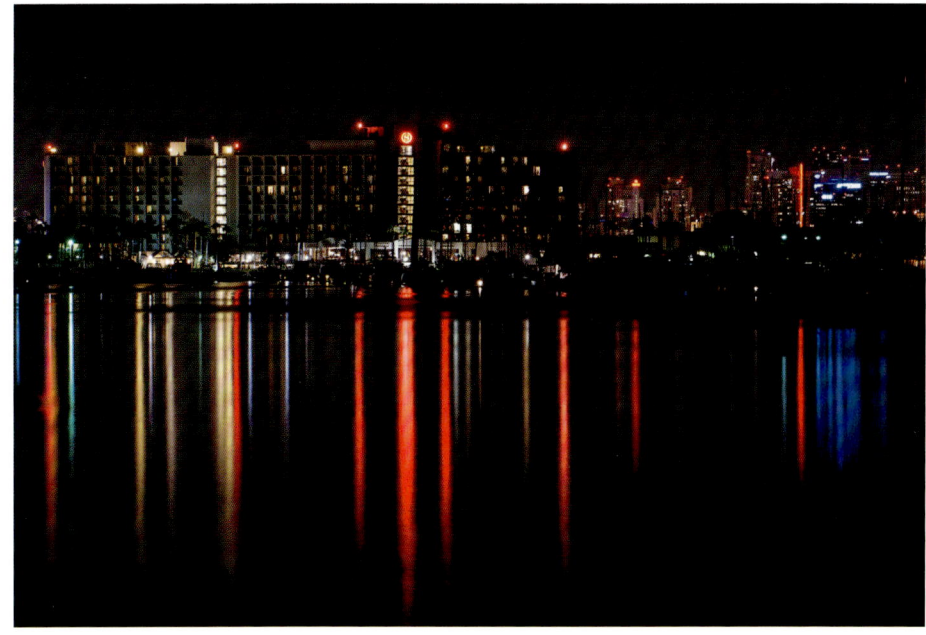

37.2 The long shutter speed made the reflections of the city lights in the water soft and blurry.
ISO 100; 65 sec.; F/16; 200mm

38. HOW TO GET THOSE STARBURST STREET LIGHTS

TO CREATE A STARBURST effect around the visible light sources in an image you simply need to use a very small aperture, like f/18 or smaller. This effect works best when there is a light that is very bright compared to the surrounding area, and it depends on the construction of your lens. The starburst effect is created when the blades that are used to adjust the aperture are really close together, as opposed to when the aperture is wide open and the blades create a more circular opening.

Figures 38.1 and **38.2** show the same scene photographed with two different apertures. You can see that using a small aperture greatly enhances the starburst effect around the lights.

Because I needed to use a longer shutter speed to take the photo in **Figure 38.2**, I used a tripod and cable release so that that everything was in sharp focus.

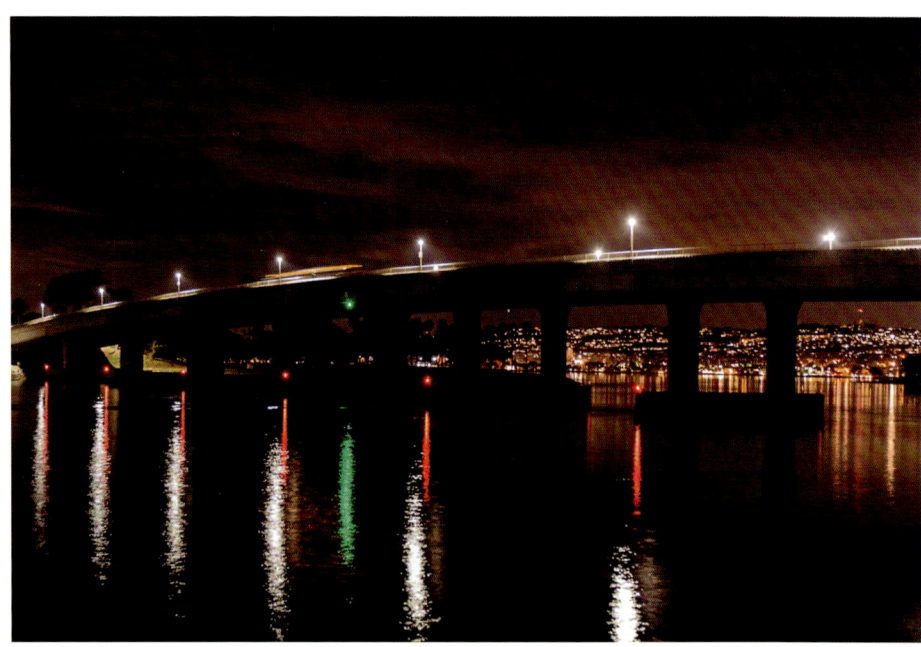

38.1 Even at f/5.6, the aperture is too wide to create the starburst effect.

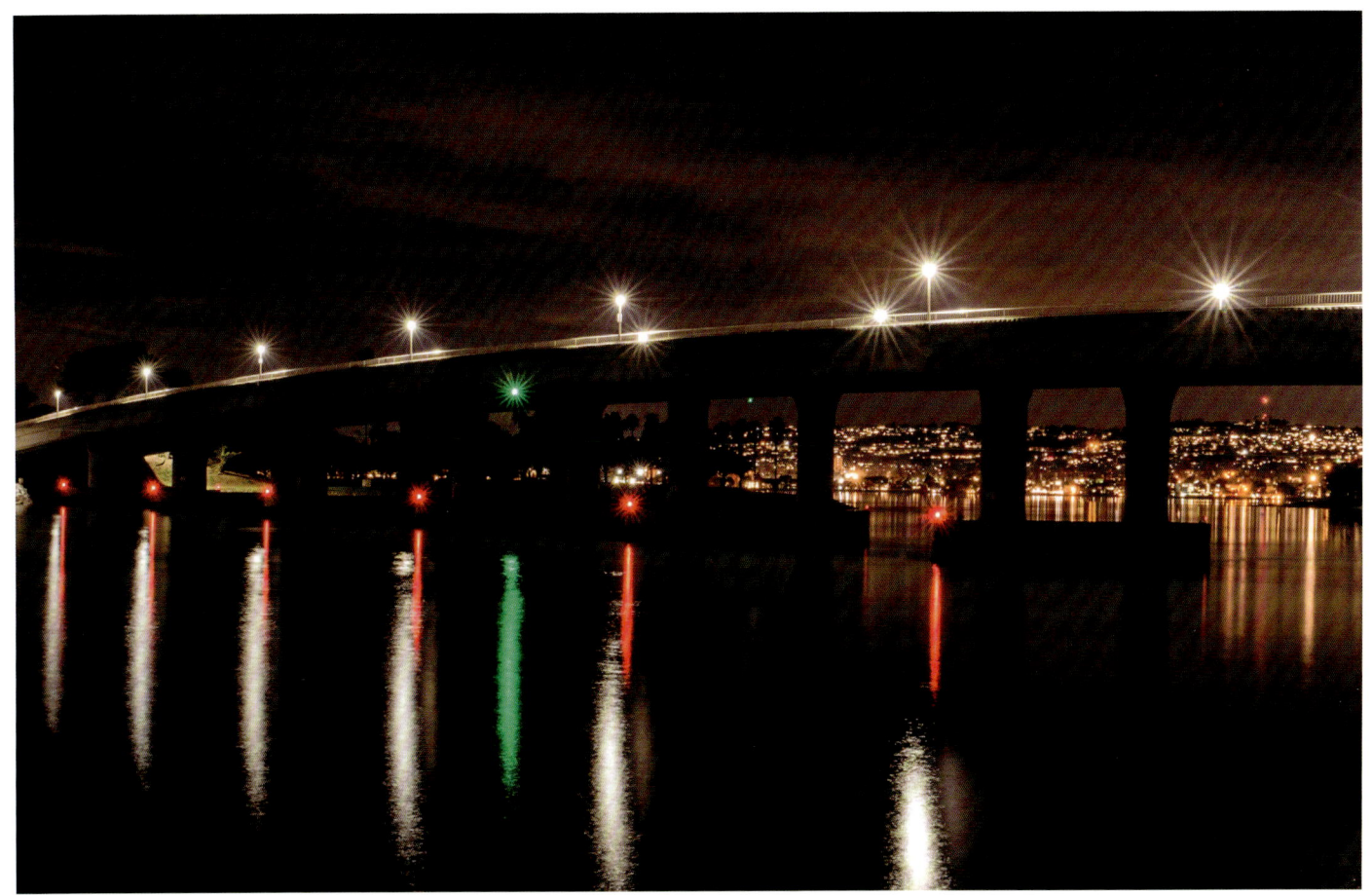

38.2 The starbursts are easily seen in this image, which I shot at an aperture of f/22.

39. PAINTING WITH LIGHT

LIGHT PAINTING is a technique whereby you use an external light source to selectively expose part of a scene with the camera shutter open. It's very simple to start painting with light, but to get good at it, it takes practice, patience, and the ability to imagine the outcome before the lights are turned off.

To paint with light, you will need a camera, lens, tripod, dark room, light, and an interesting subject. Then just follow these steps:

- Mount the camera on the tripod.
- Focus the camera on the subject.
- Turn the autofocus off so that the camera doesn't try to refocus when you press the shutter release button.
- Set the exposure mode to Manual.
- Set the aperture to f/16.
- Set the shutter speed to Bulb.
- Turn off all the lights.
- Use a remote or cable release to trigger the camera shutter.

- Use a flashlight to illuminate the subject by painting it with the light.
- Close the shutter.
- Check the image.
- Repeat these steps until you're satisfied.

You can see a sample setup in **Figure 39.1** and the images I captured in **Figures 39.2** and **39.3**.

Light painting can be a little frustrating because no two images will ever be exactly the same. After some practice, it becomes easier to determine how much light to use and where to use it. When you first start experimenting with this technique, keep the camera locked in the tripod and use a subject that isn't going to move during the exposure. If you want to try a more advanced technique, use a person as a model for the images, but make sure they stay as still as possible when you are painting them with the light.

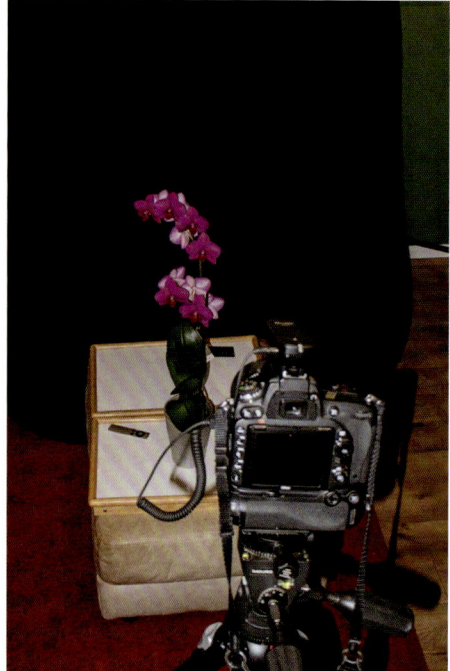

39.1 The setup for the light painting of an orchid.

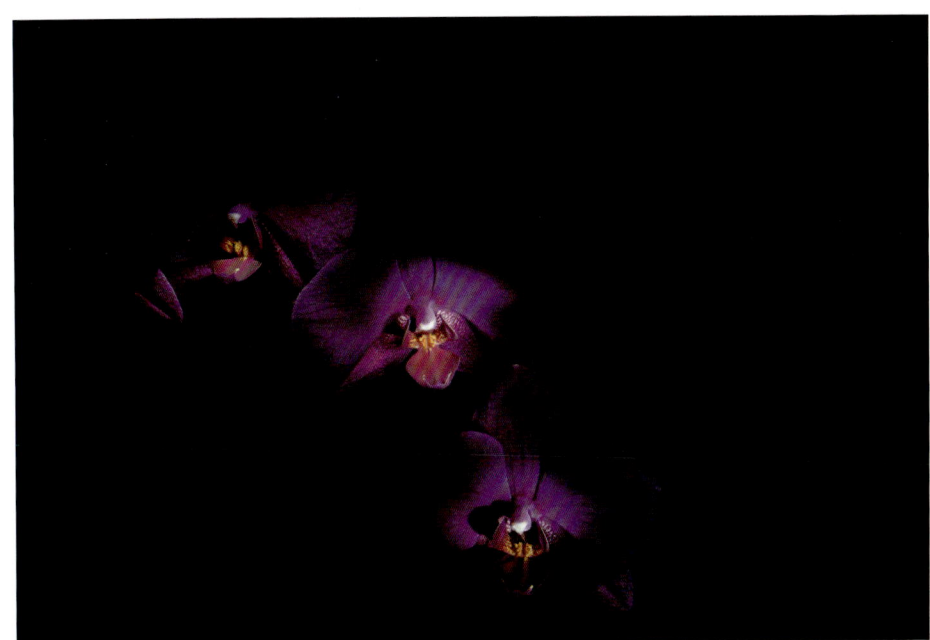

39.2 The orchid painted with a small, bright flashlight.

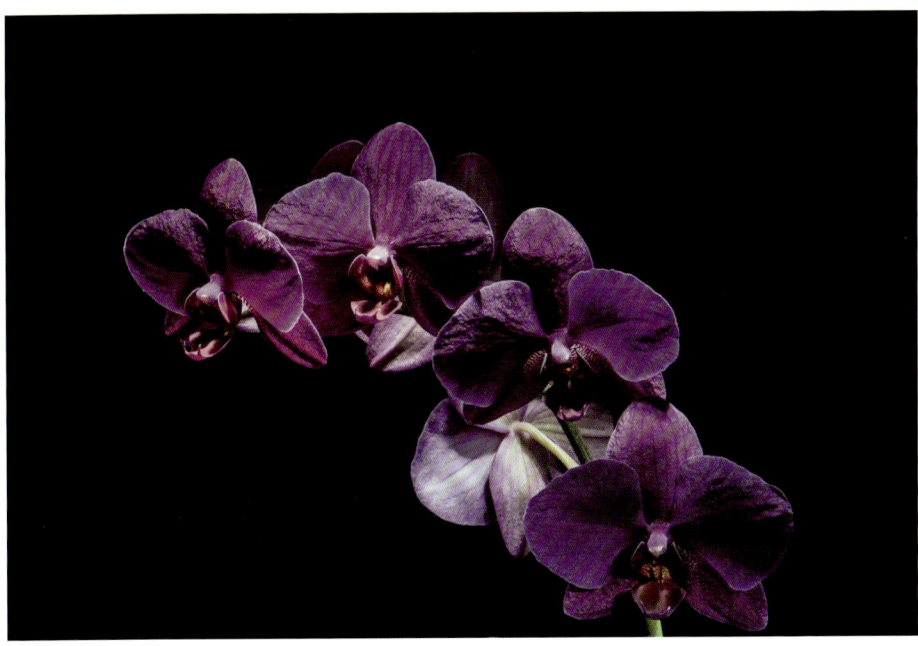

39.3 The same orchid painted with a bigger, softer light.

40. PHOTOGRAPHING THE MOON AND THE NIGHT SKY

WHEN WE LOOK UP into the night sky and see the full moon, it not only commands our attention, it can also inspire our creative side. The fact that humans have traveled to the moon and even walked on its surface is awe-inspiring. All these things make the moon a great subject, but most people who point their cameras at the moon end up disappointed with the results. The main reason is that the moon is smaller than you think when shot against the night sky.

To capture a good photograph of the moon, you need to use a lens with a large focal length, such as 600mm or more. In November of 2016 while I was writing this book, I photographed the largest supermoon since 1948 (**Figure 40.1**). On that night, the moon was closer and brighter than it had been in 68 years. However, even the biggest moon doesn't look very impressive in my photograph, and this was shot at 400mm on a crop-sensor camera (equivalent focal length of 600mm). Really, if you use anything less than 600mm, the moon will look a little disappointing and it will be hard to see the detail.

So how do photographers get those really cool photos in which the moon looks huge? A lot of that has to do with where the moon is in the night sky and the focal length of the lens. When the moon is coming up or going down, it looks a lot closer and bigger than it does when it is overhead. In lesson 16, I talked about the compression that happens when you use long lenses. This compression can make the moon look closer and bigger due to its relationship to the items in the foreground and middle ground (**Figure 40.2**).

Getting a sharp, clear photograph of the moon isn't difficult if you understand what is going on. The moon is very bright and is always moving, so you need to use a pretty fast shutter speed to freeze it. Because the moon takes up such a small amount of the frame, the camera's built-in light meter won't have enough information to create a proper exposure, so it's best to use Manual exposure mode. Start by setting the camera to ISO 400, 1/250 second, f/5.6. After you take a photo, check the exposure on the back of the camera and zoom in to 100% to examine the focus. If the moon looks too bright, increase the shutter speed. If it's too dark, increase the ISO. If you use a shutter speed slower than 1/250 second, you run the risk of ending up with a slightly blurry moon.

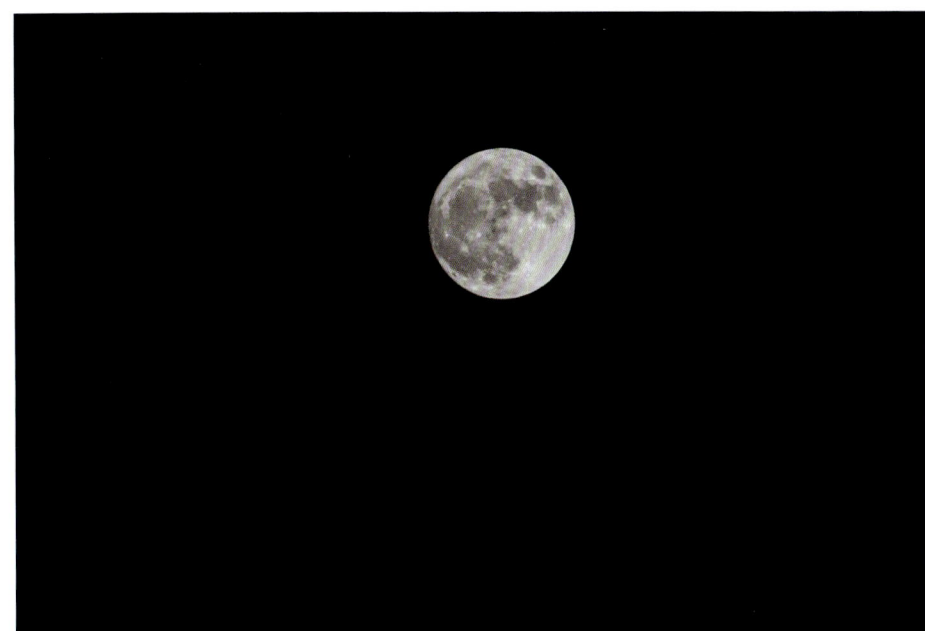

40.1 Even this supermoon shot with a 400mm lens on a crop-sensor camera looks small in the frame.
ISO 400; 1/250 sec.; f/8; 400mm (600mm equivalent)

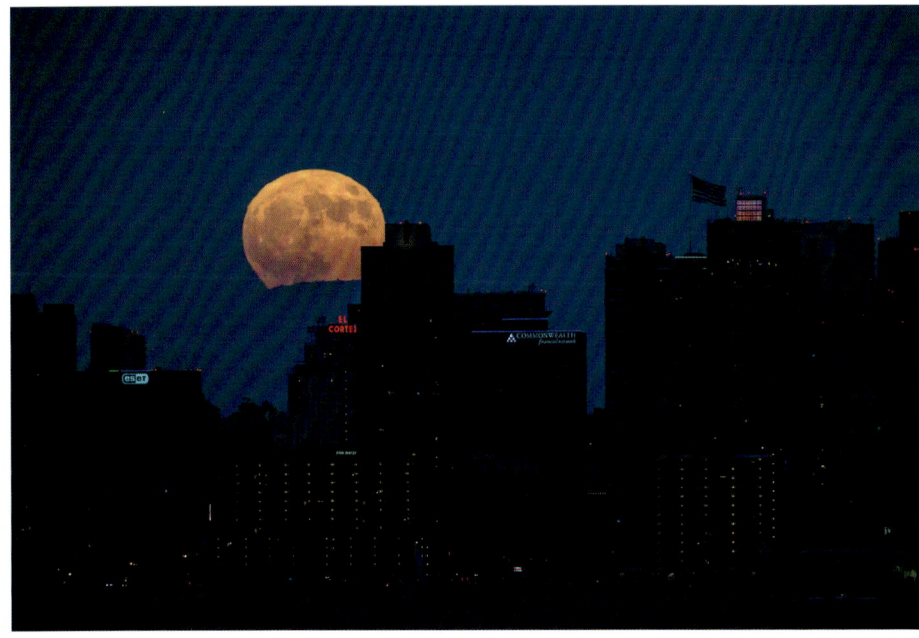

40.2 The moon photographed from a low angle with the city skyline in the foreground. The position of the moon and its relationship to the buildings in the foreground makes it seem bigger. Image © Daniel Knighton, Pixel Perfect Images
ISO 400; 1/30 sec.; f/5.6; 600mm

The stars are another wonderful subject just waiting to be photographed, but capturing good star trail photos is a little more complicated. You need a tripod and a cable release to keep the shutter open for a period of time. You also need a clear sky without any of the light pollution you get from nearby cities. For example, when I aim the camera at the night sky in San Diego and leave the shutter open, the lights from the city start to bleed into the frame.

There are two different methods for getting images of star trails. The first is to just set the camera up, aim the lens at a part of the night sky, and leave the shutter open to capture the stars. This is what I did to capture **Figure 40.3**, which I took in the Anza-Borrego Desert State Park where there is very little light pollution.

When you use this method, the main issues you'll face are how to determine the amount of time to keep the shutter open and what ISO and aperture to use to get a proper exposure. The best option is to use the concept of equivalent exposures to get the best settings. Start with a short shutter speed and a high ISO to get a proper exposure, and then adjust the shutter speed and ISO until you get a long enough exposure to create star trails. Follow this example, but remember that your exposure settings will be different because your night sky will be different:

- Set the camera to Manual mode.
- Set the ISO to 6400.
- Set the aperture to f/5.6.
- Set the shutter speed to Bulb.
- Use the cable release to take a 90-second exposure.
- Check the exposure on the back of the camera. If the image is too dark, double the shutter speed to 3 minutes. If the image is too bright, try a shutter speed of 45 seconds.
- Take another shot and check it on the back of the camera again. Continue adjusting the shutter speed until you get the image you want.

Once the exposure looks right on the back of the camera, you can change the ISO and shutter speed to get a much longer exposure and more movement in the stars. The idea is to drop the ISO from 6400 to 200, which will require a huge increase in the amount of time the shutter is open. There is a little math here, but it's not that difficult. The difference between ISO 6400 and ISO 200 is 5 full stops (6400 to 3200 to 1600 to 800 to 400 to 200). Each full stop reduces the amount of light reaching the sensor by half, so you need to increase the length of time the shutter is open by 5 full stops. For example, if you ended up with a proper exposure at 1 minute and ISO 6400, you will need a shutter speed of 32 minutes at ISO 200.

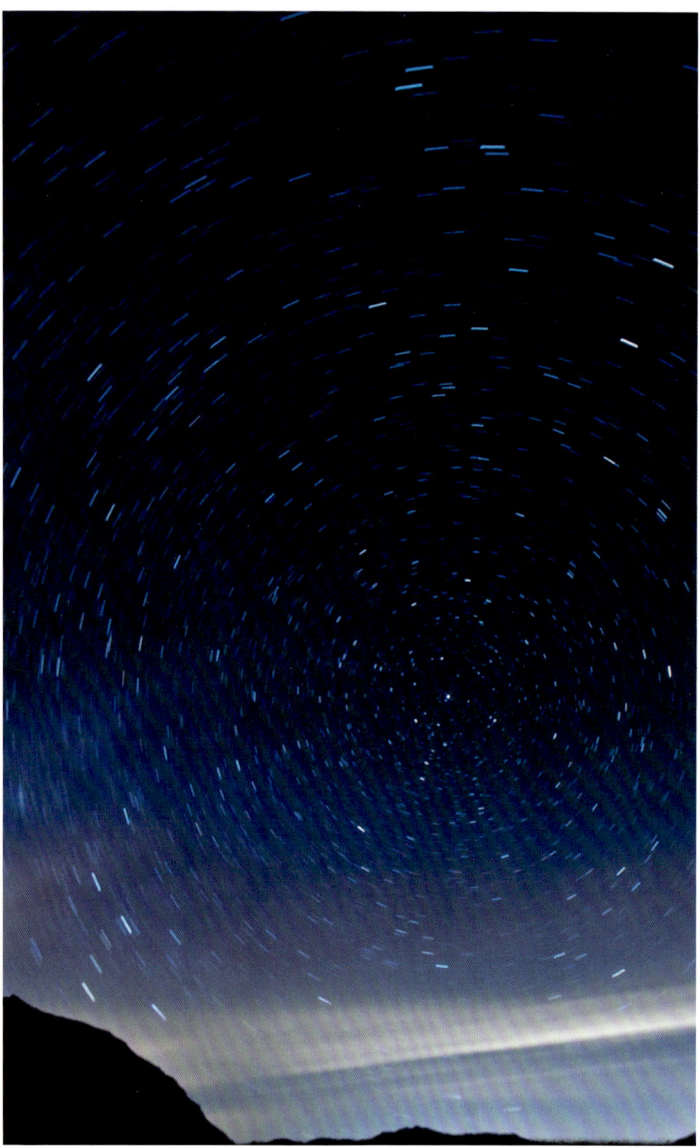

40.3 I took this star trail photo in the Anza-Borrego Desert State Park where there is very little light pollution. **ISO 400; 600 sec.; f/5.6; 20mm**

The second method for capturing star trails is to take a series of images of the same area and combine them during post-processing, which is what my nephew Tyler did to create **Figure 40.4**.

The idea behind image stacking is to break up one long exposure into smaller pieces. For example, instead of an hour-long exposure, you would take two 30-minute exposures. You can then combine individual images with the statistics script in Photoshop to create a single image file. Here's how to do it:

- Open Photoshop.
- Go to *File > Scripts > Statistics*. This opens a menu that allows you to select the files you want to combine and the method to do so.
- Select the images you want to stack together.
- Change the Stack Mode to Maximum.
- Click OK, and the file will open in Photoshop and can now be edited.

To get the best results when you're shooting star trail images, keep the following tips in mind:

- Point the camera at the North Star (Polaris). This will give you the circles that look really good.
- Use a long exposure time, regardless of whether you're shooting one frame or multiple frames to combine later. You will want at least a 30-minute exposure. This allows for lots of movement, which results in longer trails.
- The further away you can get from city lights, the better. This cuts down on any light pollution bleeding into the image.

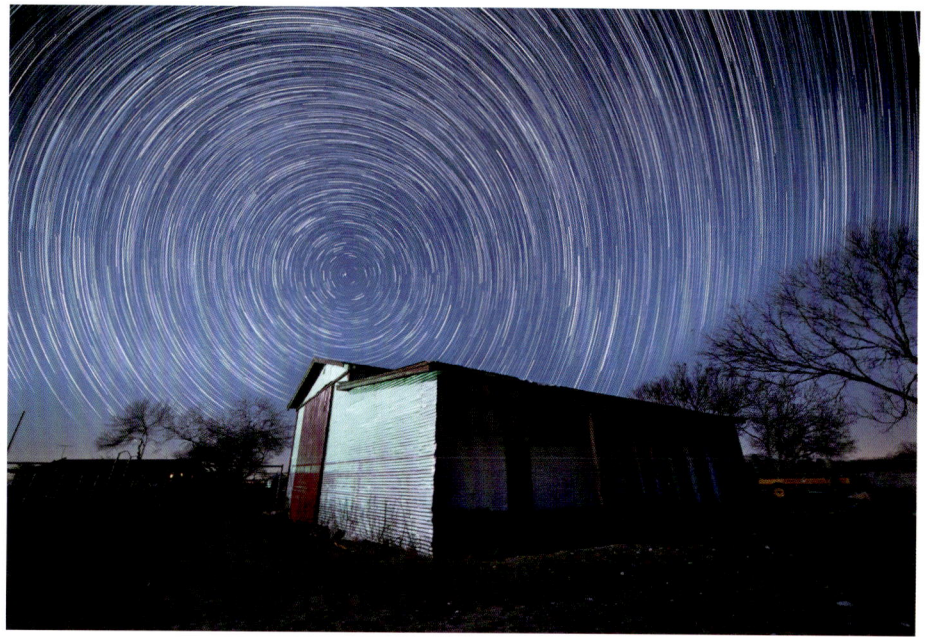

40.4 My nephew Tyler shot this star trail photo in South Texas. To create the final photograph, he used a set of 211 images and combined them in Photoshop. Image © Tyler Torwick
ISO 800; 24 sec.; f/2.8

41. SUNRISE, SUNSET, AND THE DIFFERENT TWILIGHTS

TWILIGHT ISN'T JUST A BOOK and movie franchise about werewolves and vampires; it's also the time period after the sun has set or before the sun has risen. The sky goes through color changes after the sun drops below the horizon and before it is night. These same changes occur as the sun comes up in the morning before it breaks over the horizon. There are three different twilights as the sky goes from day to night or night to day, and there are different ways to judge which twilight you are in.

- Civil Twilight: This is when the sun is 6 degrees or less below the horizon. In this twilight, you can still easily see the items around you. You don't need to add any light to be able to see things and the horizon is still easily distinguishable in clear conditions.

- Nautical Twilight: This is the middle twilight when the sun is 6–12 degrees below the horizon. During this time, it is difficult to accurately determine the horizon and sailors cannot navigate by existing light alone.

- Astronomical Twilight: This is when the sun is between 12 and 18 degrees below the horizon. For most practical purposes, this twilight period is indistinguishable from night.

The same scene can look quite different as the sun sets and the sky goes from twilight to night (**Figures 41.1–41.3**). Most of the time when I photograph the night sky, I start during twilight and keep going until after the sun has set.

It has often been said that the best light is during the golden hour, which is right before the sun sets and right after it rises. The sky takes on a more red tone at this time of day due to the way the light waves travel and everything just looks better in this light. The golden hour can actually be a combination of the time right before the sun sets (or after it rises) and the civil twilight. If you are out photographing, don't stop once the sun has dropped below the horizon because the best light might still be to come. I started photographing the shack at Windansea Beach before sunset, but the winning shot of the night was taken 20 minutes after the sun had set (**Figure 41.4**).

Share Your Best Sunrise or Sunset Image!

Once you've captured your best sunrise or sunset image, share it with the Enthusiast's Guide community! Follow *@EnthusiastsGuides* and post your image to Instagram with the hashtag *#EGLowLightSunrise* or *#EGLowLightSunset*. Don't forget that you can also search that same hashtag to view all the posts and be inspired by what others are shooting.

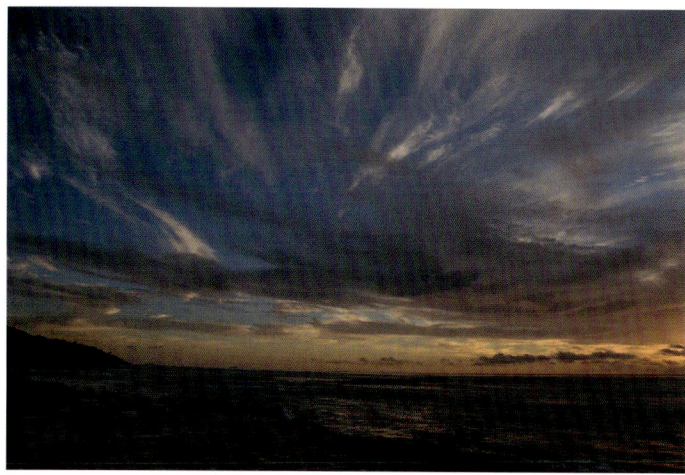

41.1 I took this image right before the sun dropped behind the horizon.
ISO 200; 1/200 sec.; f/16; 20mm

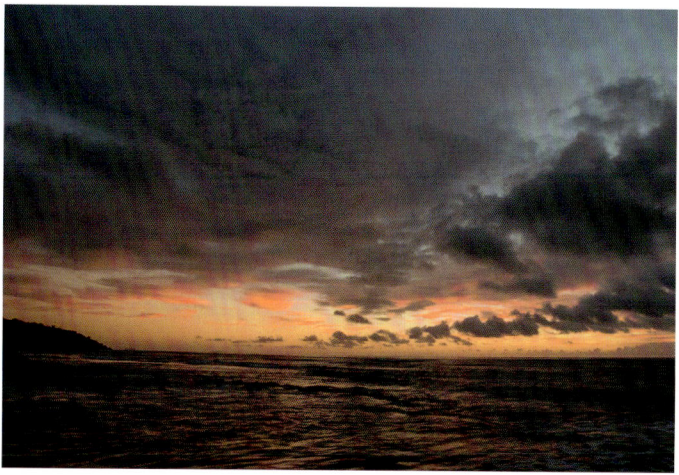

41.2 About 25 minutes after the sunset, there was more red in the sky.
ISO 200; 1/4 sec.; f/16; 20mm

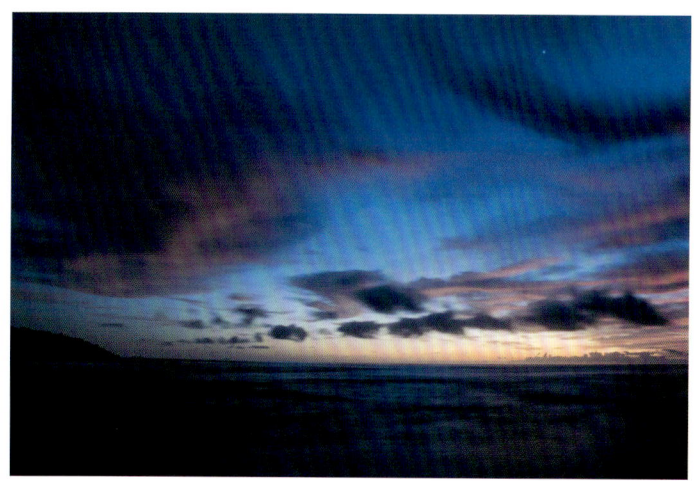

41.3 I shot this image 35 minutes after the sunset. The sky had turned a much deeper blue and while there were still traces of red in the clouds, it was very close to being fully dark.
ISO 200; 25 sec.; f/16; 20mm

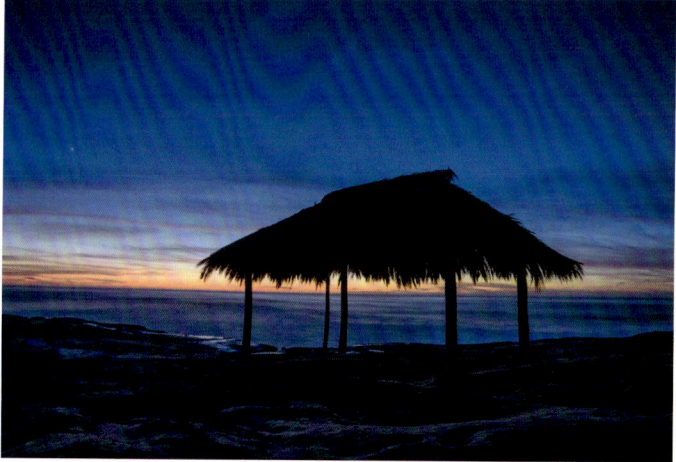

41.4 I shot this photo of the shack at Windansea Beach in San Diego 20 minutes after the sun set.
ISO 100; 30 sec.; f/13; 20mm

Photographing during sunrise takes a little extra planning because you need to set up your equipment and start shooting in the dark, and then photograph until after the sun has risen. This means you have to scout the location the day before you plan to shoot or go with someone who knows the area. I took **Figure 41.5** right before the sun came over the horizon, but I was there for quite a while before that waiting for the light to be just right. When you're shooting into the sunrise, you might need to adjust the composition depending on how the sun and clouds look.

There are a few things you can do to make sure you get the best results with those rich colors when you're shooting a sunrise or sunset:

- The color of sunset light is slightly warmer than sunrise light, so if you are looking for those great oranges and reds, focus on the sunset.
- Adjust the white balance in post-production to bring back the actual color you saw, rather than the color the camera recorded. Sometimes the camera will mute the colors because it is trying to get a natural look instead of the vibrant red that is actually present.
- I like to bracket my sunrise and sunset images so that I have options during post-processing. I usually try to take a five-image bracket that goes from −2 to + 2 exposure. This also allows me to experiment with high dynamic range (HDR) photography. (I cover HDR and other multiple-exposure techniques in my book *The Enthusiast's Guide to Multi-Shot Techniques*, Rocky Nook, 2016.)
- If you underexpose the images slightly, you will get a more saturated image that can really work for sunrises and sunsets. The sky may be rather bright, so reducing the exposure a little can work wonders.

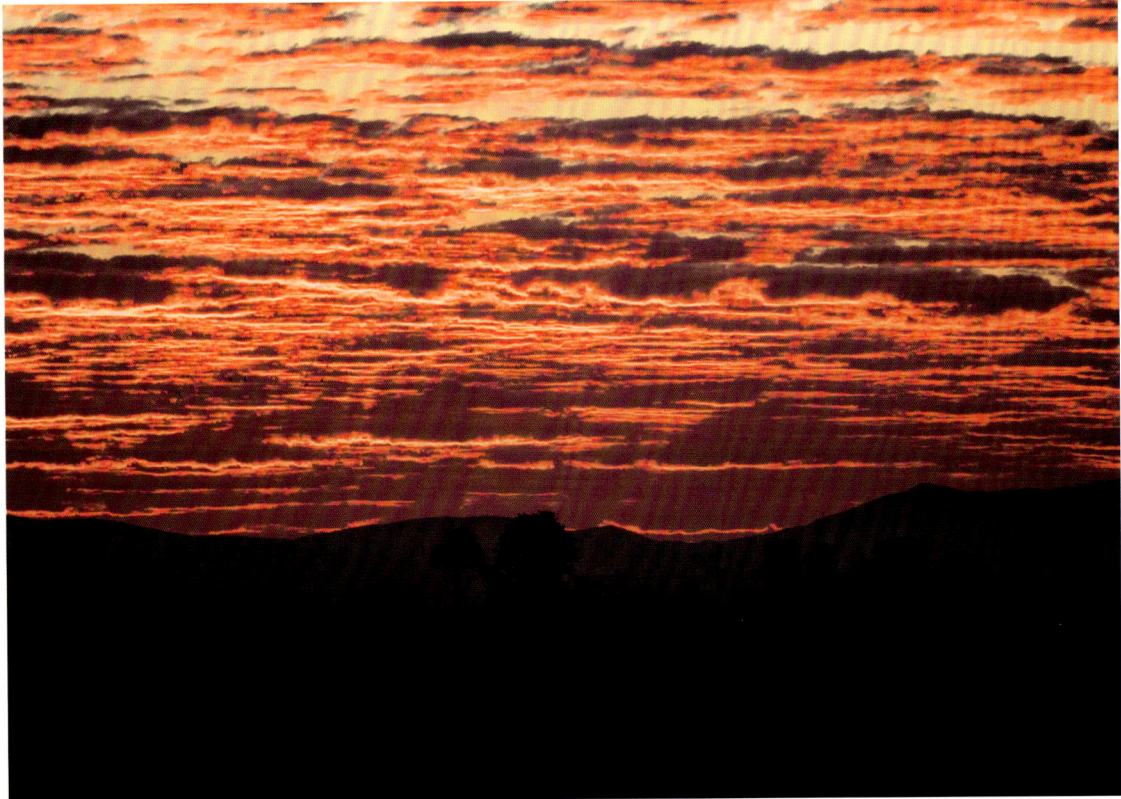

41.5 The view facing East from Point Loma as the sun broke over the horizon. **ISO 400; 1/30 sec.; f/5.6; 70mm**

42. LIGHT TRAILS AND FIREWORKS

WHEN YOU PHOTOGRAPH at night and leave the shutter open for long periods of time, any lights that move will leave bright trails that show the path they took. This is the basis of photographing light trails and fireworks—you open the shutter, allow the light to move through the frame, then close the shutter.

Photographing Light Trails Made by Car Lights

Some of the most dynamic-looking night photographs are those with the light trails made by cars traveling through the frame. These are fun to shoot and you don't need a lot of technical skill or gear. What you do need is a great vantage point from which you can see the light trails travel through a scene. These shots don't work when there is traffic or when cars are not moving, so while a traffic light is a great addition to the photograph, you will want to shoot when the light is green and the traffic is moving away from or toward you.

Mount your camera on a tripod and compose the scene as best as you can by picturing where the cars will be driving. Focus on the middle ground and then turn the autofocus off. Set the exposure mode to Manual, aperture to f/16, ISO to 200, and shutter speed to Bulb mode. Now it is just a matter of trial and error to get the streaks to look the way you want them to in the photo (**Figure 42.1** and **Figure 42.2**). The longer the shutter speed, the more time the trails have to develop. I usually start at 10–15 seconds, and then adjust as needed.

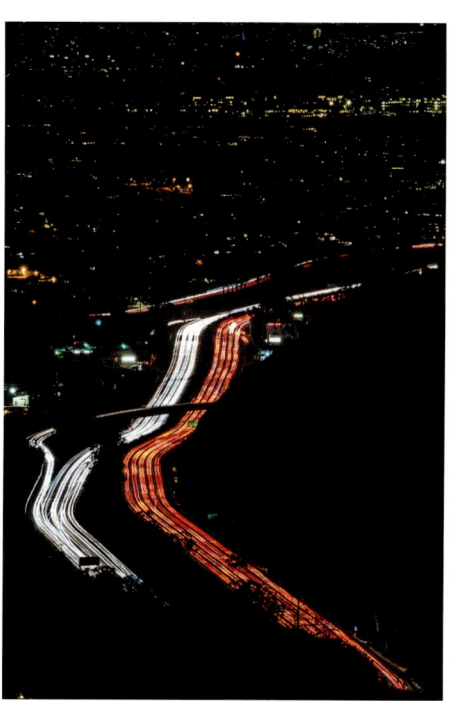

42.1 Car headlights and taillights make great nighttime subjects. I took this was from the top of a hill, capturing the rush-hour traffic in San Diego.
ISO 200; 15 sec.; f/16; 300mm

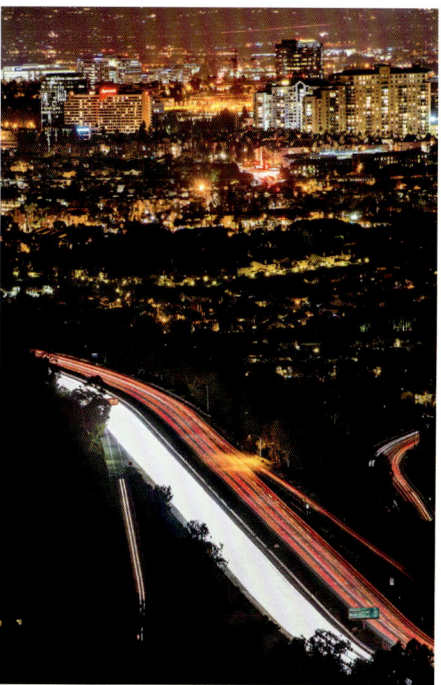

42.2 In this photo, the 30-second shutter speed turned the cars into solid white and red lines.
ISO 200; 30 sec.; f/16; 200mm

Using Sparklers to Write in the Air

It's lots of fun to run around with sparklers, and it's easy to capture cool photos of them. Before getting into the settings used to take sparkler photos, there are some important safety considerations that need to be addressed. This is literally playing with fire and is dangerous. Sparklers burn very hot and can easily burn you, your clothing, or your surroundings. They need to be treated as the dangerous items that they are.

- Make sure the sparklers you are using are legal in your area.
- Set up an area outside to shoot. You do not want to wave sparklers around inside due to the fire hazard.
- Make sure everyone is aware of what you are doing.

- Make sure there are no flammable items in the vicinity.
- Do not use sparklers in an area that is very dry. If necessary, water the area down first so a random spark doesn't cause a fire.
- This might look like a fun activity for young kids, but these sparklers can cause burns, so do not allow young kids to play with them.

For this type of photography, you need a nice dark night with little ambient light so that the sparkler is recorded but the rest of the scene stays dark. You will also need an assistant to either press and hold the shutter release or to do the writing in the sky.

Mount the camera on a tripod and have someone stand where the sparkler will be so you can set the focus. Once the camera is focused, turn autofocus off. Set the ISO to 200, the aperture to f/8, and the shutter speed to Bulb mode. Once you are ready to go, light the sparkler, and then press the shutter release button down to start the exposure. Use the sparkler to write in the air in front of the camera. Close the shutter when you think you are done. You can see some of the results I got in **Figure 42.3** and **42.4**. The speed at which you move the sparkler is important—the slower you go, the longer the shutter needs to be open and the smaller the aperture needs to be.

Photographing Fireworks

It's easer to photograph fireworks than you might think. They go off roughly in the same area, so you don't have to worry much about

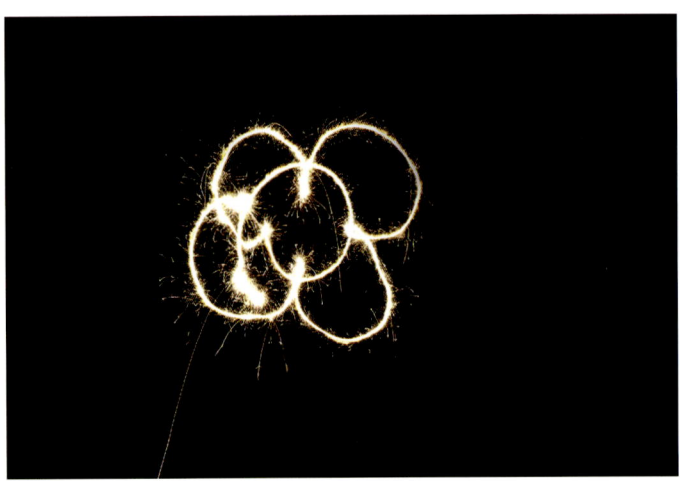

42.3 I used a sparkler to draw a flower in the sky. While this isn't the best flower ever drawn, it's harder than it looks to draw in the sky.
ISO 200; 8 sec.; f/16; 70mm

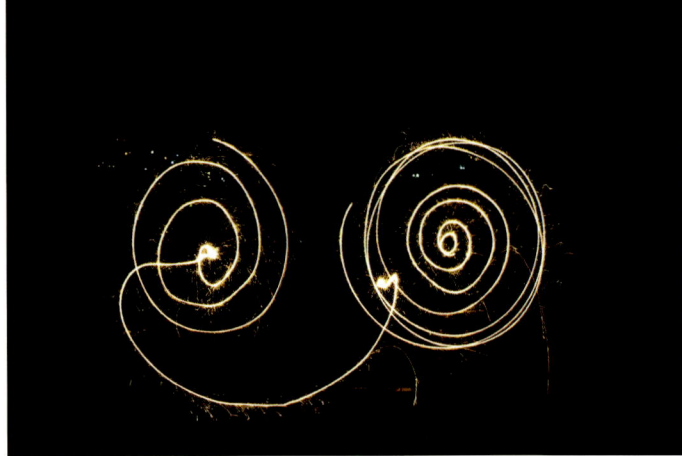

42.4 Writing very slowly in the sky allows the light to bleed more, but now you can see a little bit of the background.
ISO 200; 20 sec.; f/16.0; 70mm

focus. They are easy to time because you can actually see them go up and explode, and they are interesting subjects. Follow these easy steps to photograph fireworks:

- Find a location where you can see the fireworks clearly.
- Mount the camera on a tripod and attach a cable release or pair the camera with a wireless remote.
- Set the shutter speed to Bulb mode, the aperture to f/11, and the ISO to 200.
- When the first firework goes off, press the shutter release button halfway down until the focus is locked on the firework. Then press the shutter release button all the way down and hold it until the firework has exploded, then release it.
- Change the focus mode to Manual.
- Check the exposure on the back of the camera.
- Now all you have to do is open the shutter when the rockets streak skyward, and then close it after the firework trails are over.
- Check the composition and exposure on the back of the camera.
- Adjust the length of the exposure as needed.

The finale of a fireworks show is usually brighter and more packed with fireworks than the rest of the show, meaning you need to make the aperture smaller or shorten the amount of time you keep the shutter open. In **Figure 42.5**, you can see the fireworks exploding in the air during a Fourth of July celebration.

Including additional elements in your fireworks photographs can give the images a sense of time and place. In **Figure 42.6**, you can see the silhouettes of the spectators. All I had to do to capture them was use a wider angle and a longer shutter speed.

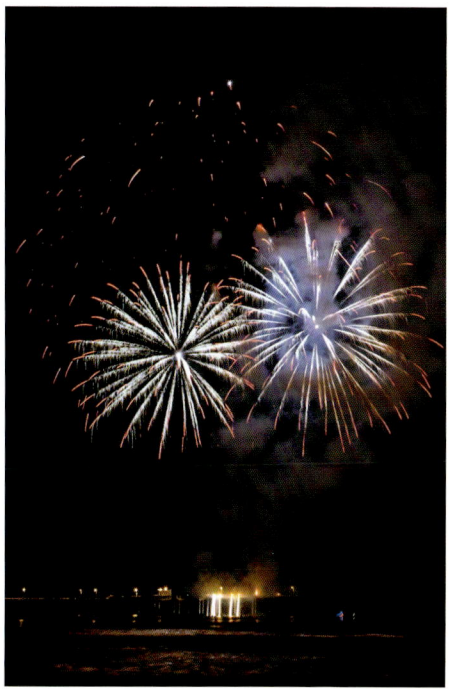

42.5 Fireworks on the Fourth of July off the Ocean Beach pier.
ISO 200; 6.3 sec.; f/13.0; 70mm

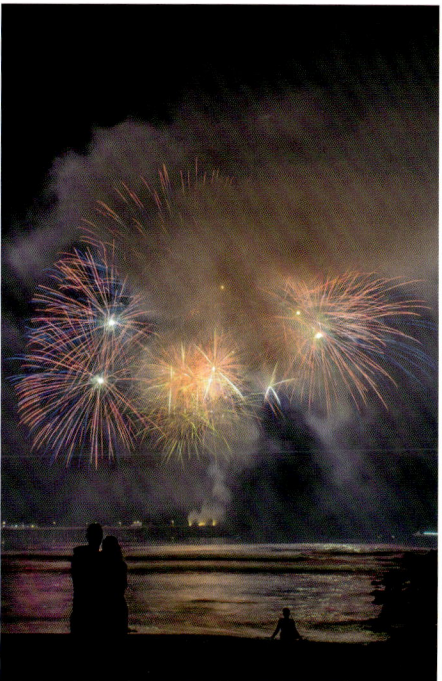

42.6 Including the spectators watching the fireworks gives the image a better sense of place.
ISO 200; 10 sec.; f/13; 24mm

43. PHOTOGRAPHING CITY LIGHTS

PHOTOGRAPHS OF CITYSCAPES are what a lot people think about when you talk about night photography, and there is a good reason for that. The nighttime cityscape is a vibrant, colorful subject that can give you great results on just about any night. When you want to shoot a cityscape, there are two great vantage points from which to shoot. The first is to shoot the city from a distance, preferably over water, as seen in **Figure 43.1**. The second is to get up as high as possible and look down on the city, as seen in **Figure 43.2**.

Getting the proper exposure for nighttime cityscapes can be a little tricky because the sky progressively gets darker, and as the lights come on, the city gets brighter. Here's what to do:

- Mount the camera on a tripod and compose the image through the viewfinder.
- Lock the camera in place and attach a cable release or remote.
- Set the exposure mode to Shutter Speed Priority.
- Set the metering mode to Matrix (Nikon), Evaluative (Canon), or Multi-zone (Sony) metering.
- Set the ISO to 200.
- Set the aperture to f/16.

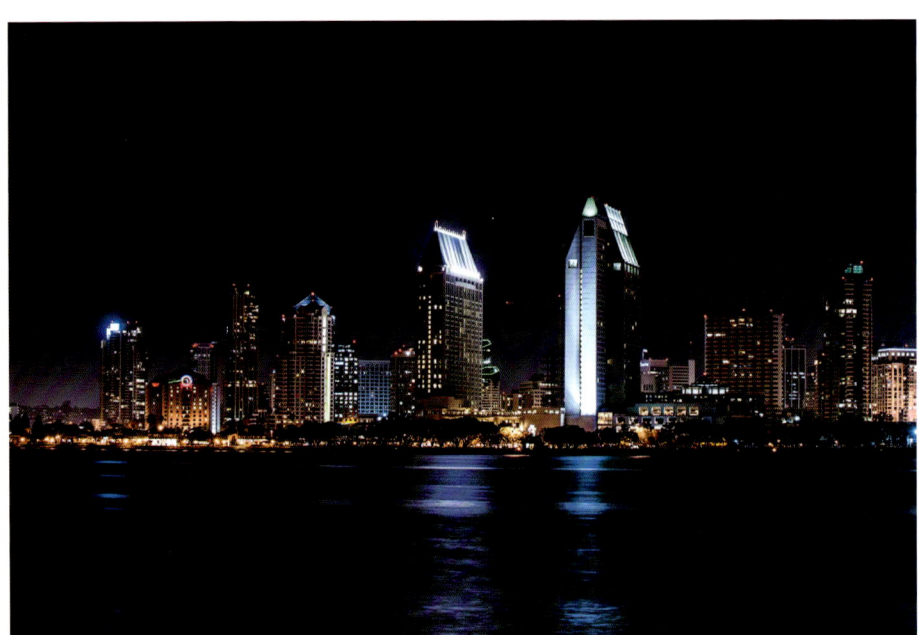

43.1 The San Diego downtown skyline photographed from across the water on Coronado Island.
`ISO 100; 13 sec.; f/10; 70mm`

- Press the shutter release button halfway down and look at the shutter speed selected by the camera.
- Change the exposure mode to Manual and set the shutter speed to the value selected in the previous step.
- Take the photo.
- If the resulting image is too light, increase the shutter speed.
- If the resulting image is too dark, decrease the shutter speed.
- Keep adjusting and checking the exposure as the sky gets darker and the city lights come on.

In **Figure 43.3**, you can see the series of images I took while adjusting the exposure until I got the one I wanted (circled in red).

When you're shooting a scene with city lights, you have to wait until the lights actually come on, which may not happen until after the sky has gone completely dark. Every once in a while the lights will come on when the sky is still light. This usually occurs right around daylight saving time when the clocks have been reset but the lights have not.

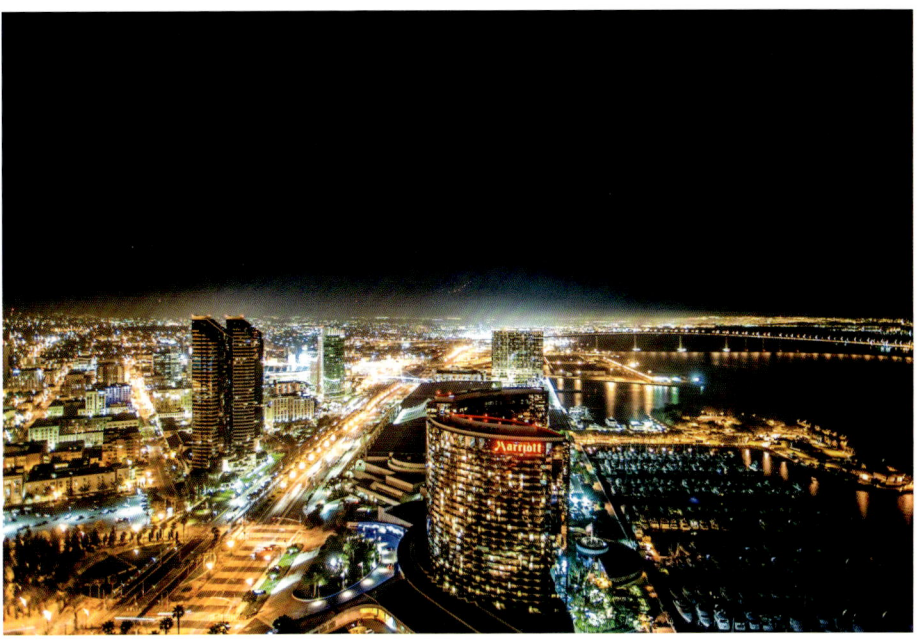

43.2 The San Diego downtown area photographed from the 40th floor of a building.
ISO 800; 5 sec.; f/2.8; 20mm

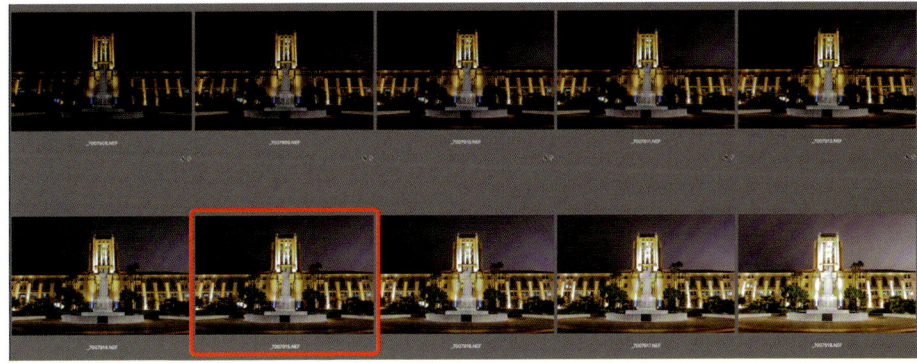

43.3 The set of images I took and the progression from too light to too dark shown in Adobe Bridge.

You can also use multiple exposures to create a scene in which the lights are on in the buildings and the sky isn't completely dark. This is a little Photoshop technique that was born out of my frustration when the sky color got too dark and the city lights hadn't come on yet.

To do this, you need two images: one with the sky at the right light level (**Figure 43.4**) and one with the lights on in the buildings (**Figure 43.5**). Then you can combine the two images in Photoshop using a layer mask (**Figure 43.6**) to create the final image (**Figure 43.7**).

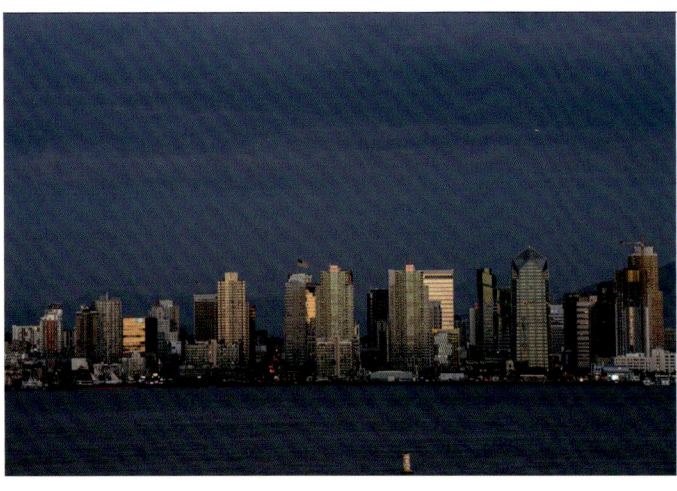

43.4 I took this photograph about 10 minutes after the sun had set. The sky looked just how I wanted it to but the city lights had not come on yet.
ISO 100; 2 sec.; f/16; 200mm

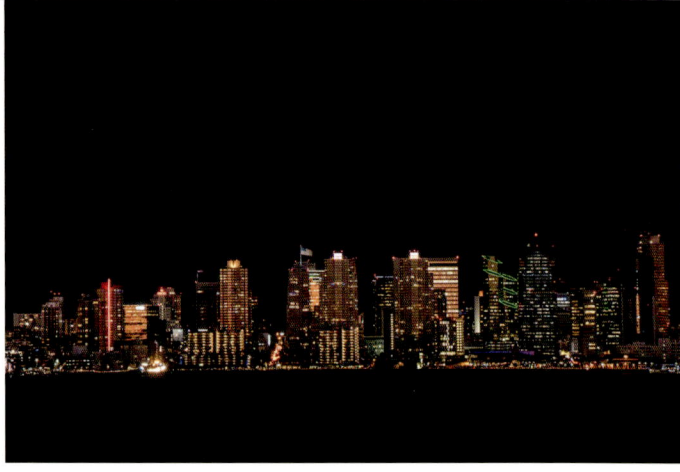

43.5 About 30 minutes after sunset, the sky was much darker and the city lights had come on.
ISO 100; 30 sec.; f/16; 200mm

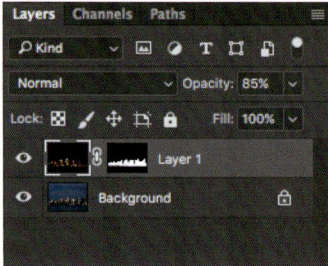

43.6 I blended the two images together by using a layer mask in Photoshop.

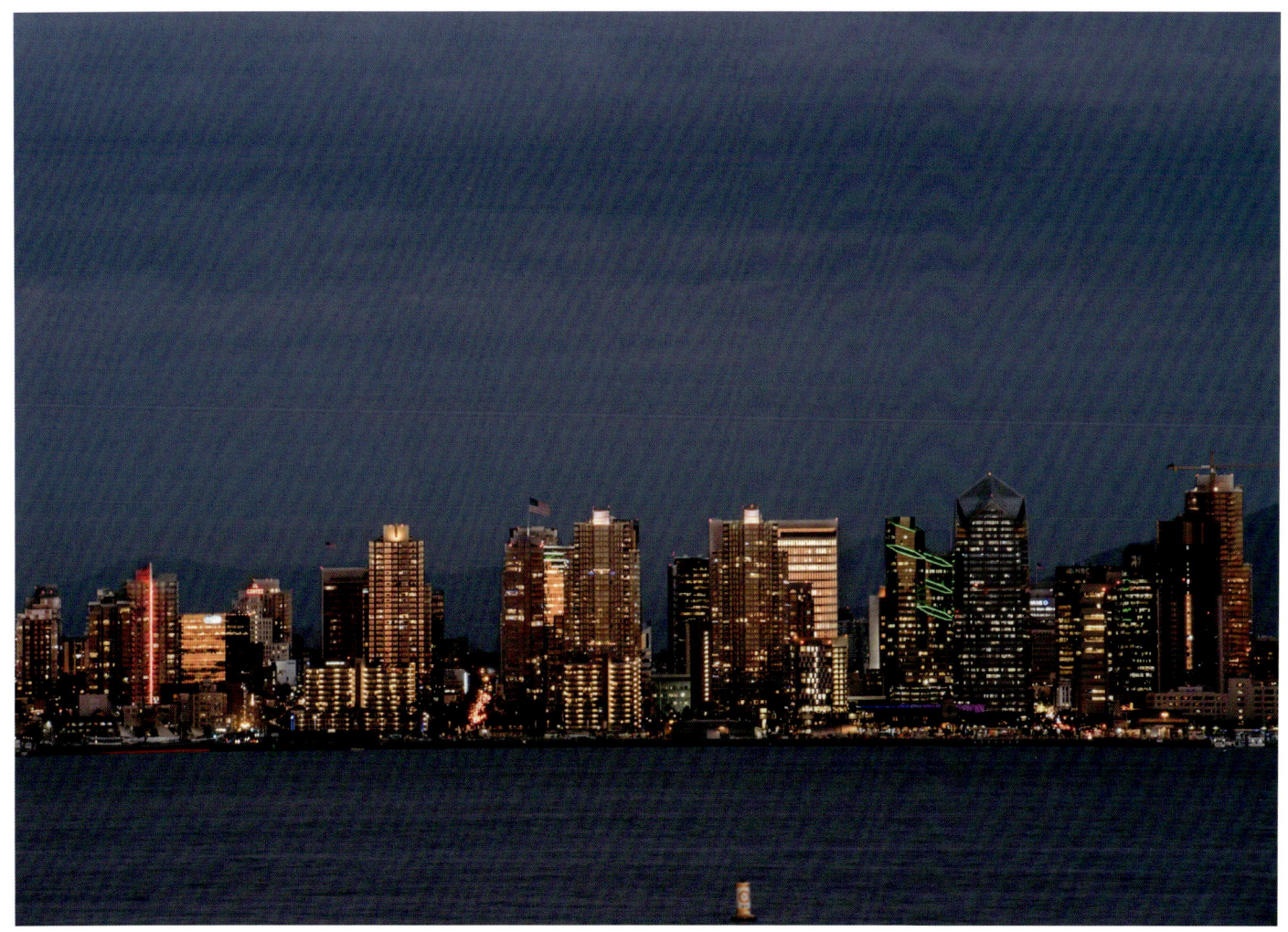

43.7 The final shot includes both the city lights and the evening sky.

5

ADOBE PHOTOSHOP POST-PROCESSING TECHNIQUES FOR LOW-LIGHT IMAGES

CHAPTER 5

Digital photography has made it so much easier to take, process, and share your images. You can shoot a quick photograph with your smartphone, edit the image right on the device, and then immediately email it to someone, share it on Facebook or Instagram, tweet it, or post it to your own website or blog. We now take image processing for granted, but it used to require chemicals, a room with special lighting, and large pieces of equipment just to get from the exposed film to a negative we could use. Now we can transfer a digital file directly to our computer and edit the image with advanced image-editing software. In this chapter, I share some techniques I use to edit images taken in low light or at night. These techniques deal with the issues that can arise when you use very high ISOs or leave the shutter open for long periods of time. In the following lessons, we'll cover how to reduce noise, fix color issues, remove dust and scratches, and adjust the tones in your images.

44. DO YOU REALLY NEED NOISE REDUCTION?

THE MAIN ISSUE that arises when you shoot action or scenic photos in low light is digital noise, or at least it used to be. Newer cameras produce much less noise at higher ISOs than they used to. However, even with the amazing advancements in camera technology, there are still times when you will want to reduce the digital noise in your images, and that is when Adobe Photoshop can really help you out.

In **Figures 44.1** and **44.2** you can see the same scene photographed with the newer Nikon D750 and the older Nikon D2X, respectively. Notice that the image taken with the D750 has much less digital noise.

Noise shows up in your images as random spots of color and it is more noticeable in areas with smooth tones. The basic idea behind noise reduction is to blur the image so that the noise blends together and becomes less noticeable, but this reduces the sharpness of the image as well.

There are multiple methods to reduce noise in Photoshop for both action photos and scenic images. In all cases, make sure that your images are properly exposed or even slightly overexposed because noise is more visible in the dark areas of an image. It's best if you can avoid having to make the photo any brighter in post-production.

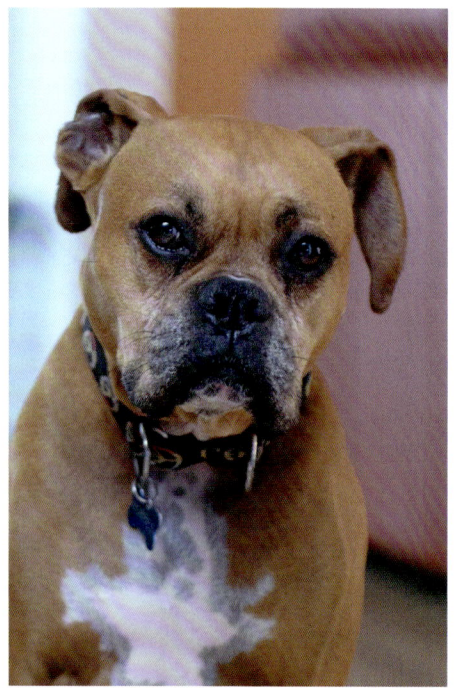

44.1 The newer Nikon D750 produces images with much less noise than an older camera, even when you use a high ISO.
ISO 3200; 1/125 sec.; f/2.8; 70mm

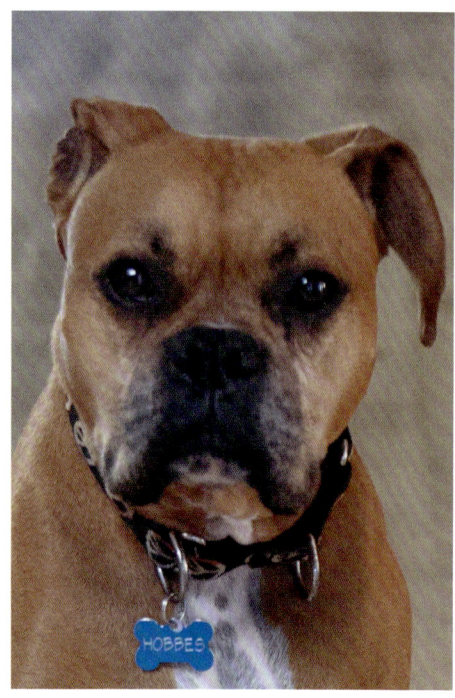

44.2 The Nikon D2X is an older DSLR, and you can see that it produces more noise at lower ISOs than newer cameras produce at higher ISOs.
ISO 800; 1/40 sec.; f/2.8; 70mm

45. BASIC NOISE REDUCTION TECHNIQUES

THERE ARE A couple of basic noise reduction techniques that can be applied easily to just about any type of image. The first technique will work for both action and scenic images, and is performed in Adobe Camera Raw in Photoshop or in the Develop Module in Lightroom. The second technique is a filter found in Adobe Photoshop.

Noise Reduction in Adobe Camera Raw

This first method is my favorite way to reduce the noise in my images. It is easy, fast, and works really well. To illustrate this technique, I am going to use a pretty extreme example, a photo shot with a Nikon D3 at an ISO setting of 25,600.

The Adobe Camera Raw (ACR) Sharpening and Noise Reduction controls are located in the Detail panel (**Figure 45.1**). These controls are grouped together because when you reduce noise in an image, you can also lose detail, so you may need to add some sharpness back into the image.

Sharpening includes four controls:

- **Amount:** Adjusts the amount of sharpening applied to the image.
- **Radius:** Adjusts the size of the details to which the sharpening is being applied. Basically, images with fine details need a lower setting, while images with large details need a higher setting. I find that a radius of 1.0 seems to work great for all of my images.

- **Detail:** Determines how much the sharpening affects the edge detail compared to the texture detail. Lower numbers tend to work better because it keeps the edges clean without increasing the detail in the noise.
- **Masking:** This is a very cool feature that allows you to fine-tune the areas to which the sharpening is applied. It controls an edge mask that ACR applies automatically. When this slider is set to 0, the same amount of sharpening is applied to the entire image, but when you increase the value, the sharpening is restricted to the areas with the strongest edges. You can see where the sharpening is being applied by holding down the Alt (Windows) or Option (Mac) key. The areas where sharpening will be applied are white and the areas that will remain untouched are black.

Noise Reduction includes six controls:

- **Luminance:** Reduces the luminance noise in the image—that is, the noise that shows up as a difference in the brightness of the pixels.
- **Luminance Detail:** Controls the luminance noise threshold. High values preserve more detail, but create noisier images. Low values reduce the noise, but also remove detail.
- **Luminance Contrast:** Controls the contrast in the image. High values preserve contrast, but result in more noise. Low values reduce noise, but also reduce contrast.
- **Color:** Reduces color noise. Color noise appears as spots of different colors that are all the same brightness.

- **Color Detail:** Controls the color noise threshold. Higher values maintain detailed color edges, while lower values can remove color specks, but also cause color bleeding.
- **Color Smoothness:** Reduces low-frequency color mottling, which appears as splotchy areas in the shadow areas of your low-light images.

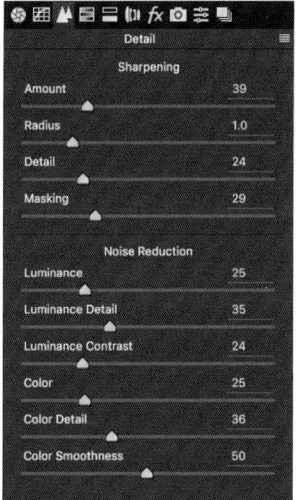

45.1 The Adobe Camera Raw Detail panel

Now let's walk through the steps to apply noise reduction in Adobe Camera Raw. I'll use **Figure** 45.2 as an example image. Keep in mind that you can open the Adobe Camera Raw controls as a filter in Photoshop, so you can apply these noise reduction settings at any time and to any type of image (JPEG, RAW, or TIFF). The specific settings might be different for your image, depending on the subject, the amount of noise in the image, and how much noise you want to remove.

1 Open the image in Adobe Camera Raw.
2 Click on the Detail menu.
3 Double-click on the Zoom tool in the upper-left corner of the dialog to zoom in to 100% on the critical area of the image. If you are not at 100%, you can't actually see what is going on. Press the spacebar on your keyboard to bring up the Hand tool, which allows you to move around in the image.
4 Set the Sharpening Amount to 25. We will come back and adjust this after applying the noise reduction.
5 Set the Radius to 1.0.
6 Set the Detail to 25.
7 Hold down the Alt (Windows) or Option (Mac) key and slide the Masking slider to the right until you can see only the outline of the image (**Figure** 45.3). This ensures that the sharpening is applied mainly to the subject of the image and not to the background. For this image, I set the Masking slider to 88.
8 Slide the Noise Reduction Luminance slider to the right until the noise starts to disappear. I never go over 50. Even for this really noisy image, I only went to 43.

9 Adjust the Sharpening Amount a little if needed. I moved it to 36.
10 Now adjust the Masking to see if you can further reduce the noise by adjusting the areas that get sharpened.
11 Set the Luminance Detail to 25.
12 Set the Luminance Contrast to 0. This does reduce the contrast in the image, but I get it back with the Contrast setting on the main Camera Raw menu.
13 Set the Color to 25.
14 Set the Color Detail to 50.
15 Set the Color Smoothness to 50.

These settings go a long way in terms of removing some of the noise from the image, but remember that noise reduction is just one part of the editing process.

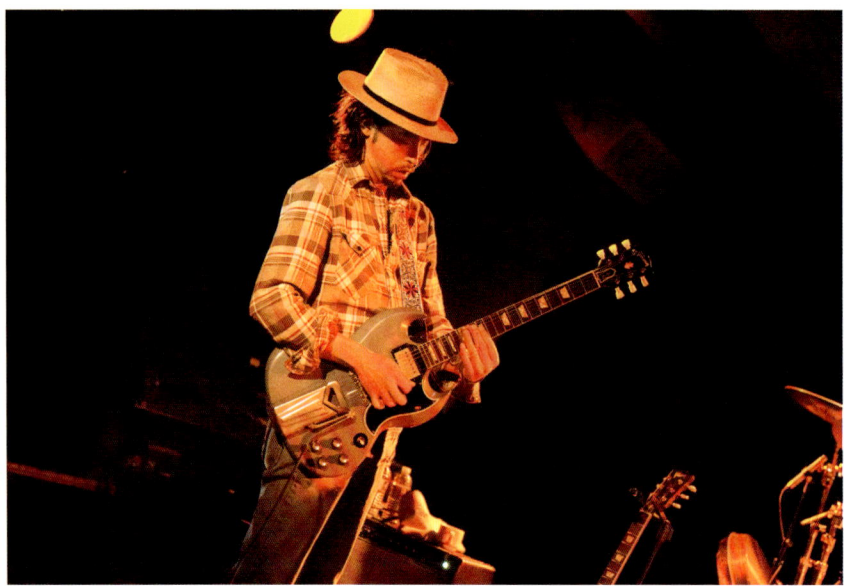

45.2 You may recognize this image from chapter 3. There was very little light inside the club, so I needed to use an extremely high ISO to get the proper exposure.
ISO 25,600; 1/320 sec.; f/2.8; 60mm

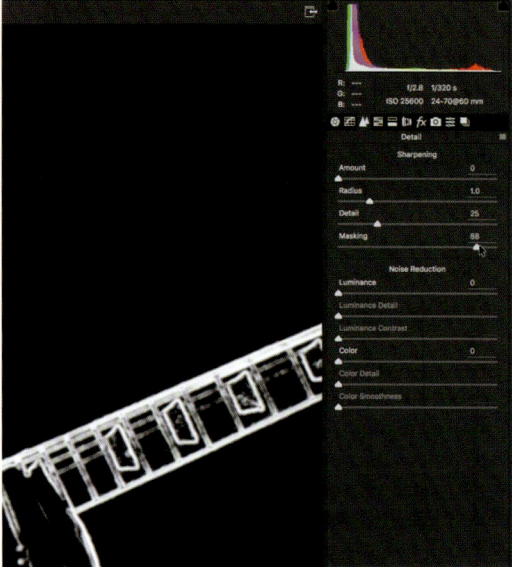

45.3 You can see the masking overlay by holding down the Alt (Windows) or Option (Mac) key while adjusting the Masking control.

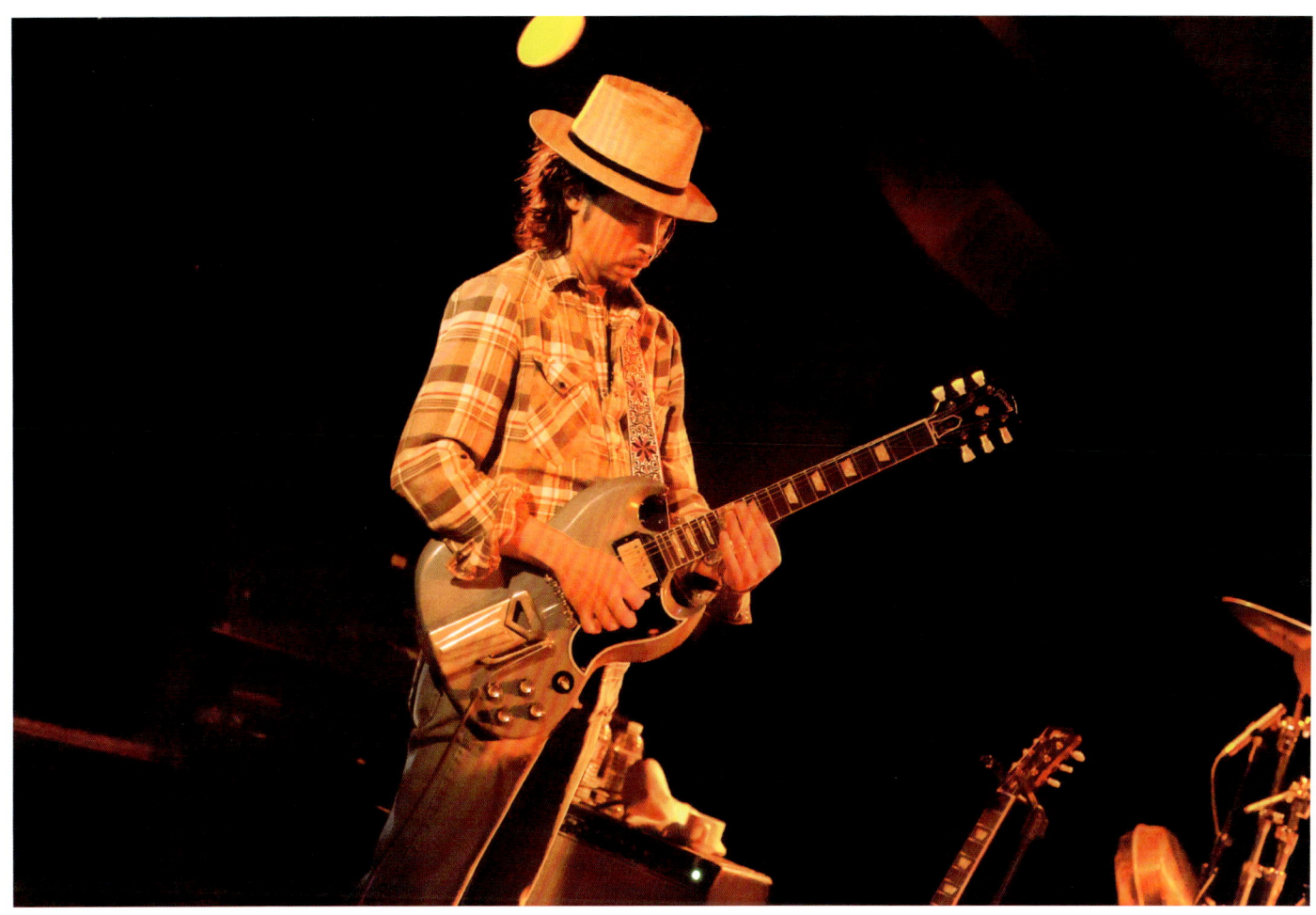

45.4 This is the final image after I applied noise reduction. You can see that the background is a lot smoother.

Reduce Noise Filter

Photoshop has a Reduce Noise filter that gives you control over the individual color channels. It is a very powerful tool, especially if you use it as an adjustable smart filter. Let's start by opening an image open in Photoshop. I'll use **Figure 45.5** as an example.

Convert the layer to a smart object by double-clicking on a background layer and changing the name to something more descriptive (in this case, Mark_ISO_12800), and then click okay. Now select *Layer > Smart Objects > Convert to Smart Object*. This allows you to apply and fine-tune the noise reduction using the power of a smart object, which means the editing you perform on the layer is adjustable. Now go to *Filter > Noise > Reduce Noise*, which will bring up the dialog box shown in **Figure 45.6**.

When you select Basic in the Reduce Noise dialog, you are presented with four sliders:

- **Strength:** Reduces Luminance noise.
- **Preserve Details:** Balances out the Strength slider by preserving the details in the high-contrast areas. In doing so, it also increases the noise.
- **Reduce Color Noise:** Reduces the color noise in the image.
- **Sharpen Details:** Maintains details by sharpening the high-contrast areas.

The real power of this filter is in the Advanced section, which lets you look at both the Overall settings and the Per Channel settings. In the Per Channel view, you can apply noise reduction to the Red, Green, and Blue channels separately by adjusting the Strength and Preserve Detail sliders. You can see these controls in **Figure 45.7**.

It's a balancing act to reduce the amount of noise in an image and still keep the detail. Because we converted the layer to a smart object, you can always go back and adjust the setting if you need to. **Figure 45.8** shows the final image after I applied noise reduction to the three different channels.

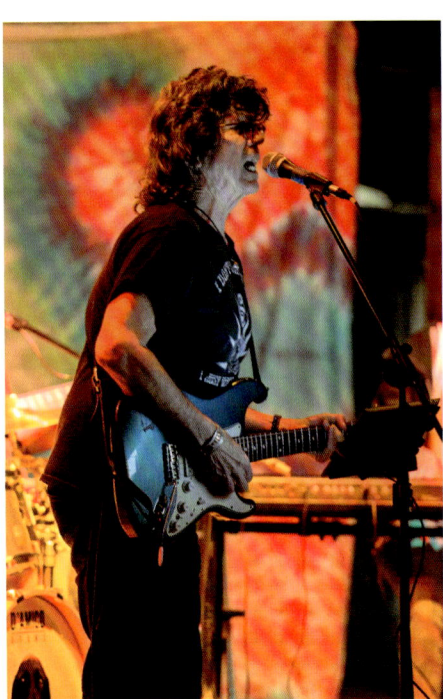

45.5 This is the original image before I applied the noise reduction. **ISO 12,800; 1/80 sec.; f/2.8; 185mm**

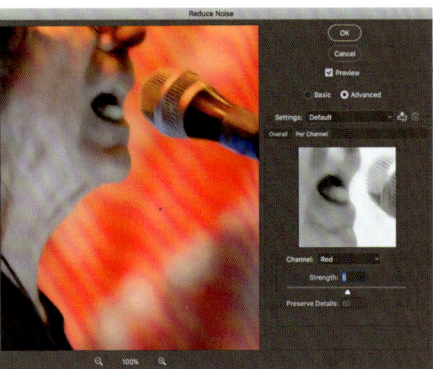

45.6 Photoshop's Reduce Noise dialog.

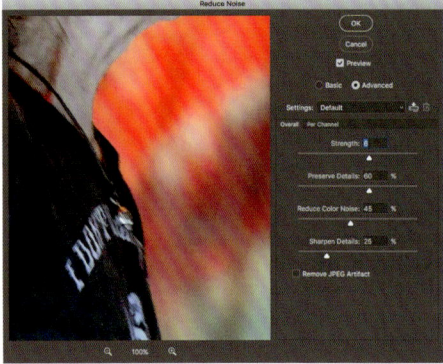

45.7 You can use the Per Channel controls in the Advanced tab of the Reduce Noise filter to apply noise reduction to the Red, Green, and Blue channels separately.

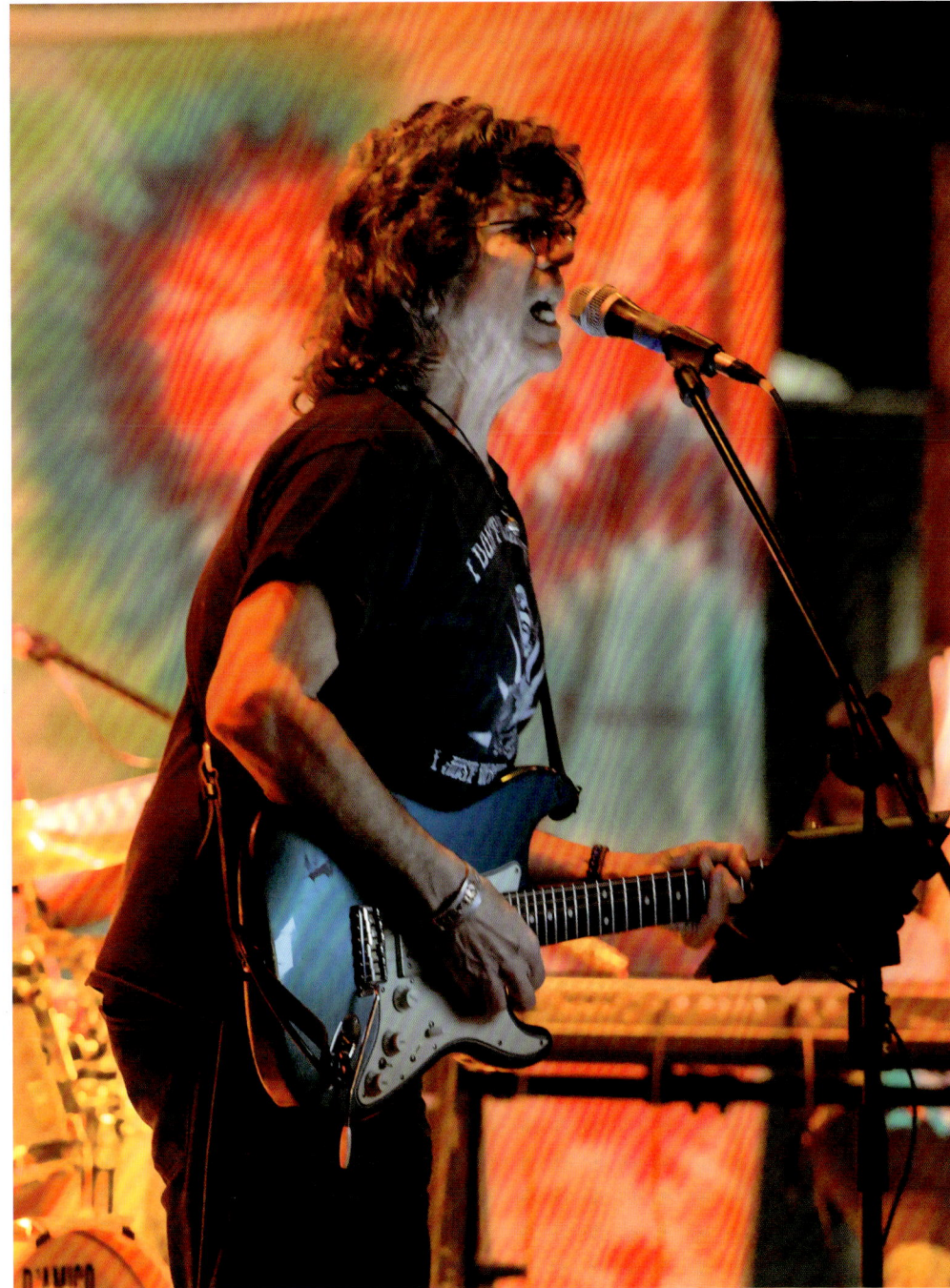

45.8 This is the final image after I applied the Reduce Noise filter in Photoshop. The image is much smoother overall.

46. NOISE REDUCTION TECHNIQUES FOR SCENIC PHOTOGRAPHS

I HAVE FOUND that the following noise reduction techniques tend to work slightly better on images in which neither the subject nor the camera moved. The third technique in this section—combining multiple exposures to reduce noise—only works when you have multiple images of the exact same subject, so you need to plan ahead and have this in mind when you're out shooting.

Surface Blur Filter

This method works really well when the noise is heavy in one of the color channels. You reduce the noise by using Photoshop's Surface Blur filter on one of the color channels, and preserve details by leaving the other color channels alone.

First, you need look at each color channel separately to see which one has the most noise. This is easy to do; just open the image

in Photoshop and click on the Channels tab. Then click on each channel to view it by itself and note which one has the most noise. In **Figure** 46.1, you can see the image with a lot of noise in the center of the screen and the selected color channel over on the right.

Once you have decided which channel you want to apply the blur to, make sure it is selected, then go to *Filter > Blur > Surface Blur*.

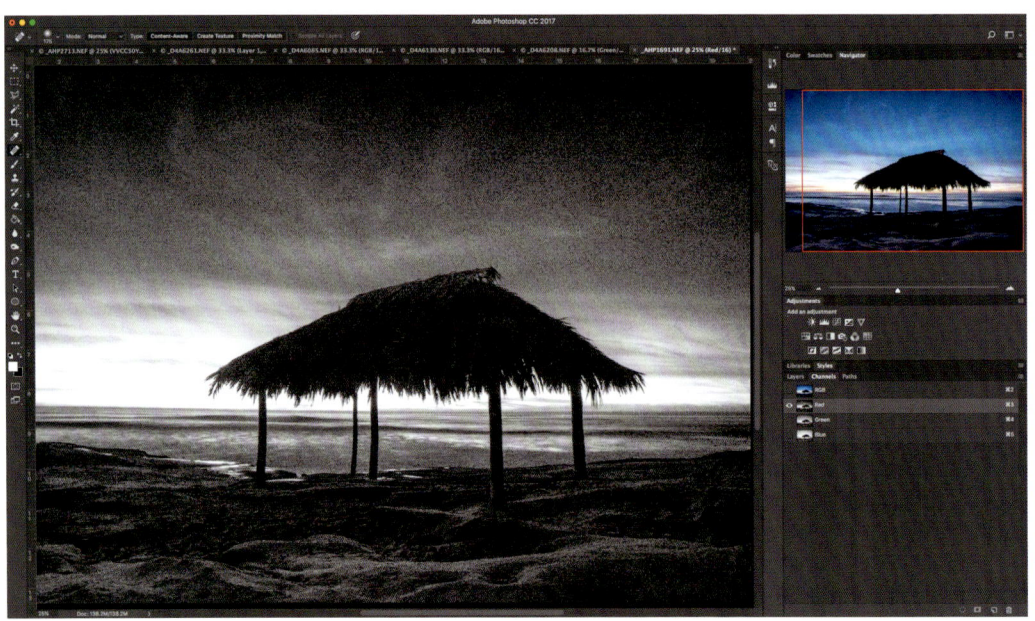

46.1 I took this photo after the sunset at ISO 128,000, which resulted in a lot of noise. Here you can see how noisy the Red channel is, so this will be the channel to which I apply the Surface Blur filter.

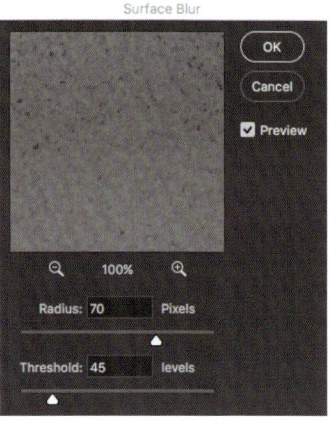

46.2 The Radius and Threshold sliders allow you to control the amount of blur that will be applied to the selected layer. Because my image had a lot of noise, I selected a Radius of 70 and a Threshold of 45.

The Surface Blur filter smoothens large areas that have the same tone, but maintains the edge sharpness, which makes it perfect for reducing noise. There are two sliders that affect the amount of blur: Radius and Threshold (**Figure 46.2**). The Radius slider defines the size of the area sampled for the blur, and the Threshold slider controls how much the surrounding pixels must change in tone to be affected. I like to push the Radius up to 60 or higher to smooth out the tones in the entire image, and then I use the Threshold slider to control the edges, starting at around 10 and moving it as needed. These values will change depending on the subject, the amount of noise in the image, and your preferences.

Once I have applied the Surface Blur filter to the first and most heavily affected color channel, I can then do the same thing to the other channels if needed. I usually select a much lower Radius and Threshold for the second and third layers because they need less smoothing and I do want to keep the image looking sharp. Many times I just apply this filter to the worst channel, and then go back and do a small amount of noise reduction with the Adobe Camera Raw filter.

Because this technique actually blurs the image, it is easy to go overboard and blur too much. But you can also use it to give an image a more painterly feel. In **Figure 46.3**, you can see the before and after of the same image with the noise reduction applied to just the Red and Green channels. In this example, I pushed the blurring in the two channels to create a more surreal image.

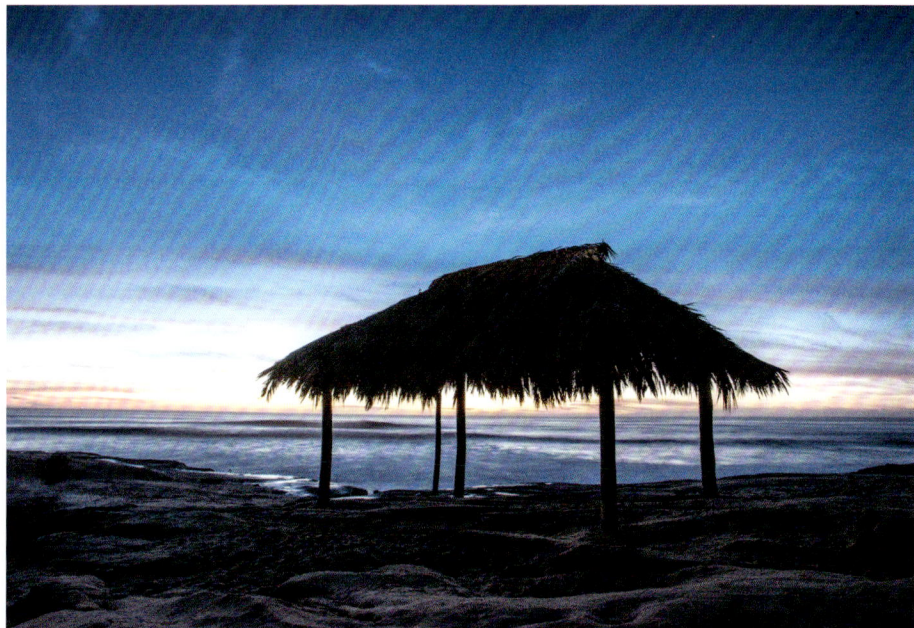

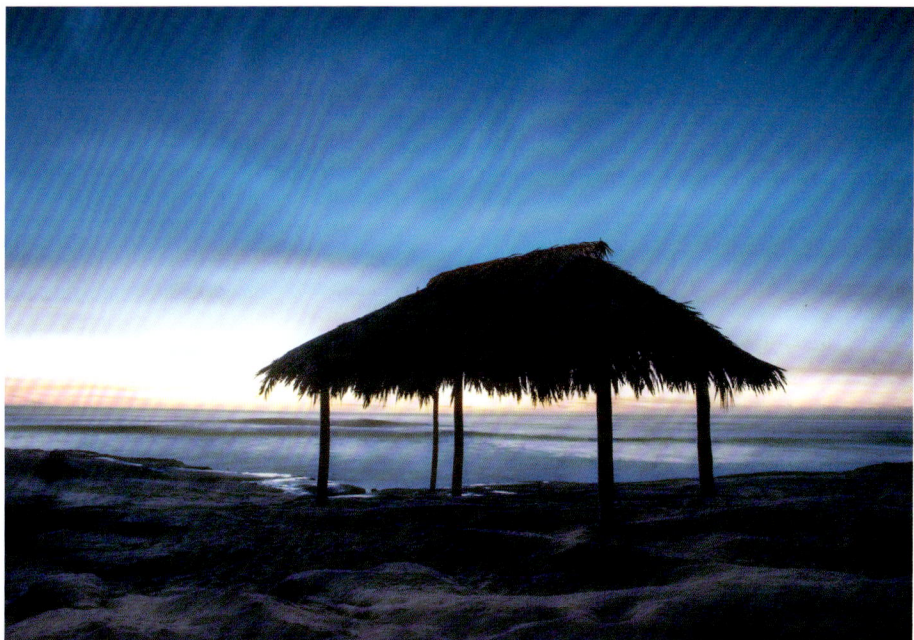

46.3 I applied the Surface Blur filter to the Red and Green channels in this image, giving the entire image a slightly ethereal look.

The History Brush

Sometimes the noise in certain parts of an image is more distracting than it is in other areas, and instead of performing noise reduction on the entire image you just want to deal with a small part. The History brush allows you to selectively and easily paint away some of the noise. This might seem like a lot of steps, but it's pretty simple once you get going:

1 Open the image in Photoshop.
2 Select *Filter > Blur > Gaussian Blur*. I use a Radius that is enough to blur the image slightly, about 1 to 1.5 pixels.
3 Open the History panel by selecting *Window > Show History*.
4 In the History panel menu, click on History Options (**Figure 46.4**).

5 Check the Allow Non-Linear History box.
6 In the History panel, click on the box next to the Gaussian Blur state and the History Brush icon will appear.
7 Highlight the state above Gaussian Blur, which will return the image to its noisy state.
8 Select the History Brush.
9 In the top menu bar, change the History Brush Mode to Color and the Opacity and Flow to 100%.
10 Paint over the noisy areas.

The History Brush uses the Gaussian Blur state as its source, so you are effectively painting blur onto your image (**Figure 46.5**). The Color blend mode retains detail, but hides the blurriness and at the same time desaturates the color noise pixels, making them less noticeable.

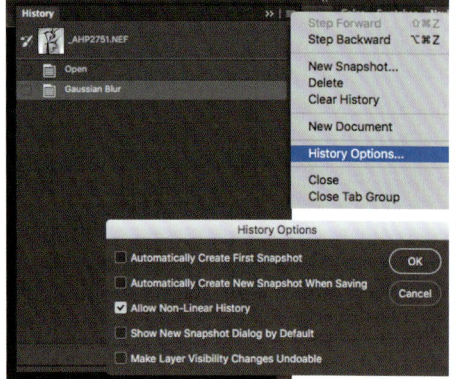

46.4 In the History Options dialog, you can choose to Allow Non-Linear History.

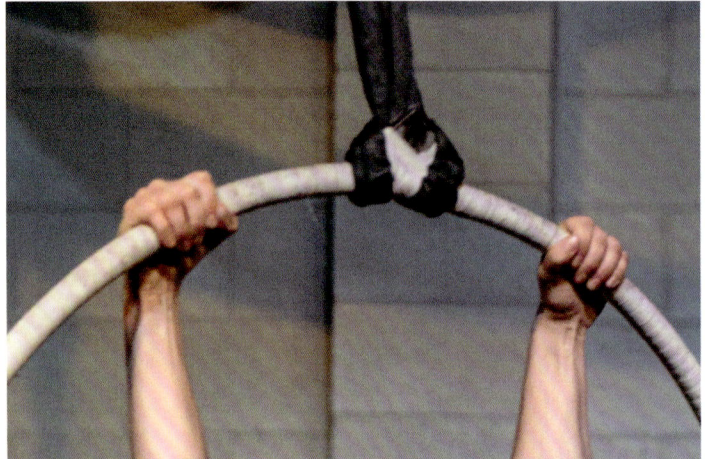
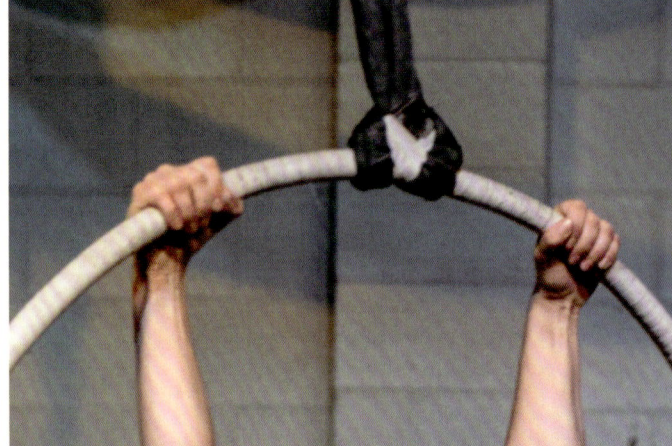

46.5 The left image shows the noise at 100% and the right image shows the same area after I used the History Brush to paint on the noise reduction.

Combining Multiple Exposures to Reduce Noise

Combining multiple exposures is a great way to reduce noise in low-light scenes, but you have to plan ahead and take multiple images of the exact same scene. This works because digital noise is random, which means that if you take a series of photos of the same scene, the noise will be different in each image, while the subject will be the same. When you combine the exposures, the noisy pixels from each exposure will be averaged with the good pixels from the other exposures.

You will need a set of images that have the identical composition, so it is best to shoot all of the images with your camera mounted on a tripod, and make sure neither the camera nor the subject moves between frames. There are two methods you can use to combine the exposures—you can manually average the frames together or you can let Photoshop do it automatically.

Method 1 – Averaging Layers Manually

The idea here is to stack each image on a different layer and blend them together so that each layer contributes to the final image equally. Open the images in Photoshop, and then copy and paste each image onto the same document. Each layer's opacity setting determines how much of the layer beneath it gets let through. I like to use four separate images with the following layer opacities:

- The background layer is set to 100%.
- Layer 1 is set to 50%.
- Layer 2 is set to 33%.
- Layer 3 is set to 25%.

Figure 46.6 shows the four separate images in the Layers panel. **Figure 46.7** shows the image before and after I reduced the noise by combining multiple exposures.

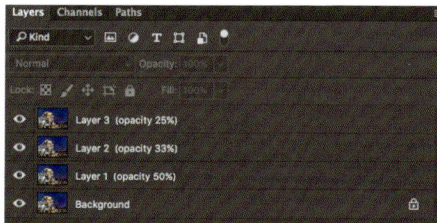

46.6 I combined four exposures and varied the opacity of each layer to create the final image.

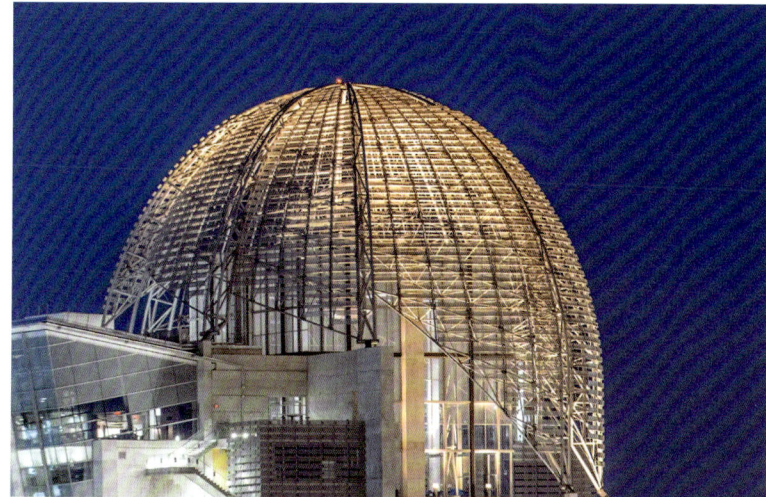

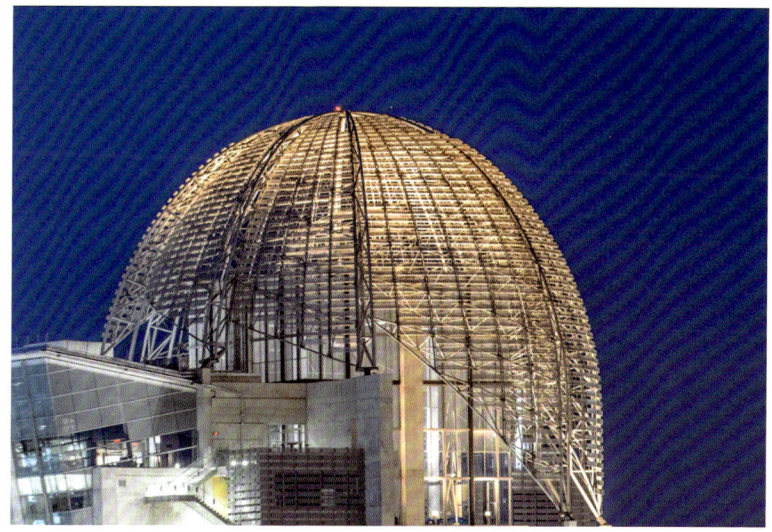

46.7 The noise in the final image is greatly reduced.

Method 2 – Using the Photoshop Stacks Feature

Photoshop can combine images automatically with its Stacks function, which is mathematical magic. Again, you need a set of images that were all taken at the same time and place, and it works best if you shoot the images with the camera mounted on a tripod. You will load the images into a stack and then apply one of the blend functions to the stack of images. Because the noise is random, it will appear in different areas in all the images, so Photoshop is able to get rid of it when it blends the images together.

- Open Photoshop and go to *File > Scripts > Load Files into Stack*.
- Click Browse and select the images you want to use in the stack (**Figure 46.8**).
- Check Attempt to Automatically Align Source Images and Create Smart Object after Loading Layers.
- Click OK to create a single Smart Object from the multiple exposures. You can double-click on this Smart Object to see the layers separately.
- Now go to *Layer > Smart Objects > Stack Mode > Median* to blend the exposures (**Figure 46.9**).

Photoshop has now combined the exposures to create a single image with reduced noise. This is a very easy way to reduce noise if you can plan ahead and take multiple images when out shooting.

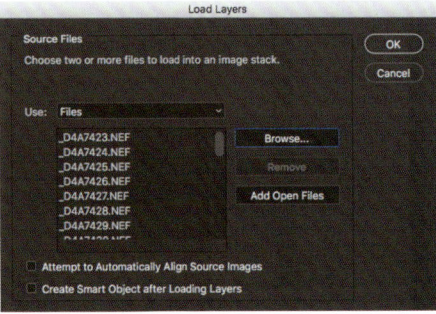

46.8 The Load Layers dialog where you select which images you want to use in the stack.

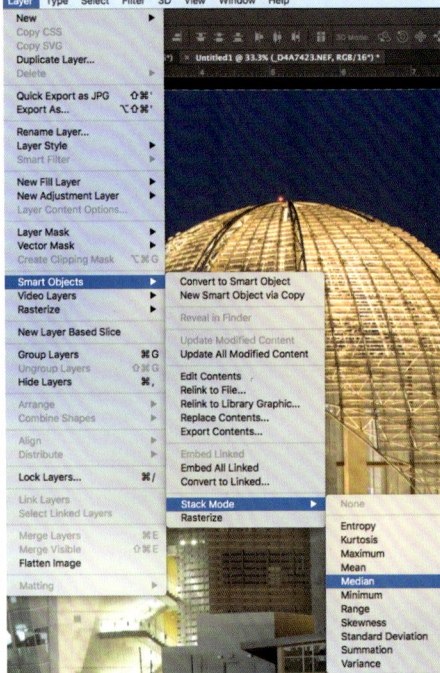

46.9 You can apply a variety of mathematical algorithms to the stack of images, but to reduce noise, use the Median setting.

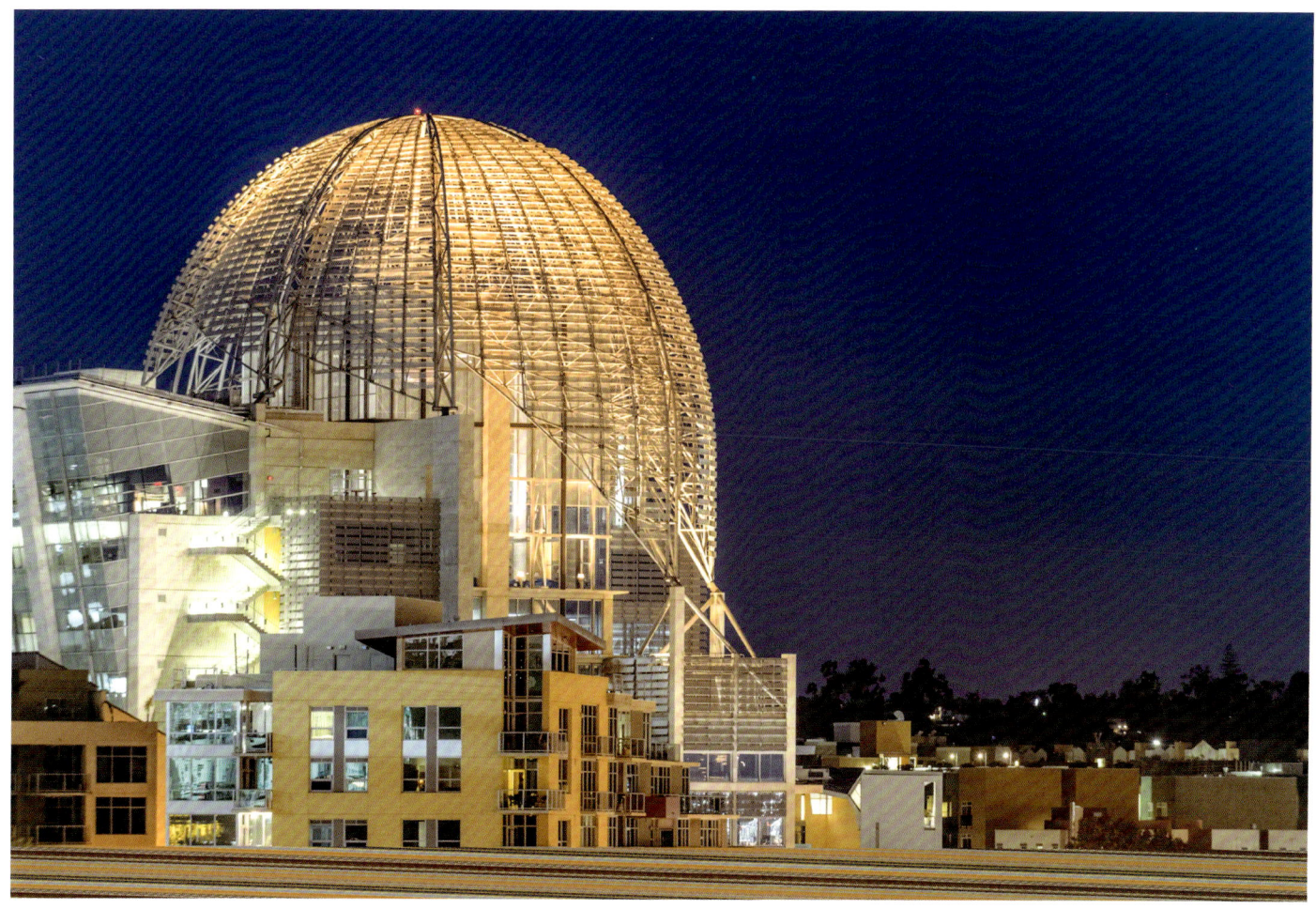

46.10 The noise in the final image is greatly reduced.

47. CORRECTING CONTRAST AND DODGING AND BURNING

JUST ABOUT EVERY image needs some contrast adjustment. This is especially true for images shot at high ISOs or long exposures. There are many different methods for adjusting the contrast and exposure of images in Photoshop; in fact, there are whole books written on just this subject. In this section, I cover the basic steps I use to adjust the exposure and contrast of my images in Adobe Camera Raw, as well as how I use the dodge and burn tools, which are a throwback to working in the darkroom.

Contrast Adjustments

I find the easiest way to adjust the contrast of the images I shoot at night or in low light is in the Adobe Camera Raw module, with its basic editing adjustments. When I work with an image, I tend to follow the same steps every time, even though not every image needs every adjustment.

My basic workflow is to adjust the white balance first, and then start at the bottom and work my way up (**Figure 47.1**). I adjust the Clarity slider, followed by the Vibrance and Saturation sliders. Then I use the sliders for the Blacks, Whites, Shadows, Highlights, and Exposure. And finally, I adjust the Contrast.

- **Clarity:** This increases (or decreases) the contrast in the midtones of the image and can really sharpen (or soften) the look of the entire image. A little can go a long way here, and while I do adjust it first, I tend to come to this control at the end as well to give it a final tweak.
- **Vibrance:** This controls the saturation of the image, but tries to leave skin tones untouched.
- **Saturation:** This increases or decreases the total saturation of the image.
- **Blacks:** This adjusts the black clipping.
- **Whites:** This adjusts the white clipping.
- **Shadows:** This control is a lifesaver for concert photos in which the performer is backlit or is wearing a hat or cap that casts a shadow over his or her face. When you slide the control to the right, the shadows are lightened, opening up the dark areas. If you slide the control to the left, the shadows are closed down, making the darkest areas darker.
- **Highlights:** This control adjusts the brightest areas in the image. If you drag it to the left, it decreases the brightness in the highlight areas and reduces the blown out areas, which may allow you to recover lost details. If you slide it to the right, it brightens the brightest parts of the image.
- **Exposure:** This controls the overall exposure of the image. You can adjust the image from −5 to +5 stops.
- **Contrast:** This controls the overall contrast of the image.

A little goes a long way here. When you adjust images taken with long shutter speeds, you can really push the clarity. When you're working with people, you need to be a little more restrained.

In **Figure 47.2** you can see an image I took of Windansea Beach, which was a little dark and needed to be adjusted to reflect the scene as I saw it. I edited the image with the basic image correction controls in Adobe Camera Raw (**Figure 47.3**) to get the final image shown in **Figure 47.4**.

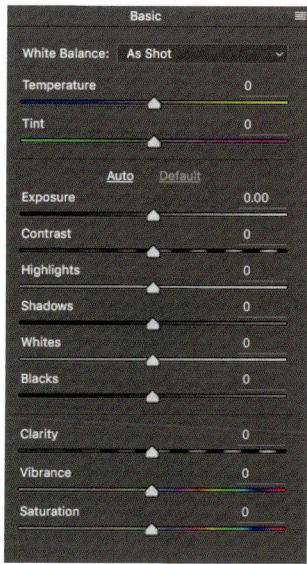

47.1 The basic image correction controls in Adobe Camera Raw.

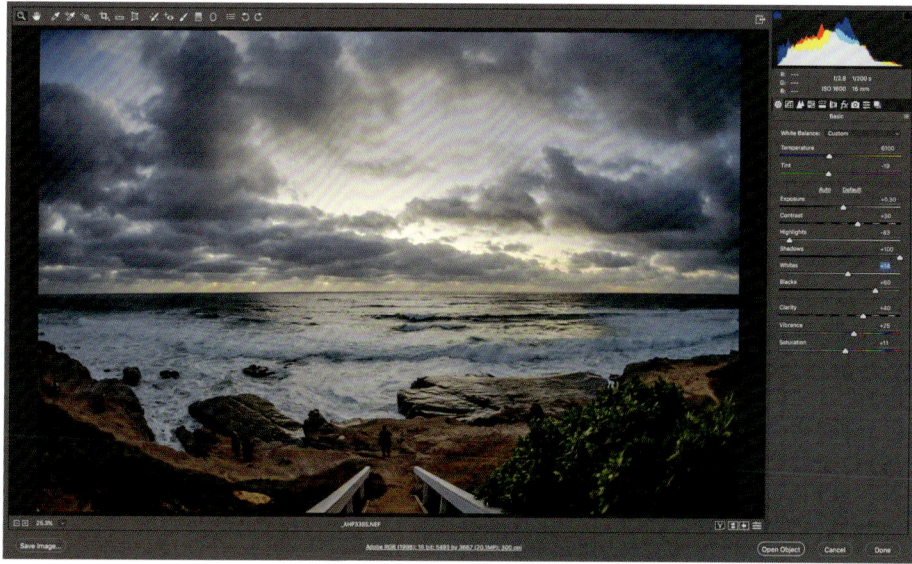

47.3 The adjusted basic image correction controls in Adobe Camera Raw.

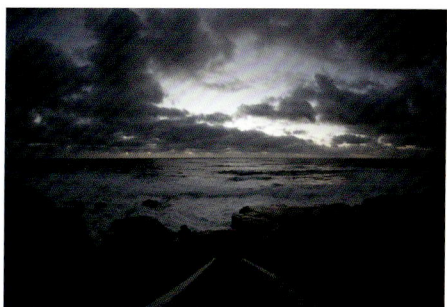

47.2 This photo of Windansea Beach needed some basic adjustments to make it look more like the scene I saw in front of the camera.

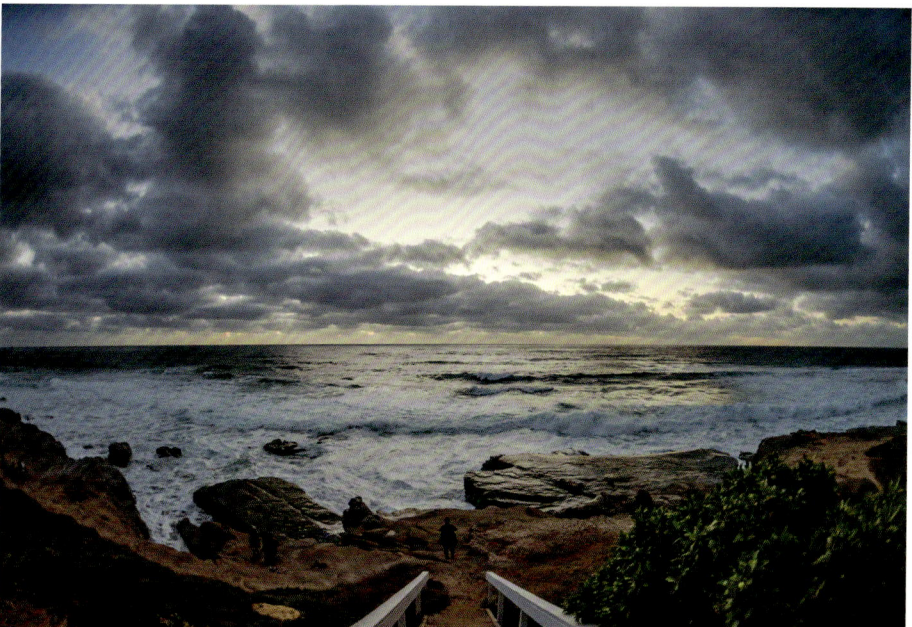

47.4 The final image with the basic corrections applied.

Dodge and Burn

This is my favorite technique for adjusting images taken at night. It's probably because when I started doing photography, I processed my images in an actual darkroom and these tools are really familiar to me. When you combine Photoshop's Dodge and Burn tools with the power of a touch-sensitive Wacom tablet, the editing is easy.

I always start with the same settings (**Figure 47.5**). For the Dodge tool, I set the Range to Highlights and the Exposure to 10%, and I turn on Protect Tones. For the Burn tool, I set the Range to Shadows and the Exposure to 10%, and turn on Protect Tones.

Begin by duplicating the layer so that you can adjust the opacity and fine-tune the effect. Once the layer is duplicated, all you have to do is use the Burn tool to paint the areas that need to be darker and use the Dodge tool to paint the areas that need to be lighter. For example, **Figure 47.6** lacks contrast, so I used the Dodge and Burn tools to make the dark areas darker and the light areas lighter. You can see the areas I painted in **Figure 47.7**. (The black represents the burn areas and the white represents the dodge areas.) **Figure 47.8** shows the final image, which has increased contrast.

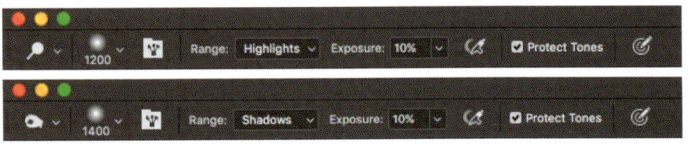

47.5 I always start with these Dodge (top) and Burn (bottom) tool settings.

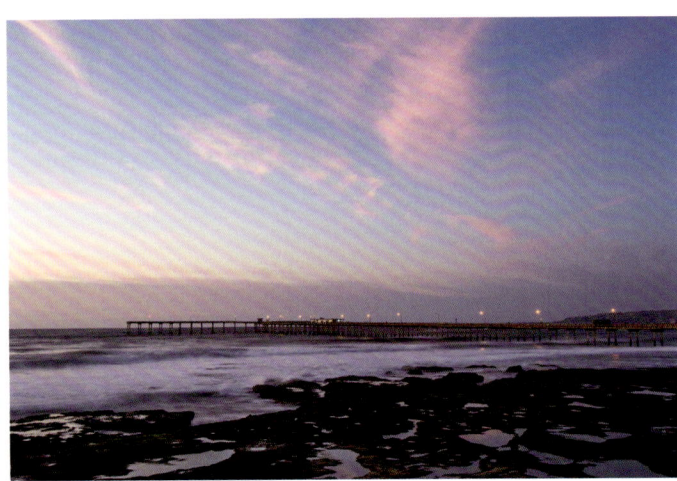

47.6 The original image lacked contrast.

47.7 I used the Dodge and Burn tools to increase the contrast in the image.

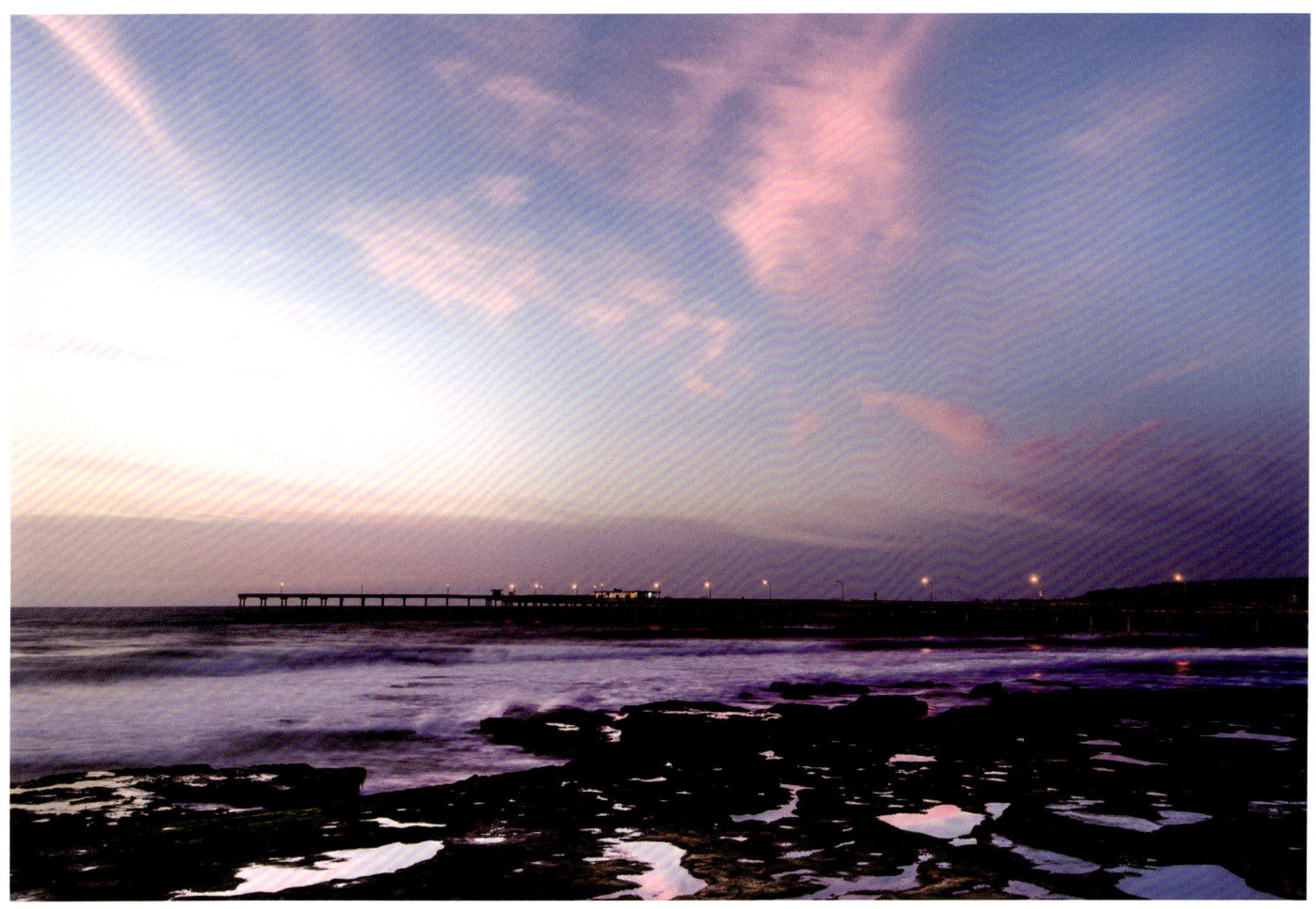

47.8 The final image has more contrast.

48. ADJUSTING WHITE BALANCE AND USING CURVES FOR BETTER COLOR

THE WHITE BALANCE setting tells your camera what color the light is under which you are photographing so that you get accurate colors in your images. It is really easy for the camera to be fooled when it uses the Auto white balance mode, especially when you're shooting at night under mixed lighting conditions. Luckily, there is a very easy way to adjust the white balance during post-processing with Adobe Photoshop.

The Adobe Camera Raw module allows you to adjust the white balance in couple of different ways depending on the file type. You can use an eyedropper to pick a neutral spot of color in the image (**Figure 48.1**), you can use sliders to adjust the colors (**Figure 48.2**), or you can use a drop-down list that contains presets for the different lighting types (**Figure 48.3**). Since you can open the Camera Raw module as a filter in Adobe Photoshop, you can adjust the white balance of any individual layer, but in this case, the drop-down list of presets includes only three options: As Shot, Auto, and Custom. The powerful part of adjusting the white balance of individual layers is that you can adjust different parts of the image and combine them easily by using layer masks.

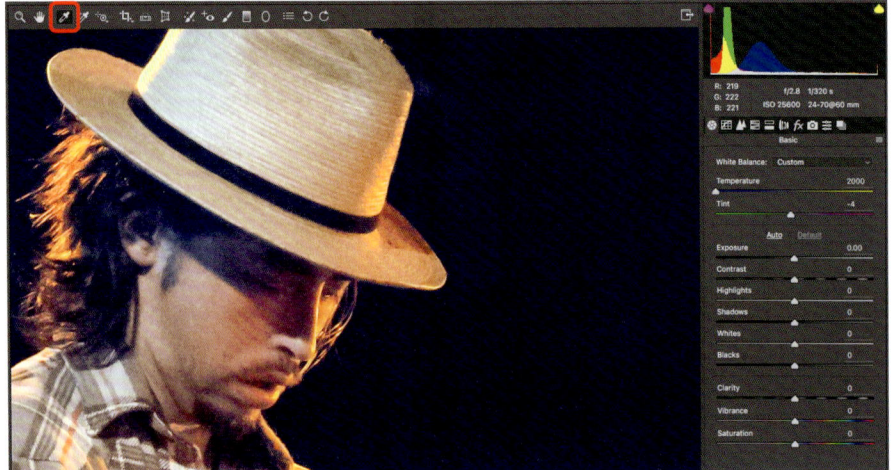

48.1 The eyedropper tool lets you pick a spot in an image to set as neutral, and the rest of the colors are automatically adjusted.

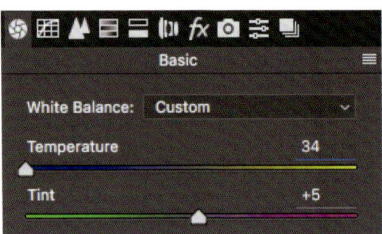

48.2 You can adjust the white balance of an image with these two sliders. The top one adjusts the temperature from cool to hot (blue to yellow), and the bottom one adjusts the tint from green to magenta.

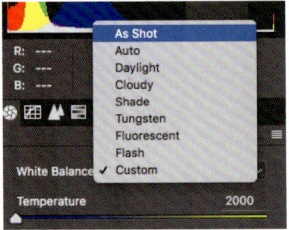

48.3 The White Balance drop-down menu lets you quickly pick the type of lighting under which the shot was taken from a list of presets. If you open Camera Raw as a filter in Photoshop, or if you are adjusting the white balance of a TIFF or JPEG file, this menu will include only the As Shot, Auto, and Custom options.

I shot **Figure 48.4** at a very high ISO, which caused some color shifts to occur, and the LED lights made the image look too warm. I used the color picker to pick what I thought would be a neutral spot and all the colors improved (**Figure 48.5**).

Another way in which you can quickly adjust the colors in an image is by using the Curves adjustment in Photoshop, which allows you to remap the colors in your image by picking a black point and a white point. You can also use this method to tone your image by purposely introducing a colorcast. The steps to do this are pretty easy, and the adjustments can range from very subtle to really blatant.

1 Open the image in Adobe Photoshop.
2 Click on the Curves adjustment layer to open the Curves adjustment panel (**Figure 48.6**).
3 Change the channel to Red in the Curves adjustment panel.
4 Select the Sample Black Point eyedropper (**Figure 48.7**) and click on the area that is pure black in your image, or at least the area you want to be black.
5 Select the Sample White Point eyedropper and click on the area that is pure white in your image, or at least the area you want to be white.
6 Repeat this process for the Green and Blue channels.

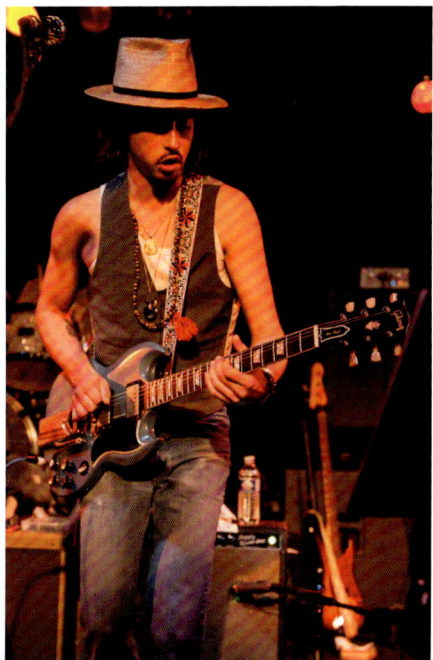

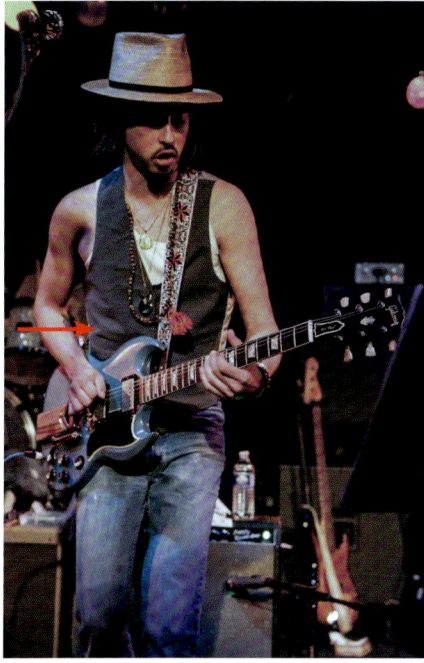

48.4 Before I adjusted the white balance, this image looked too warm.

48.5 The red arrow points to the spot I selected as neutral. After I did this, all of the colors in the image improved.

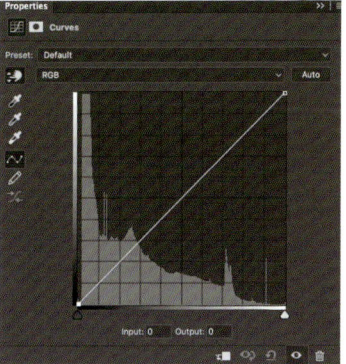

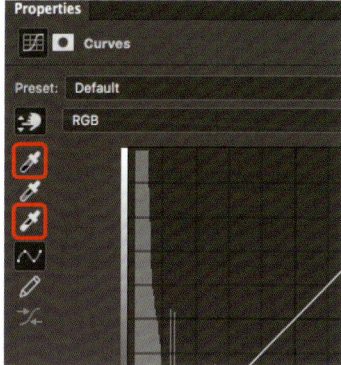

48.6 The Curves properties

48.7 The Sample Black Point and Sample White Point eyedroppers

You can change the color of the black and white points to introduce a colorcast into the image. For example, I change the black point for **Figure 48.8** from pure black to red, which gave the image a red colorcast, as you can see in **Figure 48.9**.

To change the black point, open the Curves adjustment panel and double-click on the Sample Black Point eyedropper. The color picker will open, allowing you to remap the black. You can do the same thing to change the white point as well.

48.8 The colors in this image look natural.

48.9 By changing the black point from pure black to red, I gave the image a red colorcast.

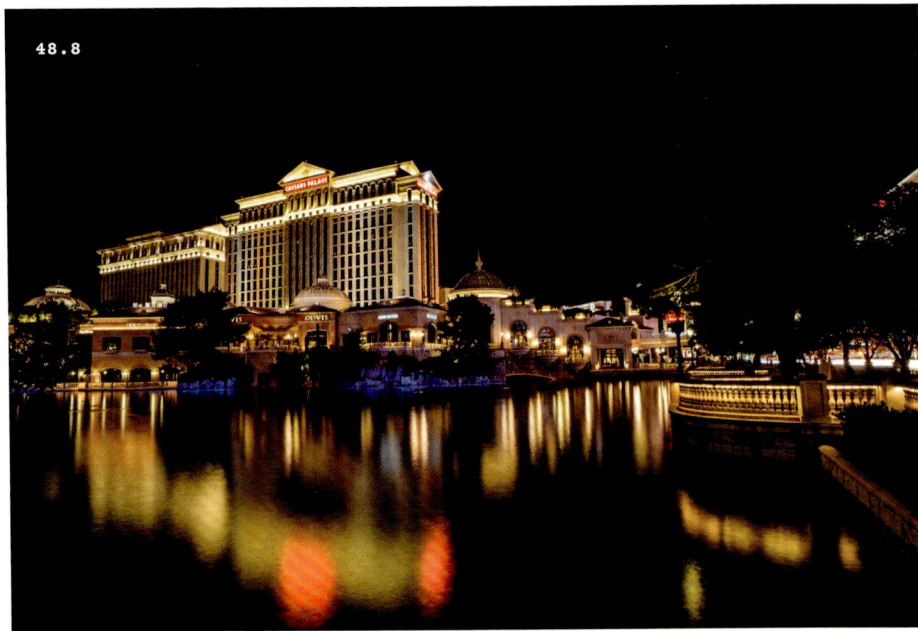

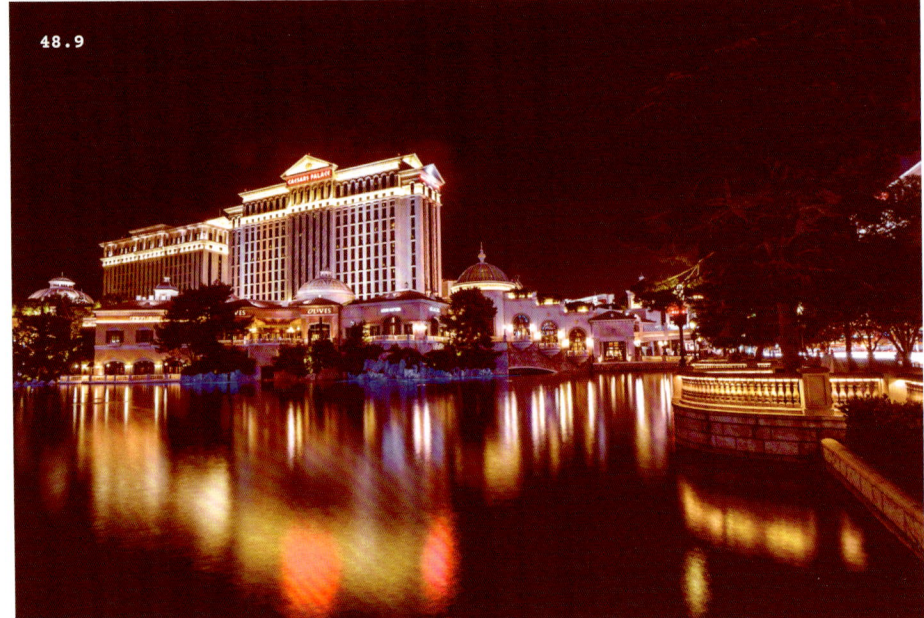

49. REMOVING DUST AND SCRATCHES

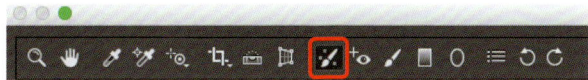

WHEN YOU PHOTOGRAPH with wide open apertures like f/2.8 or f/4, you don't see any of the dust and dirt that could be on the lens. But when you start to shoot exposures with a narrow aperture like f/16 or f/22, every piece of dust and dirt on your lens shows up in your images. No matter how clean I think my gear is, a 30-second exposure at f/16 will show me how wrong I am.

I usually try to remove the spots left by dust and scratches after I do noise reduction because the noise reduction often helps to minimize the smaller spots. The Adobe Camera Raw module has some of the best tools for dealing with dirt and scratches, particularly the Visualize Spots setting, which will show you what you need to fix. This can be run when you open a RAW image in Photoshop, or it can be run as a filter on any image.

Start by clicking on the Spot Removal tool shown in **Figure 49.1**, and then turn on the Visualize Spots selection at the bottom of the panel on the right side of the screen. When you slide the control over to the right, the spots in your image will start to show up in white (**Figure 49.2**).

49.1 Click on the Spot Removal icon to open the Spot Removal tool.

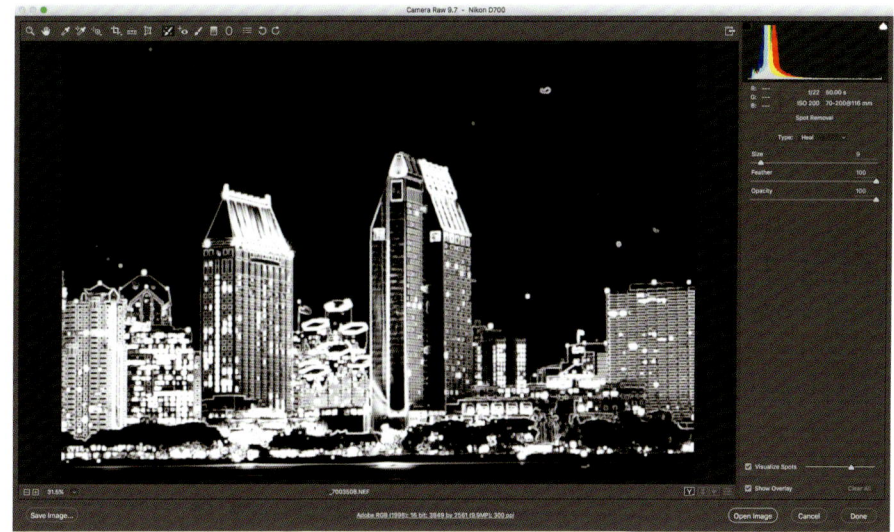

49.2 Turning on the Visualize Spots setting and sliding the control over to the right allows you to see the dust and spots in the image.

You can now select the Heal Brush or Clone Brush from the Type drop-down menu and use it to remove the spots. You can adjust the size of the Brush to get rid of the smaller bits of dust and smaller scratches. Take your time because it can be difficult to see all of the spots and dots and dust. I prefer to remove the dust and dirt by running the Camera Raw filter in Photoshop instead of trying to remove everything when I first open the image in Adobe Camera Raw. I just don't want to spend the time doing all this work until I know the image is one that will meet my needs. Use the following steps to remove dust and scratches with the Camera Raw filter:

- Open the image in Adobe Photoshop.
- Duplicate the layer so that the original image stays as the background and the adjustments are made on the duplicate layer.
- Make sure that new image layer is selected, and then go to *Filter > Camera Raw Filter*.
- Click on the Spot Removal tool.
- Turn on the Visualize Spots view and move the control to the right so you can see all of the spots.
- Select Clone or Heal from the Type drop-down menu and use the brush to fix the spots. You can switch between the two brush types as you work, and you can also adjust the Size, Feather, and Opacity of the brush for use in different areas of the image.

I have no idea how so much crud got on my lens and into my camera, but the Spot Removal tool really saved my image, as you can see in **Figures 49.3** and **49.4**.

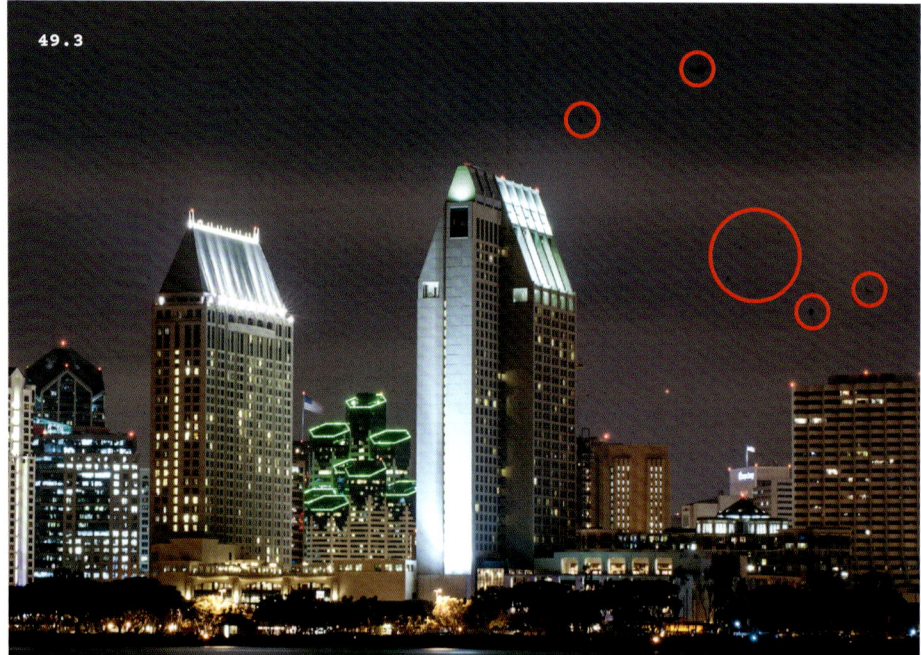

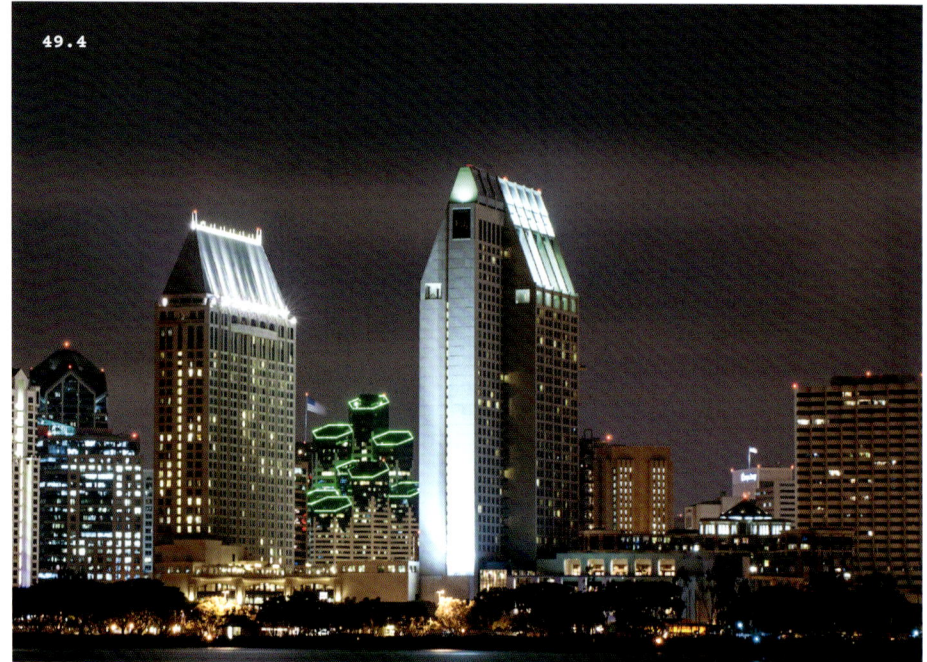

49.3 There were some really large pieces of dirt and dust on my sensor or lens, which showed up in this image as dark spots in the sky.

49.4 I was able to remove the spots in Adobe Camera Raw and the image looks much cleaner.

50. A QUICK CONTRAST TRICK USING BLEND MODE

FOR THE FINAL tip in this book, I am going to share a Photoshop trick that I learned years ago and still use to this day because it's easy, fast, and can really add some pop to your images.

This technique relies on the Luminosity Blend Mode, which blends the lightness values in an image but doesn't affect the color. This allows you to adjust the contrast without messing up the color of your image. I like to make a new layer with a high-contrast black-and-white version of the image, and then blend using the Luminosity Blend Mode. This makes the dark parts darker and the light parts lighter. Since I can control the opacity of the blended layer, I can adjust how much of the effect to apply. **Figure 50.1** shows my original image before I added this effect, and **Figure 50.2** shows the same image with the effect applied at 70% opacity.

The key to this technique is to not go nuts, but to keep it as a subtle contrast improvement. I usually set the opacity to about 20%, but that's a little too subtle to really see in this book. As is the case with every technique I've discussed in this chapter, it is always a good idea to start with big bold changes and then tone down the effects until you get the look you want.

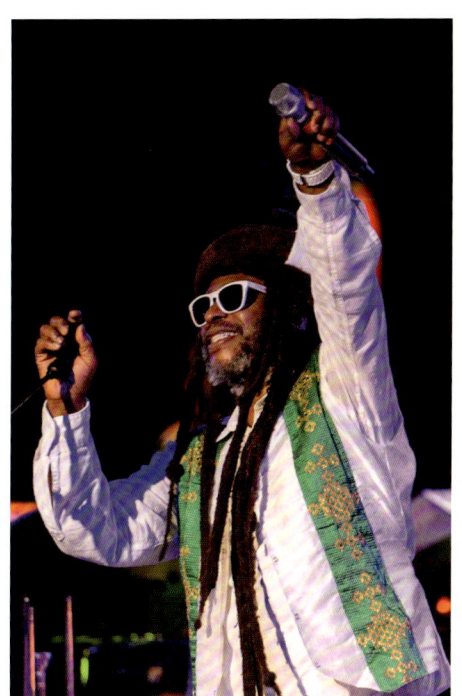

50.1 The original image after editing, but before I applied the final touch. **ISO 4000; 1/200 sec.; f/2.8**

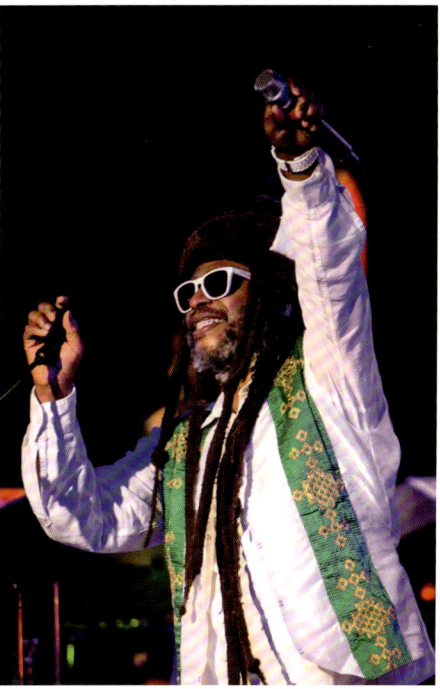

50.2 I applied the Luminosity Blend Mode to a duplicate layer at 70% opacity to adjust the contrast in the image. The final image has more punch with darker shadow areas and lighter highlights.

For this technique, just follow these simple steps:

- Open the image in Photoshop.
- Duplicate the layer.
- Make sure the new layer is selected, and then go to *Layer > New Adjustment Layer > Black & White* (**Figure 50.3**).
- Go to *Layer > Merge Down*.
- In the Layers panel, change the Blend Mode to Luminosity.
- Adjust the opacity of the layer to dial in the strength of the effect (**Figure 50.4**).

This effect can also be used on scenic photos, especially where you want the dark areas darker and the light areas lighter, and it works great for cityscapes. **Figures 50.5** shows a photo of downtown San Diego at twilight, and **Figure 50.6** shows the same scene with the Luminosity Blend Mode effect applied.

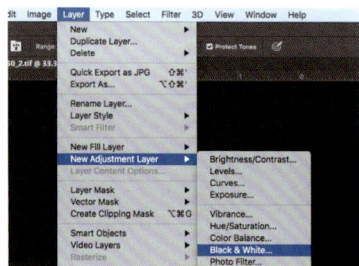

50.3 Adding a Black & White Adjustment Layer.

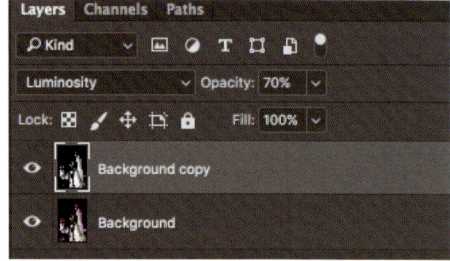

50.4 You can fine-tune the strength of the effect by adjusting the opacity of the duplicate layer.

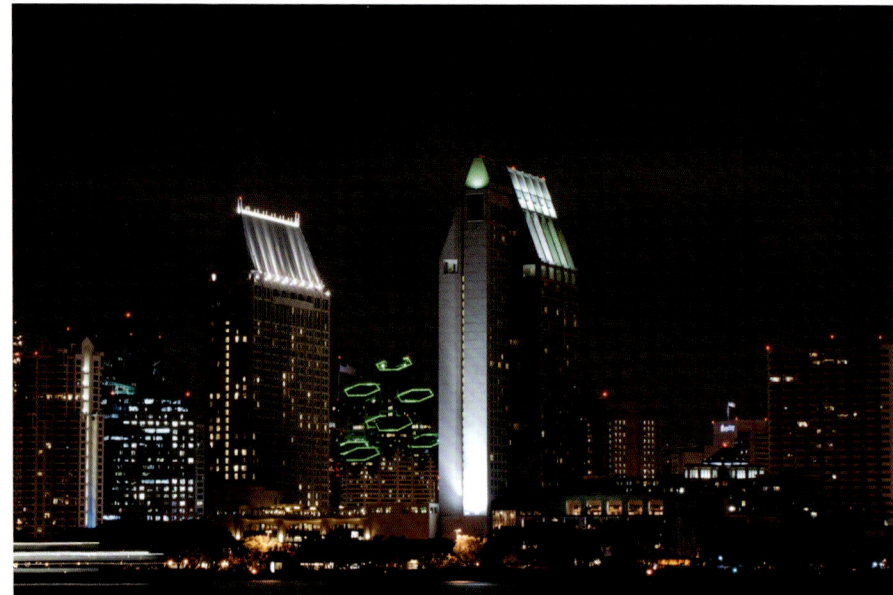

50.5 The San Diego skyline before adding the Luminosity Blend Mode layer.

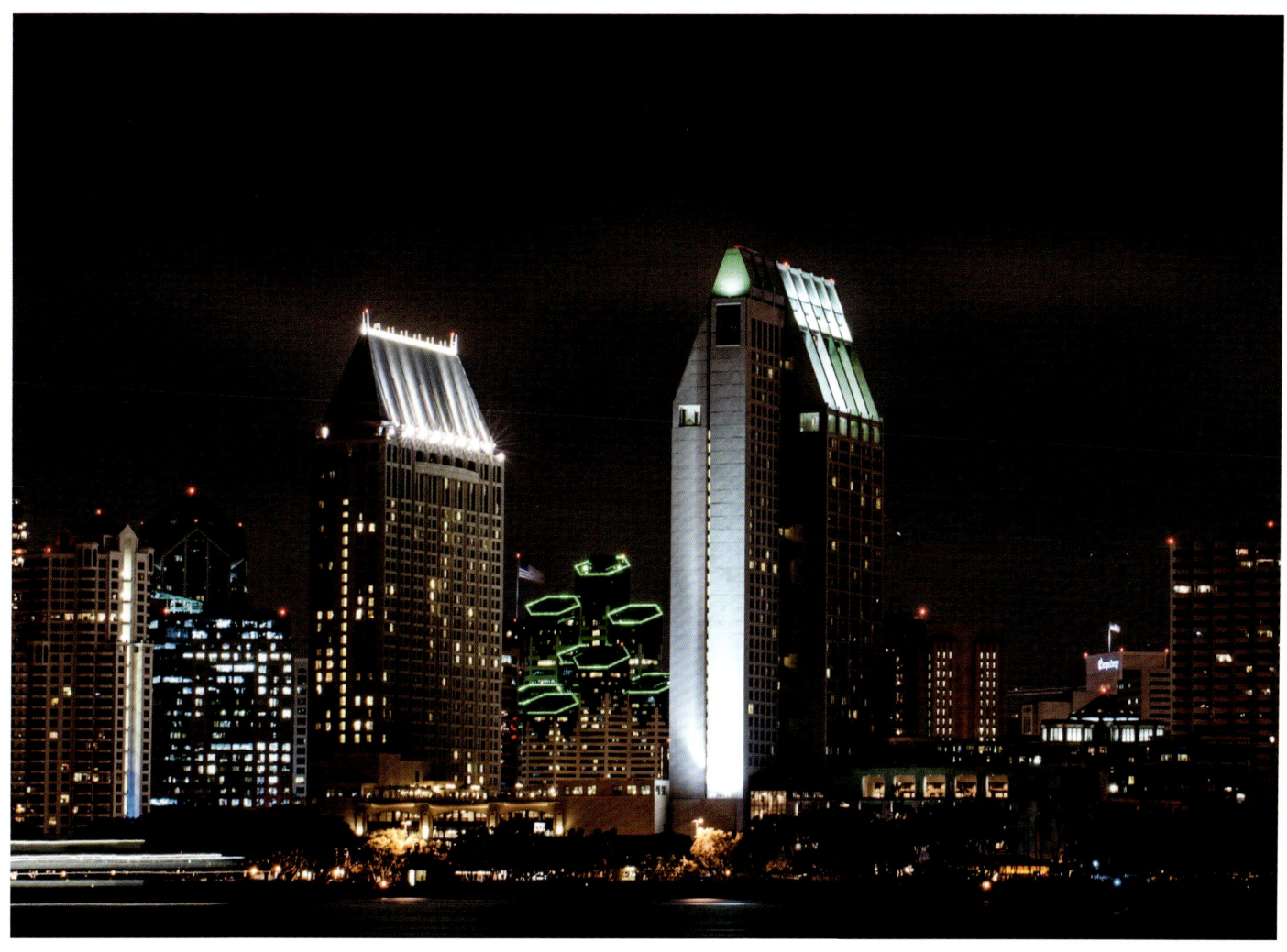

50.6 The final image with the Luminosity Blend Mode layer applied.

INDEX